# THE CHURCH SERVES
# THE CHANGING CITY

# THE CHURCH
# SERVES THE
# CHANGING CITY

By Ross W. Sanderson

For the
DEPARTMENT OF THE URBAN CHURCH
with the co-operation of
THE COMMITTEE ON FIELD RESEARCH
NATIONAL COUNCIL OF CHURCHES

*Illustrated*

HARPER & BROTHERS  PUBLISHERS  NEW YORK

Library of Congress catalog card number: 55–6788

# Contents

5

# Foreword

The demand for case studies, particularly of the churches' ministry in blighted urban areas, has been earnestly expressed for many years by denominational administrators of city work, pastors, laymen, and seminary students. After the establishment of the Department of the Urban Church of the National Council of the Churches of Christ at the close of 1950, many such requests were directed to its office. The case studies presented here are offered in partial response to the demand to know what "others" are doing in the spreading areas of urban blight.

This work was projected by national denominational administrators and other members of the Department of the Urban Church at its meeting on April 16, 1953. As first conceived it was hoped to study more churches and church agencies than are now presented. But when the plan was considered by an advisory committee of the National Council of Churches' Committee on Field Research, a unanimous opinion was expressed that to reveal the dynamics of the churches it would be more profitable to study about eight cases intensively and set them against a background of notes on similar enterprises in other areas. This procedure was approved by the Research Committee of the Department of the Urban Church.

Cases of conscious urban adaptation were selected with denominational, geographical, and functional differences in mind. Final choices were unavoidably intertwined with budgetary considerations. It was also decided not to attempt evaluations by objective criteria established in advance, but instead to allow each church and agency to be judged in the light of its own acknowledged objectives. The project as modified was begun in the winter of 1953.

It takes a man with keen analytical powers, a wealth of knowledge about church and community, ability to synthesize, and withal a warm, sensitive appreciation of the efforts of his fellow men to make objective firsthand studies of changing social and ecclesiastical phenomena. The sands in the heart of the American city shift rapidly, and an amateur observer may often find himself looking at the wrong dune, the really significant conformation behind his back. The Department had no desire to stand abashed in the revealing light of history; so it employed the dean of church researchers, Ross W. Sanderson, to make these studies of ministry in urban areas of underprivilege.

Dr. Sanderson has been parish pastor, teacher, secretary of city councils of churches, and distinguished researcher for national denominational and interdenominational bodies. He is the author of *The Strategy of City Church Planning*, organizer of the 1950 National Convocation on the Urban Church, and subsequently the first executive of the Department of the Urban Church. The Department was particularly fortunate to obtain his services for this study. No man is better qualified.

In many ways the case studies presented are incarnations of the impossible. Here are stories of strong neighborhood ministries where neighborhoods scarcely exist; of $100,000 church programs where people crawl at the brink of hunger; of talented and well-educated apostles of Christ who with their families have given the lie to the deceptive glories of suburbia and chosen to do and dwell in the stark reality of squalid slums; of strange people from many lands with many tongues, who are misunderstood, exploited, condemned, driven by fear and hostility, and yet in breaking bread together find courage and peace.

Stately vestigial edifices, murky railroad flats, and drab basement storefronts are all scenes of the slum dwellers' emerging newness in Christ. By gospel songs in teeming streets and the Word preached in rubbly lots, by nursery centers and medical clinics, by cleanup campaigns and political action, by the uplift of souls that dwell on the passion of Christ before the stations of the cross, the redemptive gospel is being made known through the churches and agencies here set forth.

Among the churches are some which have been objects of classroom criticism and round-table debate when denominational administrators have convened. Quite possibly a few of the programs and emphases may be ill advised, though the time for the final word is not yet. But here is new light on their successes and failures as they face up, unashamed and unafraid, to the changing, deteriorating heart of the city, from which countless churches have escaped to more favored locations.

As the dreams of some churches have been strangled by the slums, others have been renewed and some have come to birth. In dreams of Christian community lies the hope of the city, for without vision how can disintegration become reintegration? Without spiritual, moral, and social fiber, the city's future is dim. Pawns of chance cannot conquer the blind brutality of material forces. The world can be saved only by the leadership of God-fearing men in every walk of life.

In these documented interpretations of what some churches are dreaming and doing in some cities, there is exhibited a renewed concern of the church for the welfare of "the whole man" —body, mind, and soul. Dr. Sanderson points to "a new settlement movement" in which Christian men are identifying themselves with the lot of the less fortunate whom they would serve and with whom they would work together for justice and righteousness.

The horizons of the leaders are broad, but the focus is upon neighborhood renewal, as it was a half-century ago. Social work skills which grew out of the earlier settlement movement are being increasingly employed in the churches' neighborhood ministry. Yet churchmanship has not lapsed nor theology become irrelevant.

The years between these settlement movements have brought a realization that "the city is too much for a divided church." Churches and church agencies are generally trying to associate their efforts across denominational and functional lines, but not without pain. Established denominational patterns do not stretch easily; professional social work is exclusive, and urbanization exalts rigid specialization. The churches' interest in the whole man does not go unchallenged.

There is revealed in these studies a strong urge to be relevant to the massed needs of men in the urban "house of fear." But relevancy is heavily fraught with difficulty and with danger of misunderstanding. It is expensive too.

The inclusiveness of the church as to the racial, cultural, social, and economic status of its membership is being accepted in the changing city. The time seems not far distant when it will be axiomatic. Here is a new stirring of the gospel and of the social conscience of the nation.

Nothing emerges more startlingly out of these studies than the problems of leadership. The training of an indigenous lay apostolate, the cultivation of the active concern of Christian brothers resident in favored suburban communities, the maintenance of effective dedication and strength of group ministries in the light of inherent administrative weakness—these are a few of the aspects of leadership shown to be in need of attention.

Despite denominational and interdenominational emphases upon strategy in high places and the increasing number of specialized offices and personnel agencies, what is being done of a pioneering nature is most often the personal implementation of the dream of one, two, or three people at most—dedicated and convinced ministers, leaders of rare vision. In almost every case studied, the name or names are indelibly inscribed—names of rare souls. Can others carry on for them? Which others? Can their patterns of success be reproduced? By whom?

The inner city will not be taken by Christianity until the Church prepares ministers sufficient in number and wisdom and saints who will lead the downtrodden along an ascending path. How many will give themselves in earnest prayer and conquering action for Christ in city neighborhoods of dire poverty? Multitudes are prone to criticism and censure, but few are rushing across the abyss.

The opportunity of today may not come this way again. In these case studies are exciting glimpses of a series of partial victories in a relatively few areas of urban blight. They are skirmishes on a vast field of battle encompassing much of the population of the nation. Will the battle of this generation be won? Can the Church penetrate and win the whole city for Christ? I believe the reader will share my feeling that Ross Sanderson has in these chapters set forth beyond all statistics a warm human story of what the skirmishes have involved and has given new insights for the plan of battle.

WILLIAM J. VILLAUME

September 30, 1954

# Chapter I

# Introduction

## Purpose of This Study

[This study seeks to indicate some of the instances where American Protestantism is ministering most effectively to urban residents in areas of underprivilege. It confines its attention to churches actively at work in their own neighborhoods, or to church-sponsored agencies ministering in the name of the churches. Adequate extensive summary of the work of the thousands of city churches in scores of denominations, all caught in the spread of urban blight, is obviously impossible. Brief case studies of eight situations are here presented in some detail, in an effort to analyze their significance for the churching of the American city, and these studies are framed in a background of two dozen additional instances of somewhat similar situations, more briefly sketched.

## The Range of Coverage

[The material here presented involves participation and investment on the part of thirteen denominations: Baptist, Congregational, Disciples, Episcopal, Evangelical and Reformed, Evangelical United Brethren, Friends (Hicksite), Lutheran (U.L.C.A. and E.L.C.), Mennonite, Methodist, Presbyterian, and Reformed; also a number of agencies—educational, interdenominational, or undenominational.] Limitations of time and money have required that field work be largely concentrated in a few areas, but parishes or other activities in a dozen different cities, whether named or not, have been visited. In ten cities the writer has personally visited the work described; in two others, several associates have reported their firsthand knowledge of the situations more briefly discussed. In all this study those who have co-operated in it have been observers and students of the city church for many years, and have had exceptional opportunity to study it systematically under widely differing conditions.

As the Table of Contents makes clear, some of the cases studied are city-wide churches considered from the particular standpoint of their ministry to the underprivileged in the vicinity of their buildings, whatever the nature of that ministry. Some of the cases, on the other hand, involve social service work, either affiliated with churches or organizationally distinct from churches as worshiping units. In all such cases, however, the emphasis has been not on the details of any social work program but on the outreach of the Church, as such. In many situations the type of program carried on has not been unusual or novel; what has been most important has been that the churches have made up their mind to serve their neighborhoods, whosoever may now or in the future live in them. This study did not set out to analyze the problems of bilingual churches, or biracial churches, or interdenominational churches. It found that wherever blight has set in, people of different languages, races, and church affiliations are likely to be thrown together both as neighbors and as churchmen.

*Need for Definition of Terms*

Some central "inner city" sections are essentially metropolitan and nonresidential in any ordinary neighborhood sense. Their churches are *in* the inner city but often, at least in large part, not *of* it.

In transitional neighborhoods transition can be upward as well as downward; and to hang on to a strategic location may be excellent long-range strategy, however tough the going may be before the coming of the new inhabitants of large-scale housing. Some city neighborhoods are actually becoming more Protestant because more Southern, or more Negro. Newcomers to Northern cities are too often thought of as a problem when they should be regarded as a Protestant asset—unless we intend by our neglect to encourage their becoming either Roman Catholic or pagan.

In all the areas covered by these studies their "common denominator is low income."

What is "the Church"? Is it a fellowship for worship or a service agency, or both? Should these functions be kept structurally distinct? Or should they be inextricably interwoven in theory and in practice?

## Limits of the Study

The cases and the background material covered in this report have not represented whim or fancy, or subjective preference. The whole field was successively modified over a period of months, and still further as field work progressed. Such earlier titles as "Experimental Types of Parish Ministry in Depressed Urban Areas" seemed less appropriate as the visits to suggested churches were actually made. In fact, the evidence mounted that the very word "experimental" was regarded with disfavor by those who felt that the Church should never have abandoned its most difficult urban opportunity.

This report has sought to present a few facts, and to attempt to establish some of their meanings. Wide areas of fruitful investigation have had to be neglected. There has been little or no opportunity to study the question of the *church and industry,* a field entered experimentally by several denominations with new vigor recently. Both *social welfare* and *social engineering* aspects of the whole problem of the changing city are among those at which this report can only hint. Perhaps Chicago's Church Federation has moved farthest in this direction. Likewise the relations of the *church and labor,* whether organized or unorganized, have had no adequate consideration in this report. The problem of huge *apartment house areas* also deserves more detailed study.

As blight gives way to "high housing," new techniques are slowly being developed for more adequate ministry to dwellers in our modern "box culture."

The general program of the central church, with its city-wide, widely scattered parish, has not been featured; neither has the church in the prosperous or relatively static or stable residential neighborhood. Transitional areas have been recognized as a major unsolved problem for urban Protestantism. In practice, is any part of any sizable city free from transition these days?

Private enterprise, adequately planned, has one advantage over public housing. It is able to avoid the "one-class neighborhood." Monocultural and one-class communities are alike distasteful to the real builders of neighborhood. People come to church as "to the settlement, as people with a need to be met that often has nothing to do with the cultural group to which they belong." One cannot avoid the regretful conclusion, however, that broad as is the gap between classes or races, such gaps are easier to bridge than the canyons separating some of our varieties of ecclesiasticism. May it not be that the frequent indifference of the people at the grass roots, as on the foreign mission field, to denominational distinctions representative of Western cultural divisions is in the providence of God evidence of the *unity and mission* of the Church?

No church or community could be comprehensively analyzed in a report of this length. What has been attempted has been a *documented impression* that would show the reader with reasonable accuracy what some churches are doing in some cities. If church leaders responsible for urban strategy are moved to raise further questions, and seek their answers, this limited study has accomplished its purpose. Here is no complete sociological, psychological, or ecclesiastical blueprint for the better churching of the city, or any portion of it, but only some more or less detailed sketches of the way in which Protestantism has achieved constructive results in problem areas. These pages reinforce the truth of Samuel C. Kincheloe's statement (personal letter, February 1,

1954) : "The penetration of the inner city, really a pagan country, is exceedingly costly and very difficult."

## Other Necessary Limitations

Readers of this report will know of many other parishes and activities, some of which may be similarly effective or even more effective than those cited in this report. It is hoped that adequate documentation of all such ministry to urban underprivileged people will promptly be supplied to the Department of the Urban Church, for the benefit of all the co-operating denominations and of the ecumenical movement at large.

Resources of time and money have sufficed for only a quick study of situations nominated chiefly by denominational city work executives or local interdenominational consultants. Obviously such a study could be pursued for years, and represents a process that might well be co-operative and continuous.

## The Utility of This Study

[In the midst of kaleidoscopic urban change some institutions migrate. Some, in order to survive at the old stand, adapt themselves to the swift social changes which have come upon them and their neighborhoods. Some adaptations have been slight, others have been radical. Facing similar problems, with motives strikingly the same, there are widely differing views, now increasingly articulate, as to what ought to be done by the churches to meet the needs of the changing city.] In the pages that follow is the story of some actual ministries that have come to the attention of national church leaders.

It is hoped that these chapters will be of value to administrators as they compare notes as to successes and failures, to theological students as an introduction to some of the realities of urban church life today, and to pastors and loyal lay persons whose insights and labors are essential to the conquest of the city in behalf of any worthy type of churchmanship.

*The Turn of the Tide*

Twenty-five years ago Professor H. Richard Niebuhr [1] saw that "the religiously neglected poor, who fashion a new type of Christianity which corresponds to their distinctive needs," are likely to "arise in the economic scale under the influence of religious discipline, and . . . in the midst of a freshly acquired cultural respectability, neglect the new poor succeeding them on the lower plane" (p. 28). And, he records, "Wesley himself faultlessly described the process whereby other churches of the disinherited, and his own with them, sloughed off their original character. 'Wherever riches have increased,' he wrote, 'the essence of religion has decreased in the same proportion. Therefore I do not see how it is possible in the nature of things for any revival of religion to continue for long. For religion must necessarily produce both industry and frugality, and these cannot but produce riches' " (p. 70).

So Protestants have climbed up and out, and less privileged persons have moved into the inner city. But just to run away, just to leave the neighborhood of surviving churches unshepherded, no longer leaves the denominational conscience free, still less that of the ecumenical fellowship. Some Protestants who worship in good residential neighborhoods, urban, suburban, or rural, have a new sense of responsibility about the changing city. Herewith is part of the story of what the churches have tried to do about it.

*Increasing Co-operativeness*

Every day it grows more and more clear that the city, like the world, is too much for a divided, non-co-operative Church. This study has been made possible by administrative co-operation at the national top, among many denominations. It has been carried forward through the co-operation of denominational and interdenominational administrators in city after city. It could not have succeeded without the willing and eager help of pastors and lay

[1] *The Social Sources of Denominationalism*, New York, Henry Holt, 1929.

persons in dozens of local churches. Even the World Council of Churches has shared one of its significant but unpublished studies. The writer has had the counsel of a committee appointed by the Field Research Committee of the National Council of Churches, and the entire report has been submitted to the Department of the Urban Church, of the National Council's Division of Home Missions. The devotion of many, many people lies behind these pages.

## Chapter II

# Great Central Parishes and Their Neighborhood Ministries

First of all, this study seeks to document the fact that not every central city church neglects its neighborhood, however great the temptation to do so. Not all centrally located churches are rich; many of them are without adequate endowment. A few, by reason of accumulated capital funds, are able to spend twice as much as or more than they could without such exceptional resources. Among these is a historic parish, now presented as

### Case I—Trinity Church, Boston

Among the recognizably great churches of America is Trinity Church, Boston. Always associated with the name of Phillips Brooks, is it indelibly stamped with his spirit.

In 1869, at the age of 33, Phillips Brooks came to Boston from Philadelphia to be pastor of Trinity Church. Organized in 1729, as an offshoot of King's Chapel, Trinity was worshiping at its Summer Street location, near Washington Street, in a building erected in 1829. Soon came the fire, and the move to Copley Square was accelerated. The new rector labored for years in the erection of a great building and became one of the greatest preachers in the world; but when he came to Boston, according to his biographer, A. V. G. Allen, "a significant change in his ministry" had occurred. Here "he sought to know the people to whom he preached, to study their needs, to share in their joys, to lead them into larger conceptions of the mission of a parish to the church and to the world." [1]

A colleague "had an appointment to meet him at the rectory at eight o'clock. . . . Not until nearly eleven did Mr. Brooks return. . . . He had been detained at a hospital by a colored man who had been injured in some affray and had sent for him." When a dying colored girl sent for him on Sunday morning, an assistant was sent to explain "why he was unable to come. But the assistant returned with the message that the girl had declared she would not die until he came. When the service was over Mr. Brooks himself went according to the request." [2]

"He had a great gift for inspiriting people who were depressed or had lost heart for their work. A word from him would send them back to their tasks again with renewed energy. . . . The letters he wrote to people in affliction, if gathered together, would form a considerable volume. He seemed to attract them, as he did the poor, the sick, the outcast, by some force which he did not consciously exercise, and yet of whose existence he was aware." [3]

That was the kind of man he was. That is the sort of tradition he left. Is this not the authentic opportunity of the church in the inner city, now as then?

Succeeding rectors have included such men as the presiding bishop of the Protestant Episcopal Church, Rt. Rev. Henry Knox Sherrill, and the present pastor (since 1942), the Rev. Theodore P. Ferris. Men like these do not merely use the Prayer Book words concerning "all sorts and conditions of men"; they tune their ministry to the needs of all those whom it is their privilege to serve, both those of the neighborhood and those of the wider community in which their leadership is exercised. Such men unavoidably become nation-wide figures. Such churches are city-wide parishes; Trinity attracts regular Sunday attendance from

[1] *Life and Letters of Phillips Brooks*, New York, E. P. Dutton, 1900, II, 9.
[2] *Ibid.*, II, 673.     [3] *Ibid.*, II, 807.

as far away as Providence, which is 48 minutes from Boston's South Station by the fastest New Haven train.

Roughly Trinity Parish is said to consist of three concentric circles: first, a fifth or more of the total constituency, those who live within a mile of Copley Square; second, maybe three-fifths of the total, those who live within fifteen or twenty minutes by public transportation, or less by private automobile—in Brookline, Cambridge, or other close-in communities; and third, approximately the final fifth, those who reside on the outer rim—in Needham, Dedham, Wellesley, the Newtons, Wakefield, Reading, and other places just inside, outside, or astride Route 128, the circumferential highway that roughly bounds an area with a fifteen-mile radius (sometimes less) from the State House dome. By car, coming in along any one of the spokes, even from this far rim, to the center of the Hub is a matter of half an hour or so. Accordingly six or eight boys may travel twice a week to Trinity Church choir rehearsals, as well as on Sundays, from a town on the outer edge of the metropolitan district. This is a typically metropolitan parish. Then, too, at a church like this there are always a host of visitors from all parts of the nation, and of the wider world, attracted by a historic spot and a famous pulpit.

By and large, parishioners who live farthest out may have the best economic status, or at least enjoy the best living conditions for families with children. In the second or closer-in circle there are people in fine houses or comfortable and expensive apartments, and people in quite other neighborhoods, just as loyal to Trinity but materially at the other end of the spectrum. Then within walking distance there are all sorts of parishioners. Between the church and the Charles there are still some well-to-do people, but nowadays rooming houses are more characteristic of the area. Such territory houses many people who have known better days economically, now living frugally but representing all that is best in New England culture. Others are young people, mature students and couples on their way up, who in due time will arrive; for the moment, their resources are sometimes as limited as their hopes are legitimately high.

Across the tracks it may be quite different. Boston's South End is an area of vanished glory. From its earlier high residential status many a family has migrated, first to the Back Bay, later to the suburbs. Here, too, however, are many of Trinity's parishioners.

Accordingly Trinity's parish is cosmopolitan. It draws important people, "proper Bostonians," from many miles; it also serves people not yet important, including students (graduate and undergraduate) from the region's numerous colleges and universities; and it ministers lovingly too to many persons who never were important and maybe never will be, persons stranded in little urban pockets, with the great city swirling all around them. Perhaps three out of four, maybe four out of five, are persons referred to the parish by the diocese, by individuals, by groups or agencies, all of whom have come to know that Trinity is set in the heart of the metropolis to be as one who serves—or maybe they just came in on their own. Fortunately there is a modest endowment which enables the staff to be more helpful than they could be without this resource.

These days, however, such money does far more than meet the emergency needs of individuals. Trinity does not do social work that can be better done by established social agencies. What Trinity seeks to do is to become the sort of friend who can put at the command of the individual or family all the resources of a highly organized urban community. One of the clergy makes it his business to know who can help, and in what manner. Requests from Trinity can often expedite the slow processes of social work or governmental agency. Sometimes a lay person or couple can provide just the lift needed—of counsel or "know-how."

In Boston everybody knows about Trinity. It has prestige. When it makes a request, it is a reasonable one, humane and understanding. It seeks not favors for its own, but assistance for those who need it. As a result, everybody lends a hand, wherever possible.

This is not the place to rehearse specific kinds of needs that Trinity has to face. Occasionally the need is just plain financial. Without help, *now*, not next week, somebody will be evicted. On their own resources alone, a couple may not be able to put a bright youngster through school. More often, even when there is economic need, the real trouble goes deeper. Personal counseling is largely used. The rector is accessible, and does his full share of this part of the parish work. When he passes a person along to a colleague, it is because in the particular instance the colleague happens to know the available resources better. Nobody gets the "run-around" if he comes in real quest of help.

Once in a while it turns out that a situation is of a sort that keeps recurring. At this point Trinity can help organize a civic force, bigger and broader than itself, inclusive perhaps of Roman Catholic and Jew, to fill a gap in the social work structure. Here Trinity has the tremendous advantage, far more important than its material assets, of being able to command some of the ablest personnel in Massachusetts as volunteers, only part of them from its own membership. Trinity has become known as a place from which new needs are seen, new agencies are incubated, new social competence is organized. In at least two cases, its sincere request for help has enabled much-needed new civic groups to get started, make a demonstration of their worth, and take their place in the fabric of the larger community life. Several other opportunities seem now to be ripening. One need may be adequately met by processes already under way; but if not and a new agency proves desirable, Trinity could spark-plug another program, during the critically determinative period of its infancy. Of course, behind all the referrals or the organization of new agencies is the long, patient, face-to-face contact of clergyman or other parish worker with parishioner—or, perhaps in four cases of five, with the stranger whose sole reason for appealing to Trinity is his sheer sense of need. The applicant may be referred to this agency or that, or to this expert or that, but always it is with the firm friendliness of a parish that seeks to be neighborly in the midst of a city's loneliness and desperate personal inadequacy.

This chapter does not attempt to tell picturesque details of what in the nature of the case is confidential. It seeks not at all to praise the work of this one parish for what it seeks to do. Trinity itself is deeply convinced that it is only trying as best it can to serve all the children of God who look to it for guidance, mindful of the fact that God loves them all, alike. Students from the ends of the earth are made welcome. Among worshipers, neither color nor status bars one from the church's ministry. Rich as it is, and famous, this is a house of God for *all* people—in deep intent and in practice recognized by all those who seek to serve humanity in this seaboard city. What Trinity seeks to do, it regards as normative for any church similarly located in any city: to minister to all who come, from wherever, for whatsoever reason.

It will be understood, of course, that these brief pages have made no effort to describe the work of Trinity's varied parish organizations, or even to present its worship and preaching ministry. As in scores of churches, in Boston and in other cities, the fact that its pulpit is literally of nation-wide significance only adds to the contribution it makes to the residents of the neighborhood. Of all that the central church does to serve its local community, no factor is more outstanding than its ability to reach people through the sermons of an able preacher. None of his Trinity staff associates would be willing to have the homiletical excellence of the rector's ministry overlooked. Dr. Ferris continues a great pulpit tradition.

*Generously Supported Mission Programs*

Sometimes a great central church extends its outreach through one or more chapels or missions, utilizing its exceptional resources for the employment of the necessary personnel and for the maintenance of work which the residents of underprivileged neighborhoods, working alone, could not possibly support. Thus, an immensely wealthy corporation like Trinity Church in the City of New York is able to operate a number of chapels.

For example, at 292 Henry Street, opposite the famous Settlement, is *St. Augustine's Chapel*, of which the Rev. C. Kilmer Myers is now vicar. Closely associated with it is St. Christopher's Chapel at 48 Henry Street, of which Father Myers, who was previously rector of Grace Church, Jersey City, is also the vicar. He is assisted by four other priests, only one of whom, the resident at St. Christopher's, is married. These men constitute "the Team." St. Christopher's is the former Jacob Riis House, whose type of service is less necessary now in this location because of the migration outward of many Jewish people and the turning of Jewish philanthropists' attention elsewhere.

St. Augustine's was formerly located on East Houston Street. When this became nonresidential, Trinity Parish sold the old building and in November, 1944, merged the congregation with All Saints, which seventy years earlier had resisted the temptation to leave Henry Street and join the movement uptown. "A century ago this [area] was one of New York's most fashionable residential neighborhoods; two hundred years ago it was verdant farm land. Today it is one of the city's worst slums. Over the years immigrants have found this section a welcome haven. Jews, Italians, Irish, Germans, Russians, Poles, East and West Indians, Chinese, Negroes, Puerto Ricans have settled there." [4]

St. Augustine's (formerly All Saints) is a lovely old building, erected in 1824. Its worship is high church, with Low Mass at 8:00 and 9:30, High Mass at 11:00, and Evening Prayer at 7:15 on Sundays; also daily early morning Mass (7:30, Monday to Friday; 9:30, Saturday) and Evening Prayer (5 P.M.). Confessions are heard at 11 A.M. and 5 P.M. on Saturday, and by ap-

[4] *Forth*, April, 1949.

pointment. Extra services during Holy Week include the Stations of the Cross. Here statues are regarded as a spiritual asset, and Passion Sunday found both Chancel Cross and Statues covered with purple veils, as a symbol of "mourning for the sins which brought our Lord at last to the Cross." Implicit in this symbolism and in the attitudes of the clergy is the confidence of victory achieved on Good Friday and Easter Day.

Some Jews are coming back into the middle-class co-operative multiple housing just to the east, erected by union garment workers. The director of the Henry Street Settlement is a member of the parish, and the Chapel and the Settlement co-operate heartily in seeking to work with the police in suppression of the traffic in narcotics. At the Settlement, 98 per cent of the patrons are said to be white; its constituency has changed less rapidly than the population. At St. Augustine's only 50 per cent of those who attend are white; the rest are Negro, Puerto Rican, and Chinese. Many of the Negroes have come from the South, via Harlem, and were traditionally Baptist.

The Chapel is eager to use social work skills. It hopes to add to its staff a community organizer, a group worker, and a psychiatric social worker. Many activities, e.g., a boys' club, are much the same at Chapel as at Settlement, with this difference: the *Church* is in the Chapel picture, and through it there is steady remembrance of relationship to God as well as to fellow men. There is a vertical as well as a horizontal dimension. Penance, the whole sacramental basis of the Chapel's life, and the influence of the priests (who are called "Father") add a *plus* to group work.

While the Chapel ministers to a few who are socially better off than their neighbors, it endeavors to serve all who are interested to come. It deliberately seeks to maintain a "Catholic Fellowship" rather than to identify itself with any one race or economic grouping. The Roman Church is not very active in the neighborhood, the small Orthodox synagogues are weaker than they once were.

An occasional Pentecostal Mission brings its own type of service. Race tension is a real problem.

An "open vicarage" tries to make its kitchen table as significant in its place as the altar in the church chancel. A major need is for a larger vicarage, so that more persons of all ages can be more adequately served.

The first vicar, the Rev. H. A. Berngen, called attention (in *Christian Social Relations*, November 15, 1948) to a number of liturgical action postulates. These included emphasis on the liturgical "we," witnessing with outward signs (e.g., processions), co-operation with neighborhood agencies and organizations, and concentration on the immediate community—"communicants resident at a distance cannot be depended upon for sustained support." In the light of 177 baptisms and 93 confirmations in three years, Father Berngen was convinced that "Anglicanism can and should attract and shepherd the masses." During the most recent year the two chapels have presented 51 persons for confirmation. Total attendance at the 1954 Easter Masses was 1,080, nearly three-fifths of this at St. Augustine's, the balance at St. Christopher's.

### "Our Neighbors Are Different Now"

There are of course many other types of effort on the part of local churches to serve their immediate neighborhoods. Sometimes the program is recreational, sometimes educational—vacation schools or weekday religious education, for example. Often a church is in one tradition, while all around it or close to it has grown up a population of quite different culture. There are well-known instances where a great city church has organized, equipped, staffed, and for many years maintained some sort of community center a little distance "across town," or very close to the church, but in a different world, so to speak. The problem of "social distance" is in such cases a very great hindrance to integration. It is easy to regret the dichotomy which divides, and the dualism which obtains; it is not easy to see how persons in groups of sharply different social status can be welded into a single sociable unit. Even if they can worship together congenially, can they find fellowship together comfortably in the weekday programs of the parish? This problem would be worthy of special study. No doubt there is something deeper here than snobbery on the one hand or inferiority complexes on the other.

# Chapter III

# Specialized Institutional Ministries

Sometimes, as part of a general parish ministry, urban churches render considerable service to their neighborhoods. Well-informed readers will think of many instances.

In October, 1942, Rev. Dan B. Genung was sent to the *All Peoples Christian Church and Community Center* at 822 East 20th Street, *Los Angeles*, to "carry out the United Christian Missionary Society (Disciples of Christ) vision of brotherhood." Here twenty clubs, each with devotions, are designed to meet the needs of all ages. "Belonging" not only means much in itself but also is said to provide many members and leaders for the church. Beginning with two small Chinese children, this church now numbers nearly 250 members, with an average attendance of 119. There is an active youth program. The youth pastor, ordained two years ago, Rev. Kay Kokubun, is one of the church's own boys. At the day nursery are 45 youngsters, ages two to five. Preference is given to children whose parents both work and to children who have no space to play. An annual camp provides a week for 100 boys and girls. There is also a vacation school. Photographs make clear that there are no racial barriers. All Peoples Church seeks to be "a church that is concerned" and it believes that "your support of our institutional missions is an expression of faith in the brotherhood of man."

The *American Baptist Home Mission Society* backs nearly sixty "Christian Centers." "A Christian Center is a church-spon-

SPECIALIZED INSTITUTIONAL MINISTRIES 31

sored social service institution through which the redemptive power of God's love works creatively to change and develop the lives of people, personally and collectively, so that they will fully understand and commit themselves to the Christian life." [1]

In characteristic Baptist fashion these Centers are associated but not centrally administered or statistically summarized. In 1951, in the foreword to a Workers' Manual prepared by the Chicago Area Conference, in which seven institutions shared, it was confessed, "The Christian Center Movement has not come of age. It is as yet quite immature in its approach to the concentrated, antisocial elements of both individuals and groups, though its objectives are basically sound and commendable. Perhaps it is time to make a special effort to get out of the candle-light age without losing perspective."

However, conference reports of the type cited now begin to formulate a significant body of experience. The 1949 report includes sixteen pages on "Program Building," with a discussion of "Group Work" techniques and a bibliography, and 31 pages on the "Role of the Volunteer," including courses for training, bibliography, etc. It lists as factors to be considered in the formulation of *objectives*:

1. The felt needs of a neighborhood or community.
2. The unfelt needs of a neighborhood which are concerns of the Center staff.
3. The concerns of others such as teachers, social workers, nurses, doctors, police, judges, business and civic leaders.

The 1951 Manual included fourteen major sections, each with bibliography. In it the question was raised: Is the denomination justified in putting money into Christian Centers? The answer was as follows:

A Christian Center is a missionary outreach of the church, in which all of the valid skills and techniques of the social sciences and

[1] From a 1949 Chicago Area Conference report.

of informal education are used by consecrated Christian leaders to minister to the physical, social, cultural, and spiritual needs of both the individual and the community: to the end that community life be enriched and that the individuals served may be led to a personal commitment to Jesus Christ as Lord and Master.

The Christian Center begins with the assumption that the "good life" is to be found in the Christian way. It is motivated by Christian purposes for Christian ends. It is sponsored by Christian people and Christian organizations. Its staff members are committed Christian missionaries who are seeking to be instruments through which the redemptive power of the love of God can reach and transform lives. It seeks to minister to the total needs of its constituency, including and emphasizing man's spiritual needs; and to this end it provides opportunities for Christian teaching, Christian fellowship, and the Christian commitment of one's life.

The Christian Center, by its location in marginal areas, by its organizational structure, and by its program is better equipped than the average church to reach people who have a negative reaction to the traditional church programs. It is better equipped to reach people of non-Protestant backgrounds. It is better equipped to reach those who live in areas of economic poverty, cultural lag, racial tensions, and nationality conflicts.

The Christian Center, by the very nature of its ministry, cannot live in a social vacuum. The Center must consider itself as being a part of the community and definitely related, consciously or unconsciously, to all social forces affecting the community's life. Therefore the Christian Center will not attempt to do its work without reference to the other community resources. The Center will welcome active cooperation with such agencies as the schools, police, courts, social agencies, government officials, and churches. Throughout the cooperative process, the Christian Center will constantly render its services in the spirit of and in a manner consistent with its Christian purpose and commitments.

In certain "Workshop Findings" it was said: "The Center should serve all the needs of the people of the community, regardless of race, color, or creed. The Center's services should be limited only by the capacity of the staff, the facilities of the Center, and the willingness of the constituency."

The movement treats the Community Chest as not a policy-making organization, interfering with program policies. It is recognized that "one of the major difficulties between a church and a church-related Center is the difficulty of budgeting staff time between the two. The church usually demands more than the staff can give directly to the church."

In 1950 a total of 139 staff members were reported by 58 Centers; and 20,000 members attended 893 groups an average of five times a week.

The 1950 financial support of these Centers may be tabulated thus:

| | | |
|---|---|---|
| Denominational societies [a] | $155,000 or | $7.75 per Center member |
| Community chests | 117,000 or | 5.85 per Center member |
| Other contributions, including $86,000 from state conventions [a] and $70,000 from individuals and fees | 156,000 or | 7.80 per Center member |
| | $428,000 or | $21.40 per Center member [b] |

[a] The sum of these items is $241,000, or 16 cents per Baptist church member.

[b] Of this, approximately $12.05 per Center member is from denominational sources.

It is argued that the Center approach is "an economical way to reach people" as compared with the reported local expenses of certain American Baptist churches in typical cities:

| City A | $36.00 per member per year |
|---|---|
| B | 23.75 per member per year |
| C | 26.00 per member per year |
| D | 24.00 per member per year |
| E | 39.00 per member per year |
| F | 68.25 per member per year |

Similarly, the cost of reaching each of the 244 persons who were baptized and affiliated with the American Baptist Convention churches, in this "least likely field," was reportedly $987.70, as compared with $1,325 in the churches of City A, $1,230, in City D, and $700 in church extension situations.

Clinical results are said to include:

1. Lives committed to Jesus Christ and his way of life.
2. Decreasing rates of juvenile delinquency.
3. Community integration.
4. Interracial co-operation—"one of the most effective channels."
5. Laboratory experience in voluntary unselfish service. Developing leaders from people served.
6. Ministering to the real needs of people where they are.
7. Speaking out on social issues and leading people to seek Christian answers.
8. Getting behind every worth-while community effort to clean up local politics and government.
9. Sending people out into full-time Christian service—four young men out of one Center.

A section of the 1952 report, entitled "The Missionary Faces Contemporary World Problems," discerningly related neighborhood Centers to the struggles for freedom throughout the planet.

A concluding section on "Proposed Criteria" outlined in some detail evolving standards as to personnel, program, housing and equipment, and results.

Against this background of objectives, standards, and expectations increasingly formulated by frequent conference, we may now examine a few individual Centers. It must be remembered that Baptist Christian Centers vary as widely as Goodwill Industries in the degrees and nature of their connection with individual churches. Often they are closely related to strong individual congregations.

A good sample of this type is *Calvary Baptist Church*, at 8th and H streets N.W., *Washington, D.C.*—right in the heart of the city. This church will be known to many as the place where Dr. Walter S. Abernethy served with distinction for twenty years, ending in 1941. He is still listed as minister emeritus, and he pronounced the benediction on the Sunday this writer attended church at Calvary. Still earlier, Dr. Samuel H. Greene had served with such acceptability that a considerable portion of the group of buildings constitutes a memorial to him. The Community Center occupies the Fraser Building, a smaller structure at the south end of the group, on 8th Street. The present pastor, Dr. Clarence W. Cranford, has served thirteen years.

Calvary Church had total budget receipts for the year ending April 30, 1953, amounting to $180,955.35. The net cost of its community service for that year was $17,264.12. Its salary item for personnel other than community service amounted to $57,084.37. There is a total staff of 21 persons. A Church Door Canteen for Service Personnel, operated on Saturday nights involves an annual expenditure of $2,525.24. (There is also a Sunday Dinner Club, primarily for service men and women.) A typical (March, 1954) week's program included 26 meetings, ranging from one to seven a day, and averaging nearly four. An additional activity is a Day Nursery, conducted in the Sunday school rooms, which has "a capacity enrollment of 30 children" and a waiting list. Last year it served 59 different children, over half of whom came from broken homes.

The parish is divided into six districts, each with ten subdivisions, and still more fine-screened units. It seeks to enlist the support of all its members. The chairman of the board of deacons said at the annual meeting: "With old-age assistance and other modern relief, every person who is sincerely interested in Calvary will be found on the roll of regular contributors." "The fact of noncontribution could be made known to the deacons as a basis for deciding whether the interest was genuine" or the member should be placed on the inactive list. There were 3,585 members, including 107 now transferred to the new Clifton Park Church, established as a colony to the northward of the city during the last five years. There are two morning services—at 9:00 and 11:15.

For the last reported year the Community Center membership was 243, an increase of 43 over the previous year. Monthly attendance exceeded 75 per cent, with a daily average of about 43 persons. Boys and girls attending Calvary Sunday school as well as the Center numbered 23. There were sixteen at the Center with no church affiliation. The rest attended one of nineteen other churches.

Activities include game room, movies, numerous clubs for boys and girls, boy choir, woodshop, swimming and Saturday night youth programs at the "Y," ceramics, archery, picnics, basketball, fishing, hikes, and camping trips. "Through each of the activities . . . we hold at the forefront the personage of Jesus Christ and the many teachings which He has given us to follow. . . . Calvary's efforts . . . over the past six or seven years have brought much fruit for the Lord." Some of those attending the Center "have never known anything but reprisal and abuse" at home.

Calvary's Sunday school enrolled 2,273, or 65.4 per 100 of its church members. Average attendance last year was 1,069. Adults enrolled numbered 1,070, or 47.1 per cent of the total Sunday school enrollment; and average adult attendance was 508. The school had a budget of nearly $6,000 and a balance of more than $1,000 in the treasury. Its gross income is nearly $15,000 a year, a third of this going for benevolences.

Thus the Community Service program is only a fraction of the total activity of this parish, which draws its strength from the entire metropolitan area but seeks to serve its immediate neighborhood.

The active program at *Park Baptist Church, St. Paul, Minnesota,* also includes a Christian Center. April 30, 1953, this church had 464 members, 362 of whom were active, a gain of ten in total and two in active membership during the preceding fiscal year. Total receipts exceeded $20,000; local expenses were $14,042.13; benevolences amounted to almost $4,000. Net surplus for the year amounted to $1,926.51.

The Christian Center employs a full-time director, a full-time boys' and youth worker, and a number of volunteers: 15 adults and 4 students, and 26 special volunteers for outings and Saturday socials in one recent month. Secretarial service is available a few hours per week. March groups numbered 16, enrolling 319. All but one group had four or five sessions; their total attendance was 798. The largest group (a junior- and senior-high Tuesday evening fellowship) had an average attendance of 43. Attendance at 29 sessions of other groups without formal enrollment totaled 766.

The Center's governing board includes representatives from the American Baptist Home Mission Agencies, the Twin City Baptist Union, the local church, and several community organizations. These last include the P.T.A.'s of two grade schools and a high school, and a Commercial Club. An Episcopal, a Lutheran, a Methodist, and a Unitarian Church, as well as a Jewish Community Center, are also represented. The Center is open to all, regardless of race, color, or creed. It "aims at youth conservation through a broad program of leisure time activities. . . . There are clubs, craft classes and recreational programs from pre-school age through high school, plus an adult craft class and a Golden Age Club for persons of retirement age." The facilities of a near-by high school, the Jewish Community Center, and the Y.M.C.A. are also available. Organized in June, 1952, the Center grew out of the work of a young couple as adult sponsors of a youth group. Work began on a limited scale during the summer of 1952, mostly with younger children in boys' and girls' clubs.

In the first year 180 children and adults registered. The sum of $4,000 was spent. Total contacts in March, 1953, numbered 654; in November, 1,366; in March, 1954, 1,708. Such figures reinforce the director's hope for a third, part-time worker. The second year's budget (1953–1954) was set at $11,200. Activities include play school, story hour and handwork, clubs and classes, games and sports, and other recreation including parties, hikes, and trips. A graded schedule includes events for eight different age groups. There is activity every weekday evening except Wednesday, and on Saturday mornings and at noon Saturdays. Saturday evening social gatherings at St. Clement's Episcopal Church have enlisted volunteer help from both congregations, with assistance provided also by one or two other churches.

In January, when the registrations (i.e., memberships as distinguished from group enrollments) numbered 372, these members were divided thus:

| 120 girls, 30 women | | 218 boys, 4 men | |
| --- | --- | --- | --- |
| *Ages* | *Number* | *Denomination* | *Number* |
| 3, 4, 5 | 17 | Lutheran | 104 |
| 6, 7, 8 | 55 | Roman Catholic | 101 |
| 9, 10, 11 | 86 [a] | Baptist | 45 |
| 12, 13, 14 | 100 [a] | Methodist | 42 |
| 15, 16, 17 | 78 | Presbyterian | 19 |
| 18 | 2 | Jewish | 10 |
| Adults | 34 | 12 other bodies | 31 |
| | | Unclassified | 20 |

[a] A number of boys in these brackets attend practically every weekday.

The special significance of this Center for this report is (1) that it is conducted by a church of medium size without unusual financial resources, (2) that it commands community co-operation, and (3) that the church as such remains unapologetically central.

In somewhat greater detail we now present

## Case II—THE BAPTIST CHRISTIAN CENTER, MILWAUKEE

In 1890, on Milwaukee's South Side, then an elite residential area, the largest Baptist church in the city was housed in the building now chiefly used as a Christian Center. In 1923, when the South Church moved farther out, a small group of people stayed on in the old building. From them started both the Center and the present Hulburt Church.

The State Convention helped, and the national Woman's Home Mission Society provided a worker. In 1934 Rev. C. Dwight Klinck came as director of the Center, which is located at 611 West Washington Street, at the corner of South Sixth Street. He stayed until 1946. To meet an obvious community need the church auditorium was remodeled to make both a gymnasium and a chapel. The latter was rented to the Hulburt Baptist Church, which is a separate organization, named after a state Baptist executive. In 1942 the Center was incorporated and became part of the War Chest; and in 1946 it was accepted as one of the "Red Feather" services of the Community Council of Milwaukee County. (This is placarded on the outside of the building.) Since 1942 the two budgets (church and Center) have been separated.

The membership of the Center was recently found to be

> 50 per cent Roman Catholic
> 25 per cent Lutheran
> 9 per cent Baptist
> 3 per cent Methodist
> 2 per cent Episcopal
> 6 per cent other Protestant
> 5 per cent no church preference.

The Center does all it can to encourage its constituents to observe the festival days of the Christian Year in accordance with their various church connections.

The articles of incorporation provided that the purpose of the Center should be to "develop better citizenship and the more abundant life as we find it in the life and message of Jesus Christ: and to that end to provide facilities for leisure-time activities, contacts with home, a spirit of Christian friendliness and helpfulness, and community programs: and to promote interest and activity in community, city, state, national and world affairs."

The nominees for the membership of the exceptionally strong Board of Directors must be approved by the executive committee of the Wisconsin Baptist State Convention, and at least two-thirds of them must be members of Baptist churches (Article IV).

Article VIII provides: "The person who is appointed by the Wisconsin Baptist State Convention in conjunction with the American Baptist Home Mission Society as Director of the Milwaukee Christian Center shall have general supervision of the work for which the corporation is responsible; and such Director shall be elected a member of the Board of Directors of the corporation and shall be an ex-officio member of all its committees."

The purpose of the Center, as publicized in recent annual reports, is now formulated thus:

1. To develop among children, youth, and adults a sound and practical attitude toward life, and a belief and conviction that the Christian way of life is The Way of Life.
2. To help our members to understand what democracy means, and to give them practice in democratic living through the group process.
3. To provide opportunities to develop creative interests, abilities, and skills through various crafts and hobby groups, such as ceramics, wood, metal, leather, photography, cooking, sewing, and hooked rugs.
4. To develop the leadership abilities of our members and to show them how to use these abilities in the Center and community.

Since 1946 Rev. John A. Craig has been director; he is also pastor of Hulburt Church. Mr. Craig served as a chaplain in the

Marine Corps and has had experience in a Kansas City, Missouri, Center. Associated with him are three group workers, an office secretary and several assistants, part-time and custodial personnel, and 24 volunteers, some of them students: a total of thirty persons.

The Center serves all ages, from three-year-olds up through the Golden Age Club for people over sixty years of age, which just celebrated its eighth anniversary. Six different age brackets are recognized, with different-colored membership cards for each. A busy schedule of activities features gymnasium and other classes (and weekly movies), from 3:30 (or 1:30) to bedtime, five days a week, also Saturday morning, afternoon, and evening. There are four two-week sessions of summer day camp.

The staff members visit in the churches, and church groups visit the Center. The director is active in Milwaukee social work and is studying for a master's degree in group work at the University of Wisconsin School of Social Work. The Center belongs to the National Federation of Settlements. Recent improvements in the building include two new furnaces and new basement facilities (a new game room accommodating up to 75). A new building is dreamed of, some day. If there were large-scale new housing, the whole situation might be somewhat changed.

In 1952–1953 the enrollment was heaviest in the 11–13-year bracket, and among adults:

| Years of Age | Number |
|---|---|
| 3 to 5 | 95 |
| 6 to 8 | 167 |
| 9 to 11 | 230 |
| 12 to 13 | 158 |
| 14 to 17 | 143 |
| 18 and up | 215 (chiefly adults) |

The economic status of the in-migrant residents is down, there is an increase of the "no church preference" type, and the returned copies of a monthly mimeographed "Leaf" show an increase turnover in population, or mobility rate. A weekly one-page bulletin, "The Bud," lists the gymnasium schedule for the ensuing week each Friday.

The emphasis is shifting. For example, an item in the October, 1953, "Leaf" declares

### The Club Is the Thing

> The days of big mass activities at our Center are over. We are placing most of our emphasis upon the friendship club. This year we have close to 30 of these group meetings each week.

This change in policy may account in part for a drop in organized club attendance, which climbed from 4,224 in 1946 to 9,991 in 1949, but dropped to 8,568 in 1951, as well as for the increase to 9,066 in 1953. (Total attendance of groups with definite enrollment amounted to 21,595; including individuals and groups without enrollment, last year's contacts numbered 64,267.)

The same issue of the "Leaf" contained the following editorial paragraph:

### Do You Teach Religion Here?

> "Do you teach religion?" is a question that we are often asked. To answer such a question, we must know what the person asking the question means by religion. Does he mean some particular creed, some denominational doctrine, such as Lutheran, Methodist, Catholic, etc.? If so, the answer would be no. If the person means by religion the difference between right and wrong, that the Christian philosophy is the way of life, the rights of others, the Golden Rule, the brotherhood of man and the Fatherhood of God, then we must plead guilty. Those are the principles on which our democracy is founded. These are the principles

that unite people. Our Settlement House is to help people to learn to live together happily.

The Center's treasurer reports the following main items of income for the last fiscal year:

| | | |
|---|---|---|
| American Baptist Home Mission Society | $ 2,030.62 | |
| Woman's Baptist Home Mission Society | 1,800.00 | 17.5 per cent |
| Wisconsin Baptist State Convention | 1,880.04 | |
| Rent from Hulburt Baptist Church | 450.00 | 14.9 per cent |
| Fees and sales | 4,428.36 | |
| Contributions | 510.85 | 3.1 per cent |
| Contributions for specific purposes | 485.35 | |
| Community Chest | 21,062.00 | 64.5 per cent |
| | $32,647.22 | 100.0 per cent |

It will now be of value to consider briefly the locale of this work. The Center is located in Block 23 of Census Tract 113 on Milwaukee's near South Side. To the east is Census Tract 114; to the south, 116; to the west, 112 and 117. A summary of some of the 1950 census data for these five tracts will characterize the immediate neighborhood objectively.

The total population for the five was 23,268—as a whole almost equally divided between the sexes, but with more males in Tract 113, and especially in Tract 114. Foreign-born included Yugoslavs (754), Austrians (428), Germans (420), Poles (418), and Mexicans (161). In three tracts (112, 113, 114), Yugoslavs and Austrians predominated; in the other two, Germans and Poles. The number of Mexicans has increased rapidly since 1950; and these have been mostly adults, to whom a larger number of children have been born in this country.

The nonwhite population in 1950 was only 120 for the five tracts; only 12 of these nonwhites were Negroes. Tract 115, large in area but with a relatively small population, lies between the five tracts and Lake Michigan. Of its 1,456 inhabitants in 1950, foreign-born numbered 234—chiefly Yugoslavs, Mexicans, and Poles.

Other pertinent data may be summarized thus: Median school years completed ranged from 8.2 to 8.6 as compared with 9.1 for Milwaukee as a whole. Three of the five tracts showed a higher percentage of people in the same house in 1949 and 1950 than did Milwaukee—85.0 to 85.9, as compared with 83.2. Median income ranged from $2,583 to $3,310, as compared with $3,340 for the city. Average rent was $31.66 to $40.88, as compared with $45.90 city-wide; median rent, $29.23 to $38.64, as compared with $43.49. Median single-house values varied from $6,399 to $7,832, as compared with $11,086 city-wide.

Just a third of the homes were owner-occupied, as compared with 43 per cent in the city. Two-unit houses led, with detached singles a close second; and houses with three or more family units made a slim third. In the five tracts the absence of private bath or the fact of dilapidation was three times as frequent as the city-wide average; crowding, as shown by the percentage of homes with 1.51 or more persons per room, was 4.1 as compared with Milwaukee's 3.1. Mechanical refrigeration was reported by 75.1 per cent, as compared with 87.2 for the city; television by 22 per cent, as compared with 23.9; central heating, 71.8 against 82.3.

Of the males employed, more than a third (33.9 per cent) were operatives, a fourth (25.1 per cent) were craftsmen, and an eighth (12 per cent) were laborers. Then came clerical workers (7.8), service workers other than household (7), managers (6.1), sales workers (3.7), and professional and technical people (3.4).

Of the women employed, almost a third (32 per cent) were operatives; more than a fourth (27.6 per cent) were clerks, almost a sixth (15.3 per cent) were service workers other than household, and more than a twelfth (8.5 per cent) were sales personnel. Professional or technical workers were 5.4 per cent; managers were 3.6; craftsmen, 2.8; private household workers, 2.5.

This Center was chosen in part because it was thought to be one not connected with a church. This proved to be misinformation. Hulburt Church is a very live organization. It had 32 accessions last year, and four during May, 1954. Of its families, 77 live in the neighborhood, 50 outside; but the farthest of these is less than half an hour away by auto. The staff help, as individuals and volunteers, in the church. The membership now totals about 150. A Spanish congregation, with an attendance averaging nearly forty, grew out of the interest of one family. There is a morning service and a Sunday school chiefly conducted in English but with one Spanish class for little children.

Hulburt Church reported an income of $5,261 during its last fiscal year, of which $3,684 was from envelope receipts; and its budget for the current year proposes that $1,600 shall be paid to missionary and interdenominational causes, out of a total of $4,665. Probably both figures will be surpassed.

The church publicizes and utilizes the Vacation Bible School of the Christian Center, open for boys and girls ages 3 to 13 for three weeks of "learning, fun, and fellowship."

On the Sunday following the 1954 American Baptist Convention, the sermon period was given over to four brief reports by three of his staff associates and the pastor. They featured the work of the denomination, especially in its world-wide missionary outreach. The minister is robed, as are the two choirs of boys and girls.

While the Center serves everybody, without restriction of faith, Hulburt Church is unapologetically denominational, but practices open membership. If more adequate quarters could be erected, the pastor would want the church somewhat separated. As it is now, either the gymnasium in the Center has to be closed or it is too noisy for a meeting in the chapel on the other side of the wall.

Whereas in some great churches a Center is a phase of their work, here a church moves forward with vigor because it can rent its meeting place from the Center and secure the services of the Center staff on a part-time or volunteer basis. Here the church wins its own members, but the Center serves all alike. Wherefore a good case worker might prove even more helpful than a church visitor. In any case, "changed kids" are regarded as more valuable than polished floors. The Center serves as an arm of the Church, reaching farther into the life of the community, to serve even those whose religious leaders may be suspicious of such nonsectarian ministry.

The director of the Center acknowledges that organized social work has great contributions to make on the technical side. At the same time he feels that in terms of motivation and personnel the Church is in a position of unique strength. He is confident that "religion is caught, not taught," and the genuine spiritual quality "rubs off" from consecrated workers. The Center specializes in individualization through group processes, which provide a sense of "belonging."

The Center is neighborhood-minded. It operates a youth fellowship on a membership basis, with half the members Baptist, others Roman Catholic, Lutheran, etc. Boy and girl relations, parents' night, and similar features are organized under competent visiting leadership. Here sectarian interest and parochial control are outweighed by community need.

The director lives next door. The staff seem very much a part of the neighborhood. Even if the population should decline, the people who remain are likely to have above-average need for social services. Were a new, more functional building available, the Center might perhaps better be located two or three blocks south on higher land with better transportation facilities. An all-purpose social hall seating several hundred, a regulation-size small gymnasium, and a variety of crafts rooms would be desirable. Such a Christian Center could continue to supplement the mass-type social services available at municipally operated centers, adding a plus of motivation, individualization, small groups, and neighborhood loyalty.

*Other Neighborhood Houses and Community Centers*

*Methodists* also are experienced in this sort of service. The Bureau of Urban Work of the Woman's Division of Christian Service of the Board of Missions of the Methodist Church reports "76 settlement and community centers and 34 other projects serving urban areas." "Our interest," says Mable Garrett Wagner, executive secretary of the Bureau, "is in the family in its neighborhood setting."

The latest annual report points out that "many long established projects have discovered new opportunities for service due to shifting populations, new housing developments, and widening community interest." For example, West Side Community House, Cleveland, fifty years old in 1954, "reports a 16 per cent turnover in school enrollment in the area during a four months' period." Likewise Wesley House in Memphis recently celebrated its Golden Anniversary; so did Wesley Community House in Louisville. Among new projects is a Community Center sponsored by the Baltimore Conference, utilizing the facilities of Mt. Vernon Place Church in downtown Baltimore.

The 1952 quadrennial institute for Methodist Settlement Houses and Community Centers featured in-service training for both board and staff members of the Bureau. Personnel policies are being increasingly developed. Board and staff from the centers are encouraged to attend regional meetings of the National Federation of Settlements. At the 1953 National Conference of Social Work a fellowship luncheon assembled twenty-two board and staff representatives of the Bureau. A 1952 three-day retreat featured group-work principles and philosophy, with special attention to group dynamics. A chief need is "alert, well-trained, experienced leaders with a sense of 'mission.'" Of such there is a "serious shortage."

One or more nationally sponsored Methodist institutions for community service are located in each of 25 states; Conference-sponsored agencies exist in 18, of which 10 states are additional to the 25. Appropriations of the Bureau for the last fiscal year totaled $522,294.

To name only some of them, these units include such agencies as

Homer Toberman Settlement House, San Pedro, California
Marcy Center, South Side, Chicago
Newberry Center, Chicago
People's Community House, New Orleans
Leslie Bates Davis Center, East St. Louis
Pearl Street Community House, Youngstown
Moore Community House, Biloxi

and a score or more of centers, settlements, schools, clinics, etc., for Spanish-speaking Americans, in New York, Florida, Texas, New Mexico, California, Puerto Rico, and the Virgin Islands.

Moreover, concludes a thirty page booklet on *Methodism and the American City*, "As the National Council of Churches in the United States grows, there are more interdenominational ways of work and wider ways of cooperation."

Likewise the 30th Annual Report of the Board of National Missions of the *Presbyterian Church U.S.A.* cites "seventy-odd Houses of Neighborly Service and community service . . . about a dozen (of them) wholly supported by the Board. For the others the Board provides guidance, when needed, serves in an advisory capacity, and usually takes the initiative in calling a conference of the directors." Statistical tables show the number of workers and activities, attendance, etc. An occasional item like "no statistics available" or "receives some support from Community Chest" attracts the attention of one who has visited the institution in question.

*Congregationalists* also have experimented with neighborhood houses and community centers, sometimes in co-operation with Presbyterians. The tendency in some quarters seems now to be to relate such agencies to one denomination rather than to two or more. Whether they should be related to a local church, or any local congregation should be separated from a social service program, especially if the latter seeks secular support, is a moot question. Some feel that the primary responsibility of the Church is religious, and that secularizing tendencies should be resisted, without detriment to social services rendered. This whole problem needs up-to-date study.

## Chapter IV

# Churches Associated with Highly Specialized Welfare Agencies

Some famous social work enterprises have grown out of parish programs. Here we consider not these specialized welfare agencies but the churches related to them, viewed from the standpoint of fellowships of worshipers. Such congregations have the very great advantage of being able to profit by the skills of secular vocations.

For example, churches with community centers have developed ways of "reaching children that might be utilized by other churches." (*The Urban Church and the Larger Community,* prepared for the Methodist Convocation on the City Church, Columbus, 1954, Panel V, pp. 11, 12.)

*All Nations Foundation in Los Angeles* is a Methodist agency participating in Community Chest funds and is a member of such national organizations as the American Camping Association and the Boys' Club of America. It operates a Boys' Club (ages eight to eighteen), a Girls' Community House, a kindergarten or play school for preschool children (morning and afternoon), a clinic (medical and dental), as well as a chapel, each with its own director. Other features include a year-round camp, a social center for boys and girls, and a youth project unit. Total clinic services in 1953 numbered 28,606. Physicians rendered 3,200 hours of volunteer service at the clinic. Similarly impressive figures could be cited for the other units of service.

This work was begun in 1917 by Bishop G. Bromley Oxnam,

who saw "this once fine old residential district becoming Los Angeles' most neglected. . . . Here is a missionary center for pockets of people caught between factories, warehouses, and Skid Row. This is the part of town where children find it hardest to be good." So much the more is camp meaningful. Clubs and activities for elementary and high-school ages are supplemented by adult recreation, library, gymnasium, and auditorium. Rev. John L. Mixon directs the professionally trained staff of 25 Christian men and women, succeeding Dr. Robert A. McKibben, who served 25 years.

Rev. John B. McGee is the minister of the *Church of All Nations* unit. Last year six preparatory members were received into full membership, and fifteen others by transfer or reinstated. Sixteen were removed by transfer or otherwise. Local church members contribute about half of the annual church budget of $10,000.

The Church of All Nations unit in Los Angeles is relatively small. It is interracial, with approximately 100 full members— 30 per cent Negro, 10 per cent Mexican, 5 per cent Japanese, the rest "Anglo." The Sunday school, which enrolls 227, with an average attendance of 58, is 60 per cent Negro. The church works primarily with the families of its children. Denominationally related and supported, it has all the organizations of any Methodist church and has available the Foundation agencies listed above. The Methodist Men seek to work among the fathers and men of the community. A Mothers' Club is sponsored through the Community House.

A large housing project is an important feature of the environment. It provides the church with three member families, and about fifty children attend weekday religious education classes conducted in co-operation with the Church Federation.

The establishment of a self-supporting church seems improbable for at least a few years. There is a rapid turnover of families, incomes are low, Mexican-Americans suffer a language handicap, the Roman Catholic Church is relatively strong, and many of the Protestants are Southern Baptist newcomers from the South.

(The Larger Parish idea is reportedly already adopted by the Presbyterians in Los Angeles and under consideration by the Methodists.)

We now quickly leap across the continent to consider another church of the same name, in a situation which Mr. McGee knew intimately for ten years, and where Bishop Oxnam once worked as a student.

## Case III—THE CHURCH OF ALL NATIONS, BOSTON

It is less than a third of a mile from the Boylston Street subway station on Boston Common to 81 Shawmut Avenue, where one is already in the "South End." There the Church of All Nations is the spiritual center of Morgan Memorial, Inc. This Methodist Church is now housed in a distinguished building reminiscent of Christian Europe; its chancel is adorned with memorial paintings, its pipe organ was a $12,000 gift. Here are color, dignity, churchliness. The front outside wall consists of stones contributed by the Unitarians when they moved from Copley Square to their present Second Church site in 1912. The completion of the Church of All Nations edifice, which was at first only a first floor and a basement, was made possible by the Methodist Centenary Movement. The finished church was dedicated in 1918, fully occupied in 1919.

Hard by, in a tenement on Wheeler Street, Mary Antin, author of *Promised Land*, grew up. In 1868, long before her time, Henry Morgan (1825–1884), a picturesque pioneer, had begun work in this area. When he died, his peculiar will provided that Morgan Chapel, built in 1869, "neither a traditional church nor a traditional rescue mission," should always be served by a Methodist minister. To this arrangement the Benevolent Fraternity of (Unitarian) Churches, which had supported him, agreed. The Y.M.C.A. later surrendered its residuary claim. As late as 1903 the Unitarian contribution to the church amounted to $2,500; total receipts for that year, including those from the Boston Missionary and Extension Society of the M.E. Church, amounted to not quite $10,000.

In 1895 Rev. E. J. Helms was named by the Methodists to develop here an institutional church. In 1901 the original building (Morgan Chapel) was condemned, and a new structure, called Morgan Memorial, was erected. It was occupied in 1903. Because Unitarian trustees feared the effect of any general solicitation on their receipts as a denomination, $50,000 was borrowed. The 5 per cent interest on this debt proved a constant source of irritation. The Women's Auxiliary continued to use money from its fairs to pay interest until 1910.

When the church was unfortunately unable to meet the remaining $10,000 mortgage on its second building, the bank foreclosed. After an expert study of the Morgan Memorial Cooperative Industries and Stores, which had meanwhile been in operation for a number of years, the Unitarians withdrew from the joint management of the enterprise. When a finance campaign secured $51,500 and the church was able to buy back the building from the bank, it became a Methodist Episcopal Church, but committed to the service of all. Individuals from at least four other denominations helped financially, and the good will of the Unitarians was maintained. When the mortgage was burned in 1912, Bishop John W. Hamilton declared: "City evangelization is a work of such large proportions that no one denomination can cope with it. Protestants must unite in its solution, as we are doing here at Morgan Memorial." Of late this enterprise could not technically be termed "interdenominational." Yet it has avoided both the sectarian and the undenominational pitfalls. Recognizing that "the handicapped know no denomination," certain non-Methodists have made noteworthy gifts to Morgan Memorial.

The church printing in those days listed all the Morgan Memorial work but distinguished between religious and social service activities. The earlier "complex and cumbersome management" (a Unitarian and Methodist joint committee had been established in 1900) now gave way to a denominationally administered church, which rented out space in its building for Morgan Memorial industrial activities. Finally, the new Church of All Nations, a third structure mentioned at the outset above, was completed in 1918.

This study deliberately neglects any further history of the early Morgan Chapel, and the unique leadership memorialized in the modern industrial and social service activities out of which in 1910 sprang the nation-wide Goodwill Industries movement, with institutions in more than a hundred cities, a resulting national association, and a denominational department. The general effectiveness of this work, locally and nationally, is not here analyzed or appraised. However, this latter development, now known locally as Morgan Memorial, Inc., has so vitally affected the fortunes and opportunity of the Church of All Nations that some of its local history and the scope of its work must here be set forth very briefly.

The situation at the Church of All Nations is now vastly different from what it was half a century ago; this church has at its very door quite unusual means of ministering to its constituency. While a Boston University School of Theology memorandum for students in the course on Church and Community, who visit Morgan Memorial each year, has termed this enterprise an "institutional church in the full sense of the word," it should be noted that in recent years the church as such has been increasingly differentiated, and has now no administrative responsibility for the very considerable industrial and social service program carried on by Morgan Memorial, Inc. An attractive sixteen-page pamphlet, issued in the forties, described the total enterprise as "A Great Institutional Church in the Heart of a Great City." Under the present regime it might perhaps be more accurate to describe the Church of All Nations as a congregation which has available the *facilities* of affiliated institutions to a quite unusual degree. Yet as a church it neither owns nor operates any of these institutional facilities. As its pastor says, "Our church, related as it is to Morgan Memorial, has many advantages and is prepared to give opportunities and to render service to its people, such as is presented by few other churches." For example, the use of day-nursery rooms is available for the very young Sunday school classes.

The beginnings of Morgan Memorial, Inc., are reflected in the motto, "Not charity, but a chance," and in the words attributed to Henry Morgan, "Never too poor to pray, never too weak to win." "Not alms, but opportunity" is what Helms, the first pastor, sought to provide for the needy. He offered self-help to "those exploited by capitalists and despised by organized labor." He was sure that "the best help is the help which helps others to help themselves by helping others"—a truth again conspicuously exemplified of late by Alcoholics Anonymous. Helms envisaged the social gospel less as a belief than as an active bond of union. Personally he held many beliefs that have not been institutionalized in the surviving agencies. His socialistic convictions, his desire to pioneer a new social order, with profit sharing, a farm co-operative, and large measure of democracy in management, were not shared by many who nevertheless supported him heartily. At the other extreme, his friendliness to Pentecostal groups doubtless greatly exceeded that of many who went happily along with him in social service and educational activities.

By 1905 Morgan Memorial Cooperative Industries and Stores had been incorporated to conduct the Goodwill Industries and other enterprises. Already "Goodwill" and "Morgan Memorial" had both become terms with a certain trademark value. Since 1917 educational, recreational, and social service activities have been differentiated from industrial activities. Something of the scope of the earlier work is indicated by a 1915 Training Institute and Children's Settlement announcement of help and instruction in two dozen widely differing subjects—music, crafts, etc.

In 1933 the Greater Boston Community Fund, an outgrowth

of the Associated Charities, gave its support to Morgan Memorial industrial work "as a nonsectarian agency . . . [especially in the light of the] increasing tendency to separate the Church of All Nations and its religious activity" from the related industrial work. The Greater Boston Community Council likewise found, in a 1943-1944 investigation, that while Morgan Memorial's motivation was "essentially religious," and this purpose was "basic," yet "the management disclaims any interest in proselyting. There is no discrimination against any individual group on any basis at all." More recently, this work, which has endeavored to maintain an entirely adaptable program, has withdrawn from the Community Fund, preferring to be freer in its policy decisions and to avoid those secularizing tendencies which have seemingly affected the non-Roman Catholic agencies jointly supported by the Fund. Morgan Memorial continues to be used by Boston University's School of Social Work, by Simmons College, and by Wheelock College as a basis for student field observation and activity. One significant factor in the situation is that the Massachusetts Council of Churches, while greatly interested in social action, does not now employ social service personnel.

Of what, then, does Morgan Memorial, Inc., now consist?

First of all, a *Day Nursery and Kindergarten* was organized in 1897. In 1938 the George E. Henry estate provided the present three-story building. There are facilities for 45 children of working mothers, and a long waiting list. The Women's Auxiliary to Morgan Memorial sponsors this work.

Second, what is now the *Youth and Children's Center* began as a phase of that activity known as the School for Applied Christianity, out of which grew the present schools of religious education and social work in Boston University. (A Morgan Memorial Academy, organized in 1918, was disbanded in 1924 in view of the increasingly effective Americanization work of the public schools.) This Center included the former Children's Settlement. Like other features of the work, it has been influenced by the decline of such foreign population groups as the Syrians and Italians in the neighborhood, and by the increase of Negroes. By 1946–1947, however, eighteen race and nationality groups were being served. The Youth Guidance Center has never had a complete staff or adequate funds. Its relation to the church and religious education has not always been clear.

Third, the *Charles Hayden Inn for Boys* began in 1932 with fifteen boys. In 1938 the Hayden Foundation provided the present seven-story fireproof building, which has a capacity of fifty boys.

Fourth, *Fresh Air Camps* were established. From 1898 to 1906 various places were utilized. In 1906 a South Athol farm was purchased, originally for the use of nursery children. This property now consists of 800 acres. The children's camps have the following capacity:

| | |
|---|---|
| Ages   2 to  5 | 80 boys and girls |
| 6 to  8 | 30 boys 30 girls |
| 9 to 11 | 36 boys 28 girls |
| 12 to 16 | 18 boys 24 girls |

By a 1940 grant of the Hayden Foundation there is also a Charles Hayden Goodwill Village, with six cabins, each with a living room and fireplace, and three rooms for three boys each, plus accomodations for their counselor. This phase of the work was begun in 1933.

There are also rest camps and an inn for paying guests, with 800 to 900 applications annually.

Fifth, the *Fred H. Seavey Seminary Settlement for Men,* formerly sometimes called the Seminary or Temperance Tower, was organized in 1915. (The problems involved in the relation of this work to the School of Theology need not here concern us.) Certain theological presuppositions of this phase of the enterprise are of interest. "The emphasis was not on the utter depravity of man as a result of original sin, and his complete dependence upon supernatural power to lift him from his plight." The objective of this institution was stated thus in 1918: "We believe Christ is in every man by virtue of his creation. We believe our job is to set the imprisoned Christ free and bring Him into control of the lost. To this end we are glad to use all that science and business and common sense may be able to contribute." This settlement was closed for a few months in 1921, and again from 1943 to 1946. Alcoholism was a major problem among stranded men. Up to 1942 there were frequent changes in employed personnel, and it was not easy to find the required type. In 1941 a study was made of 1,011 unattached men served. In those days fifteen religious services were held per week, with attendance at thirteen required. While Mr. Browning, director from 1946 to 1948, felt that "the actual success of the venture was extremely limited," the work continues against recognized odds.

This settlement is Morgan Memorial's way of promoting temperance. Its program includes

1. Self-supporting employment
2. Dormitory sleeping quarters
3. Personal guidance and counsel
4. Planned recreational program
5. Medical care, with referrals to hospitals for treatment of major maladies or diseases
6. Group activities and therapy, including religious orientation
7. Close association with other agencies such as Alcoholics Anonymous.

Under the guidance of this program an increasing number have gained and maintained sobriety and others have made definite progress.

Sixth, the *Eliza Henry Home* for employed women and B.U. student couples was established. Four floors are set aside as a home for middle-aged working women. The balance of the building provides apartments for married students, most of whom attend Boston University School of Theology. Many of them assist in the institutional program. Ministers throughout the world have received part of their training here. Student help is now decreasingly used because so much indigenous leadership has been trained out of the ranks of the handicapped.

Seventh, and in some ways most important, the *Goodwill Industries*, which Helms regarded "as a method of social change." Many readers are probably familiar with this now nation-wide movement, and its ubiquitous Goodwill Bags, which originated at Morgan Memorial. It has dealt with "broken down materials, broken down workers, and a broken down market." It has sought to provide "business plus, social service plus, religious organization plus, and democracy plus." Its original "idea of converting industry" dropped into the background in the light of the size of the nation-wide task. Emphasis shifted also from the needy and dependent as well as the handicapped to the latter only. However, it might be better to say that the word "needy" has been enlarged to include the socially as well as the physically handicapped. This shift was accelerated by the growth of public welfare services. Various "co-operative" phases of the movement were short-lived, as subsidies and contributions continued to be available. "To over 300 people every day Morgan Memorial, through its Goodwill Industry, says, 'We won't drop a coin in your hat, but we will put a tool in your hand and set you to work.' "

In the Goodwill there is a staff, a board of directors, and a corporation technically including all contributors of two dollars or more in cash or materials as members. There are five types of workers: (1) executives, (2) staff members and department heads, and (3) service workers—these three types of workers were formerly (in pre-social-security days) eligible for pension, in recognition of a "missionary assignment" of an hour per week in the program of the church—(4) special workers, and (5) opportunity workers or clients. In 1949 more than three-fifths of the first three groups were sixty years of age or older.

The problem of adequate production, from the business standpoint as over against the development of the ability of the worker to outgrow the need of scattered workshop conditions, is obvious. In December 1948, there were 84 employed in Groups 1 to 3, with 400 others belonging to Groups 4 and 5—61.8 per cent of them handicapped in some way. These latter workers are paid a minimum wage, with piece rates for the qualified.

An unemployment and social service department, which makes use of B.U. School of Social Work students, is reputedly understaffed.

The Noyes Work-Experience plan is just getting started. It is intended to provide job training for the handicapped (a majority are victims of cerebral palsy) and job placement. It is available for G.I.'s.

The fees for social service work are adjusted according to program and often consist of only a token payment. The Goodwill Industries are about 85 per cent self-supporting. There is some endowment. The gross budget for the entire Morgan Memorial program amounts to about $1,200,000 a year, with $300,000 paid to opportunity workers each year, who would otherwise be unemployed. From contributions $200,000 is sought.

The national movement, organized in 1910, was a part of the Methodist Centenary Program in 1918 and grew rapidly from then to 1929. E. J. Helms went round the world in its behalf in 1926–1927. In 1933 a National Association was organized. In 1953 there were 103 local organizations reported, with a total of $13,421,048 paid in wages (as compared with $1,730,000 in 1931), and $16,979,586 earned income. The handicaps presented among Goodwill Industries employees as of December 31, 1953, were distributed thus: 12 per cent blind, deaf, or with defective speech; 16 per cent with mental, emotional, or social handicaps; 16 per cent, handicapped by age or infirmity; and 41 per cent with orthopedic or general handicaps. The other 15 per cent of employees, who are nonhandicapped, serve usually as supervisory or executive employees.

This whole enterprise has thus become both a local and a wide-

spread corporate entity. Its vitality has been due in part to the
group need of its beneficiaries, but its administrative mechanism
is now quite other than the local church which was the occasion
and source of its origin. Structurally the church adjoins Morgan
Memorial, Inc., and provides inspiration for all its work. Admin-
istratively the two enterprises are now distinct, though closely
articulated as to program, a fact ironically emphasized by a
sign just to the left as one approaches the church: "Rear Entrance to Store."

The local leaders are proud that Edwin Markham, who once
visited Morgan Memorial, remarked afterwards, "What you are
doing here is as practical as chopping wood."

The Church of All Nations is "an ever present reminder of our
Christian purpose" throughout the entire Morgan Memorial enterprise. Thus, while it is only one of ten or a dozen phases of
the total work that can be differentiated, it has its own distinct
and central place and a growing self-consciousness as a center
of spiritual fellowship among a widely scattered membership
that is racially, economically, and educationally diversified to an
unusual extent.

Our primary concern in this study is with the (Morgan Memorial) Church of All Nations—of late the words in parentheses
have tended to drop out of use. Its present building, begun in
1917, was made possible in part by one large gift from George
E. Henry. In that year the church was separately incorporated
to conduct worship, parish visitation, and religious education.
Its present life cycle had begun, however, with the appointment
of E. J. Helms in 1895. It was that event from which flowed all
that has since happened, whether in the church or in terms
of social service. The present total enterprise is the lengthened
shadow of two men: Morgan and Helms. One pioneered, the
other built. Morgan Memorial is even more a Helms Memorial,
though not so labeled. Helms "accepted the appointment on the
condition that he be allowed to study the community and develop

a church program suitable to the needs of the neighborhood. He was especially insistent that a children's program be developed." [1]

In spite of diversity there has been a fine loyalty. People have stood by. Permanence is up, turnover is down. Witness how *the percentage of members continuing five years or more has steadily risen*:

| Five-Year Periods | Per Cent Continuing Five Years or More |
|---|---|
| 1925–29 | 6 |
| 1930–34 | 18 |
| 1935–39 | 20 |
| 1940–44 | 40 [a] |
| 1945–49 | 80 |
| 1950–52 | 87 |

[a] In 1943 there were 37 members who had been active for 25 years, since the occupation of the new church building; and 13 others were still on the rolls though they lived at a distance. "It has never been the policy of the church to try to keep its members after they have moved from the South End." They are encouraged to move out and transfer to other churches, unless willing to accept important active leadership in the Church of All Nations, in spite of the handicap of distance.

These figures should not be permitted to give the impression of an aging membership. The pastor reports with satisfaction, "We are growing at the base of our church—at the level of young members."

An effort, immediately following the erection of the new building, to increase the membership from 250 to 1,000 seems not to have reached its objective. By 1920, however, membership had reached a high plateau at more than 500. Dropping off in the early forties, it began then to recover. By 1948 there were 453 members, but only 370 were active. While half of the members were either foreign-born or children of foreign-born, the need

[1] Quoted from p. 79 of "The Development of Morgan Memorial as a Social Institution," by Charles Wesley Fisher. To this Ph.D. dissertation (B.U., 1949) this study is greatly indebted. Dr. Fisher's interest was only incidentally in the Church of All Nations; the present study makes no effort adequately to analyze and appraise the work of Morgan Memorial, Inc. Unless otherwise indicated, quotations are from this thesis.

for services in other languages had so sharply decreased that they had been discontinued five years earlier. Half of the members were white, half were Negro. The record shows the familiar pattern of close correlation between membership losses and changes in pastoral leadership or policy. At the end of the last Conference year, with a new denominational method of computation, full membership was 418.

In any fair consideration of membership figures, not only the nature but also the number of the available population must be taken into consideration. The neighborhood in which the Church of All Nations is located has long been an area of declining population, as well as one of low economic level and great social problems, e.g., a high tuberculosis rate.

What sort of community did Helms find?

By house-to-house visitation exact knowledge was acquired.[2] The South End was originally a fashionable residential district, but since 1870 the poor had moved into the area, while people of better economic status had now developed the Back Bay. Encroachment of business had probably hastened this migration. "The territory between Dover Street and the railroad (just south of the Chapel) [was] more compactly built with dwellings than any similar area of the city." [3] Edward Everett Hale called this part of the South End the most "charitied" region in Christendom—so far as he knew.

Said Helms, who had served in the B.U. Settlement in the North End, "I went into the most vicious neighborhood I have ever known. I have visited most of the slum sections in nearly all American cities but I have never seen anything quite so bad as the conditions around Morgan Chapel" (in the late nineties). On the other hand, things were not as bad in Boston as in other cities,[4] and here such "evils do not exist in their fullest develop-

---

[2] Cf. also Robert A. Woods et al., *The City Wilderness,* 1898, a study of the South End by South End House workers.

[3] *Ibid.* This social work classic describes the general area in rich sociological detail.

[4] *Ibid.,* p. 8.

ment. There is no such overcrowding as there is in lower New York; poverty has no such painful and revolting aspects as are to be seen in East London; drunkenness is of a less sodden and brutalizing character than in the corresponding quarters of many American cities; immorality is at least not obtrusive and defiant; and, amid a cosmopolitan population, representing nearly every grade of working-class existence, the labor problem is at about average degree of difficulty."

Because of the social consequences of overcrowding, day nurseries were from the first recognized as a potent weapon for health improvement.

In 1898 Woods estimated that of the males twenty years of age and over in the South End, 28 per cent were unskilled, 30 per cent were mechanics or artisans, 27 per cent were clerks or shopkeepers, 12 per cent were unemployed, and only 3 per cent were professional and mercantile personnel. There were then seventeen Protestant churches in the South End, most of them quite inadequately staffed, and there was "little cooperation" among them. Many of these churches were vestiges of the South End's earlier and better days. Only a few ministers now lived in the area and frequent staff changes were the rule in the Protestant organizations.

One of five Congregational churches in the area, Berkeley Temple, is said to have been chronologically second only to St. George's in New York as an institutional church; none of the five survives. There were two Episcopal churches; one of them, St. Stephen's, "tried to bring rich and poor into fellowship through a common experience of worship [and] . . . to have the social activities follow from the religious worship. . . . [It] tried to avoid using the activities as an incentive to membership." Other Protestant congregations included three Baptist, two Methodist, two Presbyterian, one Lutheran, one Unitarian, and one Universalist (the Everyday Church). It was claimed that two-fifths of the population were Roman Catholics—German, Irish, and French. The German Catholic church allegedly had a bar as a chief source of its revenue. Six or eight settlement houses served about 7 per cent of the population. By 1948 there were only two Protestant churches left in the immediate neighborhood: the Church of All Nations and the Episcopal Church of the Good Shepherd.

In 1900 Josiah Strong said, "St. Bartholomew's [in New York] shows what can be done when occurs the rare combination of a big brain, a big heart, and a big treasury." Fisher points out that Morgan Chapel had the first two "but was pitifully lacking in funds." [5] Its 1899 budget was only $3,180.42. The Unitarian missionary organization owned the property, and the corner was leased to a drugstore. When illegal sales were discovered, Helms insisted on the termination of the drugstore lease, though this rental was the chief source of his salary. Likewise, through arranging for the substitution of different tenement tenants, prostitution in the neighborhood was reduced.

Not only were resources meager, but policies had to be sharply changed. When Helms decided to discontinue free Sunday breakfast given to men who had been locked in, to hold them for "preaching service," attendance dropped off from three or four hundred to scarcely a dozen, who were probably more deeply interested. Professional gamblers attended the chapel service in those days in order to sell policy slips to the worshipers! Public bath facilities and a laundry were installed in the chapel basement, to supply what the "homes" in the neighborhood lacked. A bath cost five cents. A former immersion box was used to shower the people who washed in the basement, thus substituting nonsacramental sprinkling as a cleanliness device. It is said that in this neighborhood the few bathtubs did often serve as coalbins. A Saturday morning industrial school was begun. The Saturday night entertainments held in these early days have been described by Mary Antin.

In 1896 a vacation Bible school, with one helper, served 400 children. In spite of the fact that within a few days nearly every

[5] Fisher, *op. cit.*

pane of glass in the vestry was broken, this was the beginning of the permanent Day Nursery and Kindergarten, organized in 1897. The first month's enrollment was 39 children, and the average daily attendance for nine months was sixteen. The sanctuary was used. Parents paid five cents a day.

In 1896 an employment bureau was also begun. In 1900 industrial work was established in one room, later to grow into the present Goodwill Industries. In 1897 a music school was started.

By 1902 Morgan Memorial Church reportedly had 160 members, 1,000 constituents. For the next two decades its Sunday school enrollment exceeded its church membership, and even now its Sunday church school is one of the largest in the New England Conference. It enrolls 480; its average attendance for the regular year 1952–1953 was 261. Summer attendance in 1952 averaged seventy. Total church school enrollment, including evening youth groups, was 717, as compared with 450 in 1946. After the new church was built in 1918 the Sunday school continued to grow for a decade, then dropped off during the depression years, and still more sharply in the early forties, followed by recovery.

By 1912 it was said that 10,000 families of twenty nationalities lived in the area. A thousand children were attending some Morgan Memorial activity.

For many years the problem of language was a real one; later, as the number of foreign-born decreased, this became a less serious difficulty. In 1914 a New England Association of Bi-Lingual Churches was formed. Plans for the new building envisaged, besides a strong English-speaking congregation, others speaking German, Swedish, Norwegian, Italian, Syrian, Armenian, and French. Other denominations were to be invited to share the new building for their bilingual work without cost. As late as 1917 two-thirds of the congregation of 400 were of foreign birth or parentage. A school for bilingual Christian workers in the industrial centers of New England was proposed.

Great as was his interest in social service activities, Helms soon saw the need of a building to be used exclusively for religious purposes. He wanted foreigners to mingle with Americans in worship, and Americans with foreigners. He did not want immigrants who had been used to great church buildings to be "kept away from us in ugly mission halls." In October, 1921, it was declared, "In this edifice . . . the poorest and the most illiterate will be given the best that Protestantism can give in the way of loving kindness, inspiration and education. . . . While the gospel will be proclaimed in the various languages of the people living near the church, these new Americans will be helped as quickly as possible to understand English and become thoroughgoing Americans. The rich and the learned will work and worship with the poor and unlearned." These ideals are still operative.

There seems not to have been entire unanimity on the matter of language. Because the Boston City Missionary and Extension Society favored the arrangement, Italians, Portuguese, and Scandinavians were separately organized, "despite the protest of Helms." As late as 1922 a prospectus and manual made little attempt to differentiate between religious activity and social service and education. The Church of All Nations then reported Italian, Portuguese, Syrian, and now Negro departments, as well as English-speaking, Educational, and Americanization departments. Negro work had been organized in 1921, following an influx of colored population. More recently Italian, Syrian, and Negro groups had their separate additional Sunday afternoon or Sunday evening services, and their own pastors. These language and racial groups were extras. Their members were never excluded from Sunday morning worship; the chief congregation was always inclusive in its welcome and make-up. As early as 1918 it was announced that the church was "open and free to all. Pew sittings will be assigned to those desiring them."

In 1922 the Negro leadership declared: "We are not a 'mission to colored' nor a separate church; nor must we lose the identity of our racial group as a working unit in the Church. Our aim is to have an increasing colored membership with racial leaders; and with the fullest measure of group initiative and responsibility compatible with hearty loyalty to the Church and her program." Sunday vespers were only one of several activities. This was one answer, a temporary one, to some of the problems of interracialism. In order to avoid segregation, the Negro group had pro rata representation on general boards and committees. This congregation was urged to attend all church functions and services in addition to those of the group, and to strive to furnish greater numbers of new teachers for the church school. In 1925 there were 160 members of the Negro congregation, and 1,211 constituents. The loss of a beloved pastor meant waning interest. Separate Negro services were discontinued in 1948.

From 1920 to 1947 there were two groups of Methodist Youth Fellowship adolescents—white and colored—for fear of interracial marriage. In 1947 it was decided to experiment with interracial group meetings. Joint sessions led to the union of the two groups in 1948. Meanwhile there had been a transition from an entirely recreational youth program at the Youth Center. By 1945 the Methodist Youth Fellowship had been limited to Protestants who showed some interest in the Church of All Nations. Sociability and inclusiveness were both emphasized. Midweek social activities drew fewer whites; after discussion at a retreat, they were discontinued. A young adult fellowship, formerly a colored Christian Endeavor Society, was designed to be interracial but became predominantly Negro. As elsewhere it was difficult to avoid making the inclusive merely transitional.

In 1943 all bilingual work was dropped. For the twenty-fifth anniversary of the dedication there were fortunately available Italian, Negro, and Syrian choirs as well as the Chancel Choir and Carolers.

In 1923 Professor Charles M. Carroll of the Department of Social Service, Boston University, directed a Community Survey, which was reported in a bound volume of 159 typed pages and in a twenty-page printed summary. Sponsored by the B.U. School

of Religious Education and Social Service and the Parish Welfare Bureau, its foreword gave Helms a chance to say, "We now
need a social engineer."

At that time (1923) the chief foreign-born population in the
parish was reported to be

|  |  | *Per Cent of the*<br>*Total Foreign-Born* |
| --- | --- | --- |
| Russian |  | 24.0 |
| Italian |  | 16.5 |
| Syrian |  | 14.5 |
| Irish |  | 6.5 |
| Polish |  | 2.8 |

More than half of the population (55.3 per cent) was American born, but only a fifth was native-born of native parentage.

Religiously, in 1923 the percentage distribution of the neighborhood population was reported thus:

| Non-Protestant |  | 47.1 |
| --- | --- | --- |
| Roman Catholic | 23.6 |  |
| Jewish | 13.7 |  |
| Greek Catholic | 7.5 |  |
| Others | 2.3 |  |
| Protestant |  | 7.4 |
| Unknown |  | 6.5 |
| Indifferent and unclassified |  | 39.0 |
|  |  | 100.0 |

Of the Protestant population in the vicinity in 1923, Methodists were 30.4 per cent—almost twice the proportion of any other
group. Of the members of the Church of All Nations, 54.2 per
cent were white English-speaking people, and 27.3 per cent were
Negroes; but less than 4 per cent of the households in the parish
were said to be Negro.

In 1902 there were several colored clubs, and as early as 1905
Negroes were taking considerable part in the work of the church.
The Negro population of the immediate vicinity has sharply

increased. The so-called "New York" streets (zoned for light-industry redevelopment, and therefore marked for demolition) are now largely inhabited by Negroes. The Church of All Nations neighborhood as a whole is said to be only about 20 per cent Negro, and much less so than the blocks nearest to the near-by Tremont and Union Methodist churches, half a mile south. These latter two congregations are located less than two blocks apart; the first is white, the second is Negro.

Census-tract figures for 1950 are instructive:

| | *Per Cent Nonwhite Occupancy* | *Number of Blocks with 10 Per Cent or More Nonwhite Occupancy* |
|---|---|---|
| G–4 | 13.6 | 5 out of 6 |
| I–1 | 11.4 | 7 out of 21 |
| I–2 | 27.9 | 11 out of 20 |

Tracts including *Tremont Church*

| | | |
|---|---|---|
| L–3 | 52.4 | 14 out of 19 blocks with *a third or more* nonwhite occupancy |

Tracts including *Union Church*

| | | |
|---|---|---|
| L–2 | 80.7 | 13 out of 15 blocks with *50 per cent or more* nonwhite occupancy |
| *Boston* (as a whole) | 5.2 | |

The records of these other two churches and the geographical distribution of their constituents would appear to be important data for any metropolitan denominational or ecumenical strategy, along with any consideration of the future of the Church of All Nations. Parishioners of both races come into the neighborhood to attend the Church of All Nations, but probably few if any go outside the neighborhood to attend other Methodist churches.

The pastor estimates that between 50 and 60 per cent of the

people now living in the vicinity of the Church of All Nations are Roman Catholic. Thus the population would now seem to be more non-Protestant, and decidedly more Negro, than it was half a century ago.

In the years just before 1920, as earlier, there was considerable encroachment of business. While World War II stopped the construction of new business buildings, and the migration of business into the area was arrested, housing shortage and increased Negro population combined to offset out-migration; and for a while net population loss was reduced. Yet in the 1953 parish reports the religious education leaders confess that "we have noticed this year more than ever before the large number of families who have moved from the South End." It is a safe guess that replacements if any will be harder than ever to win. In all such situations the church has to strike while the iron is hot; it must make its impact *now* while the people are still in the neighborhood—next year they may be gone.

In 1949 the Greater Boston Community Survey considered the social neglect in the South End to be greater than in any other area of the city, but Fisher saw "no evidence that in the immediate future there will be a lack of population or a lack of social and economic problems in this parish." Helms had hoped for a "social engineer" to reconstruct the whole social scene; this dream is still unfulfilled. Morgan Memorial has had to be content with salvaging goods and people in an area where population has shrunk as well as changed.

Population figures for each of seven census tracts in this general section of the city were tabulated for the five decennial years 1910 to 1950. In the area bounded by Kneeland, Elliott, and Stuart streets, Arlington and Tremont streets, Dover Street, and the Fort Point Channel, total inhabitants dropped from 37,799 to 17,144 in these forty years. As would be expected, the loss was greatest in the northern portion of the area, which has been increasingly given over to business. The seven tracts, taken as a whole, show the following losses:

| 1910–1920 | 24.8 per cent |
| 1920–1930 | 26.5 per cent |
| 1930–1940 | 13.7 per cent |
| 1940–1950 | 4.9 per cent |
| 1910–1950 | 54.6 per cent—chiefly before 1930 |

If tract-decade trends are observed, from 1910 to 1940 there were increases in only two instances, as compared with 26 instances of population loss. During the last decade, however, there were slight population gains in three of the seven tracts, though these were more than offset by the losses in the other four. Taken together, the Morgan Memorial tract (G–4) and the one just south of it (I–1) increased 7.8 per cent during the decade; yet since 1910 they had lost 57.2 per cent of their population (78 per cent in G–4, 42.7 in I–1). In the tract to the north (G–3) the population loss from 1910 to 1950 amounted to 82.5 per cent; east of Shawmut (G–2), 62.5 per cent; southward and westward the losses sharply tapered off.

Statistics of housing conditions and other social data are also significant. Omitting tract-by-tract details, the figures for the areas northwest of the church, to the south, and to the southeast (including the "New York" streets) show low ownership occupation, excessive dilapidation, and crowding into small quarters to be strikingly evident. Population density appears to occur in pockets. Children are in evidence on many streets, owing to lack of play space.

Whether in terms of average or of median rent, of property values or of income, economic status is obviously low. Likewise central heating is relatively infrequent, mechanical refrigeration only less so. Television naturally is not afforded. Almost all the housing is 35 years old or older. Education also lags. This is an area of cumulative handicaps. The Police Station at Tremont and Warren streets has the reputation of being "the most arresting in the world"—even if not deserved, such words stamp the area. In 1953 the American Public Health Association found that 98.9 per cent of the dwellings in the New York section, so called, had defects making them substandard. The chief defect was single egress.

As a whole the seven tracts nearest the church reported three major types of employment:

| | |
|---|---|
| Professional, managerial, etc. | 12.3 per cent |
| Clerical, sales, craftsmen, etc. | 24.7 per cent |
| Operatives, etc. | 61.7 per cent |

In the light of such figures it is not surprising that the Church of All Nations not only has made no phenomenal growth in membership, but, like many churches, has had difficulty in holding its own, in terms of active membership. Perhaps the more significant fact is that "its flag is still there," very much so, and flying as bravely as ever.

Nor is it surprising that the pastor keeps close to the director of the Housing Authority and is interested in all recommendations for housing projects. Whatever the federal policy, all housing becomes of increasing importance to a parish like this, scores of whose families now live in projects. Likewise code enforcement is seen to require eternal vigilance. In a church of this sort a week-night "University of Life" is naturally interested in Christian social action, particularly in community terms.

In 1922 a local statement of faith was devised, but there was no requirement to subscribe to it. Provision was earlier made for affiliate members, who did not forfeit their membership elsewhere and were not required to answer the questions in the Methodist Discipline in the affirmation of their faith. In recent years this type of membership has been de-emphasized. In line with the general policy of Methodism, the roll has been cleared of inactive members (68 of them in 1952–1953, plus 16 others removed by adjustment).

Over against this loss by revision, eleven preparatory members became full members, and a dozen were added by profession of faith. The measure of commitment appears to be deepening.

"Every new member—youth and adult—has attended classes for instruction in the meaning and purpose of church membership." A major problem is: Can replacement of membership loss be rapid enough to keep the enterprise strong? Yet prospects are still at hand in sufficient numbers. "Within our neighborhood there are many who have no church connection. In a city they must be sought for; they do not come by themselves."

It is to meet this situation that the CUE program has been devised. The three letters stand for Community, Unity, and Evangelism. Neighborhood leaders provide a connecting link between the church and its staff and the people it serves. Visitation, especially of the sick and absentees, as well as of new neighbors, is organized. Here is systematic outreach, the quest for news, the building of fellowship, the development of group spirit in neighborhood and church.

The geographical distribution of the membership is of interest. There is considerable concentration within a third of a mile. The percentage living within easy attending distance has steadily risen. In 1923 only a third of the members resided within the parish. This rose to 40 per cent in 1930, and 49 per cent in 1950. The leadership is naturally more scattered. The 85 Morgan Memorial workers who help in the parish program live all over Boston. (In a way this "artificial constituency" is even more important than the exceptional facilities available.)

Nineteen members of the current Official Board are distributed as to residence as follows:

| | | | |
|---|---|---|---|
| South End | 5 | Brookline | 1 |
| Cambridge | 3 | Dorchester | 1 |
| Lynn | 2 | Medford | 1 |
| Roxbury | 2 | Somerville | 1 |
| Allston | 1 | Watertown | 1 |
| Beacon Hill | 1 | | |

In 1949 the church Board of Trustees, made up of four members of the church and four other Methodists, had not met since

1942. Five of its members were directors of the Goodwill Industries also. The Official Board meets monthly; it has the standard commissions: education, evangelism, finance, and missions. The fourth quarterly conference serves as the annual meeting of the congregation. There have been annual program conferences of the entire Morgan Memorial enterprise. The work of the church is for the most part administered by the staff.

From 1898 to 1942 Edgar James Helms was both superintendent of the developing industries and social services and pastor of the church. Often in those days little attempt was made to distinguish the church from the other activities. In his last years the elder Helms held office both in the National Association of Goodwill Industries and in the denominational department concerned with such work. After his death there was naturally a general reorganization. He had numerous associate ministers.

Perhaps the most picturesque of these was Professor William L. Stidger, professor in the B.U. School of Theology and no mean poet and prose writer. His function was chiefly that of Sunday morning preacher. His church bulletins, often featuring either his own verse or an excellent picture (religious art or an exceptionally beautiful nature scene), or both, attracted nationwide attention. On one Sunday there were more than 100 visitors, attracted no doubt in part by his interest in an Oxford Group convention. To Stidger, Morgan Memorial was "Christianity with its sleeves rolled up."

In 1949 Henry E. Helms, son of E. J. Helms who had been chaplain of Morgan Memorial and pastor of the Church of All Nations, became associate superintendent, and in 1953 the head of the total enterprise. Rev. John E. Barclay succeeded him in the dual role of pastor and chaplain. We turn now finally to further details of the work of the church as presently conducted.

A church with a budget providing even now a salary of only $2,600 (plus house, and $100 car allowance) could not afford a man of the caliber needed at the Church of All Nations, without the arrangement by which its pastor is also the chaplain of

Morgan Memorial, Inc. (In earlier years the minister's salary was far less—approximately $500 in 1910 and adjacent years, and only $1,400 in the twenties.) It would be interesting to document the spiritual opportunity afforded by this chaplaincy. One of the most rewarding responsibilities of pastor and chaplain is a morning radio program (8:10 to 8:30 Monday through Friday, now over WVOM) which features the chapel service of the Goodwill Industries. Workers attend on company time but may absent themselves if they prefer to work. Ministers from 23 denominations—perhaps 1,700 different men—have assisted in these services, reputedly the oldest religious radio program in New England.

The parsonage is not in the immediate vicinity, so that the minister can escape occasionally from his almost 24-hours-a-day responsibility. Parsonage expenses for the last Conference year (taxes, maintenance, oil, phone) amounted to $522.34.

The student associate minister is chosen from among the more mature Negro students at the B.U. School of Theology. He is paid $1,600 a year and given an apartment.

The director of religious education is also paid $1,600 and apartment; the church visitor, $1,300 plus $300 from Morgan Memorial, Inc. Both are full-time workers. The minister of music, who directs the Chancel Choir, receives $1,094; and $375 is allowed for the children's choir (the Carolers). In 1953 the choir paid $175 into the church treasury. The sexton is paid $1,300.

The Sunday school program has already been cited. During 1952–1953 weekday released-time religious education classes held in the church reached 57 children in grades 4, 5, and 6 and the remedial class at Abraham Lincoln School. Rev. John L. Bryan, who recently concluded three years as student associate, taught the sixth-grade class. Said he: "As for these children, all of them nominal Christians, their innocence concerning Christian teachings has been amazing, many of them never having heard of the Apostles' Creed, and at first only two members could repeat the Lord's Prayer. Here is an indication of Protestantism's unfinished business; and we had better take care of it, in the face of a more militant and aggressive Roman Catholicism." (While unapologetically Protestant, this enterprise has been remarkably free from anti-Catholic belligerency.) This last year 107 children have been enrolled.

Church school workers had a planning conference at Henniker, New Hampshire. Eighteen teachers attended a fall training course. Home visitation was undertaken by the teachers. The co-operation of the School of Theology has enabled students to earn religious education credit. The parish Board of Education meets regularly. A 1952 vacation school enrolled 60. There was new emphasis on decision days.

Two weekday church clubs, one for boys, one for girls, enrolled thirty members.

Intermediates and young people met in Sunday morning class sessions, and there were Sunday evening fellowship groups, as well as weekday activities. Young adults met Sunday evening. Total youth enrollment was 48.

The church visitor, formerly called parish director, saw to it that 2,162 calls were made in the parish. Of these, she made 1,378—a fourth of them (310) in the homes of nonmembers. She helped organize the work of 24 neighborhood groups. Visits to shut-ins and worship services in homes are important parts of the church program, in which even the children sometimes share.

A Woman's Society of Christian Service meets monthly. It received nearly $800 for the year ending March 31, 1953. It gave $250 of this to the local church, $220 to missions. Besides its 59 active members, it enrolled 24 inactive. The president lives in Everett, but the vice-president near by in Yarmouth Street. Three-quarters of the participants are from the neighborhood—most of them from disadvantaged homes.

The Wesleyan Service Guild is made up of working girls and women, ages 19 to 27, holding monthly evening meetings. It raised more than $200 and contributed half of it to the church.

Envelope collections for the last reported year were $6,528.69

for local work, plus $1,214.85 for World Service. Toward various apportionments other than World Service, $908 additional was received. (Over $10,000 has been subscribed for the current year.) Loose collections amounted to $756; the church school contributed $453.45. Morgan Memorial, Inc., paid $1,500 for the use of the church, an amount slightly more than offset by cost of heat, light, and power—$1,630.12. The New England Conference Board of Missions provided $4,416.67, or nearly a fourth of the total receipts, $18,401.82. This Board undertakes to cover the cost of the local missionary workers: the student associate, religious education director, and parish visitor.

There is an endowment, amounting now to nearly $30,000 ($28,491.56 at last report). Investment income amounted to $1,206.63 for the last Conference year. Most of that expected this year was earmarked for major church repairs.

At the time the new church was built, World Service giving rose to nearly $4,000, then dropped off. The Church of All Nations is now fifth in the Conference in the amount of World Service contributions, having overpaid its apportionment.

So, without moving from its tracks, this church has now swung a full cycle from the pioneering chapel program organized nearly ninety years ago, through a transitional period of federated sponsorship, into the life of a regularly constituted Methodist parish. In the last six decades the industrial and social service phases of its ministry have been separately organized, and have been reproduced, at least to some extent, more than a hundredfold over the country. The central ministry of worship and religious education, of parish calling and evangelistic outreach, and of world-wide church extension grows more and more pivotal. As the institutional phases of Morgan Memorial, Inc., have expanded, the determination of the local church to "be the church" has deepened.

This Boston history is in sharp contrast to developments in other cities, where no such survival value of the church has been achieved. By the time the Church of All Nations comes to its centennial, the distinction between services rendered and commitments made, between manifold activities and the spiritual powerhouse by which the members and workers are energized to serve, in whatever capacity, is likely to have become even more clear.

Here is a clinical experiment in church social service, of prime importance to American Protestantism. Here also, in Boston at least, whatever may be true of other Goodwill Industries, is proof of the enduring values of the local church fellowship and its historic spiritual functions. This church is interested in the total person, in terms of evangelism as well as social service. It gears its program not down to human status but up to higher potentials.

The population in the immediate neighborhood continues to shrink, through changes in land use. While for years to come there will be plenty of people to serve in the vicinity of the Church of All Nations, it seems likely that this church may find itself at the center of an increasingly scattered parish. Yet it cannot move, for it is anchored to an enterprise that occupies two city blocks. If it can continue to attract a third of its members within walking distance, may it not fairly seek to enlist the other two-thirds from the metropolitan area?

This church would seem to be a laboratory in which Methodists and other Protestants willing to serve under the Methodist banner for a period of years may work away at all the problems of a truly inclusive fellowship in the inner city, adapting its ministry to whatever ethnic groups live near it. If strong Christians can be induced to work here for a period of from two to five years, a certain percentage of them will continue to find the Church of All Nations the object of their continued loyalty. Others will have been trained for more competent, imaginative, and sympathetic service in outlying churches, or in congregations elsewhere. Only the few can be expected to live in such an area. Some of the more stalwart of those who live more comfortably elsewhere may prove strong enough and unselfish enough to lend a hand in the work of such a church, much to their own benefit.

In the absence of any centrally located Methodist church with a famous metropolitan pulpit, the Church of All Nations might well prove to be a shrine that Protestants from all over America and elsewhere will want to visit. If able preaching, satisfying worship, and actually inclusive fellowship can be combined down the years, is there any reason to doubt that a church of approximately 500 members can here be maintained indefinitely?

One cannot foresee the social changes that may impend in the longer future; one may guess that any short-range strategy will utilize this sturdy fortress of the faith as a part of the militant battle line not only of Methodism but of ecumenical Christianity at the heart of a constantly changing city. Says the pastor, "Our greatest problem is sin!" Only from such vigorous centers can organized Christianity ever make effective sallies into the secular paganism of life at the heart of urban America. The New England Conference may well continue to back this work in behalf of all Co-operative Christianity.

# Chapter V

# Parishes Adapt to Neighborhood Change

This chapter considers various churches which have proved adaptable to changing neighborhood conditions.

Sometimes a neighborhood is only slowly invaded by change, which affects it around the edges especially but leaves a solid core of residential need, even where the character of the population has become quite different. The near east side of Cleveland furnishes an example.

*North Presbyterian Church*, at Superior Avenue and East 40th Street, is of significance as the only Protestant church in a considerable section of the city. No other is located north of Superior from the Public Square to East 79th Street. In fact, there is only one small Protestant congregation on Superior between the center of the city and East 108th Street. This main thoroughfare is thus quite different from Euclid Avenue, slightly to the south of it.

Negroes live for the most part south and east of this area, but a few reside near St. Clair and 30th streets, and some colored children attend North Sunday School. The church's parishioners are a scattered lot, second only to Old Stone Church's in this respect. Many who begin their Cleveland residence near by join up at least for a while. In 1952, from one to ten households in ten communities in the county outside of Cleveland and three places beyond the county line, were represented on North's membership list, as compared with 216 households in the city. More than 100 census tracts were represented on the mailing list. One tract near the church was represented by 41 addresses; two others by ten; another by seven; several by six. Each of 66 widely scattered tracts had one North household. In early 1954, 258 addresses were distributed thus, by postal zones:

| | |
|---|---|
| Zone 3, including the church | 90 families (more than a third) |
| Zones 4, 5, and 15, south of the church | 11 families |
| Zone 8, along the Lake | 16 families |
| Zone 6, south of Zone 8 | 13 families |
| Collinwood and east | 24 families |
| East Cleveland | 12 families |
| Heights and beyond | 20 families |
| Zone 14 (west of the church) | 24 families |
| West Side and Lakewood | 42 families |
| Outside of the county | 6 families |

Organized in 1870, all of its members bringing letters from Old Stone, this church has loyally held the line during the last half-century. There are now ten Roman Catholic churches within half a mile, a fact which in itself witnesses to the heterogeneity of the population. Relations with the Irish parish (Immaculate Conception) have been cordial.

For more than thirty years, up to 1946, North Church was subsidized to a total of $90,000. The depression meant the reduction of its larger program, and aid was reduced to $600 a year. Then the congregation, under the leadership of Rev. Arthur R. Kinsler, Jr., who has been its pastor for 24 years, said, "Let's try to go it alone." As a result, the budget has doubled, and the membership, which had been cut in half between 1910 and 1940, has increased 20 per cent. More important still, "We kept it a church." The Sunday school had made a slower recovery, but it has increased in recent years. Recently nearly $5,000 has been spent on building improvements, and an $8,000 local expense budget has been paralleled by a mission quota averaging 10 per cent or more in addition.

The present closely pruned roll numbers 374 members. There

has been an average net increase of about 10 per cent from the inner city each recent year. The second-floor sanctuary, as recently altered, seats 300, plus 150 in the balcony. Average attendance is 100; on Easter Day 350 came, and 250 on Mother's Day, when a new pulpit was dedicated. The Sunday school now enrolls 159, as compared with only 89 at the end of 1952. The policy of conducting church worship and Sunday school simultaneously has increased attendance at both. Out of a total of 28 new church members, all but five came from the neighborhood, the rest from a mile or two east. Nine older people were baptized. Of fifteen recent accessions from the Sunday school, eight were by baptism. There were 39 infant baptisms last year.

The junior-high age group has increased, but the senior-high group is still small; there are only a baker's dozen young people in both groups. Thirty younger women make up the Ladies' Guild; the group of older women is falling off. Quite a number of displaced persons have come into the neighborhood, have stayed, and have joined the church. Its facilities are limited. One large main-floor room has to serve all recreational purposes, including the activities of a large Scout troop.

The neighborhood, while relatively near the heart of the city, is one of good economic status, though factory labor suffers some unemployment just now. This section of the city has fewer rooming houses than the Hough Avenue area to the east. Many a duplex owner rents the other half of his house. There are also many small homes, especially on the side streets. Apartment houses are located chiefly on Superior Avenue.

In the area (12th to 55th streets, Euclid Avenue to the Lake) there are over 25,000 inhabitants. "Scarcely a church in the Presbytery does not have one or more members whom it has received from North."

Presbytery feels that this church is its "definite responsibility." The area, while decreasing in population since 1910 and increasingly given over to warehouses and small industry, "still serves as a port of entry for the lower-income group." North Church is proud of its ability to go it alone but could use to advantage the services of a part-time woman, to serve as children's worker, educator, and visitor. It would be glad to share such a person with one or more other churches, if necessary. Presbytery plans to contribute a worker as soon as the proper personnel becomes available.

As over against general Protestant retreat, the success of North's "holding operation" has been marked by the long tenure of "a minister who was willing to see in this [inner-city opportunity] a permanent vocation rather than a stepping-stone to a church in an area where success would be easier."

Far more radical change has affected the *First Baptist Church of Chicago*, in the South Side Kenwood section of the city, which was built up between "The Fire" and the 1893 World's Fair.[1] The oldest church in the city, it had repeatedly moved. Then it stopped running. With a Caucasian tradition, even in a time of great tension just after Pearl Harbor, it employed a Japanese-American minister, who later became its senior pastor; it has now won an outstanding place as an interracial demonstration.

Reportedly, this church had lost its earlier community before the life of the organization showed it. In spite of a strong group of supporters able to underwrite any deficit, the situation in 1942 became highly precarious. A new pastor introduced the Every Member Canvass method. A famous Nisei episode was successfully weathered. Then Negroes began to move in. Just east of the more dense "black belt," this church now began to be one of mixed race. However, the congregation contains many members of relatively high professional status, and this is still in a real sense a prestige church.

This is shown by $78 per capita giving, as contrasted with only $40 at an interracial church of another denomination, where white-collar white members have been joined by Negroes of lower-middle-class status; or as over against a middle-bracket, racially

[1] See Lincoln B. Wadsworth, "In a Changing Community," in *The City Church*, Sept.-Oct., 1953.

mixed congregation of a third denomination in Chicago. First Baptist is still financially above average in its Association, as evidenced by building fund expenditures especially, and by exceptionally numerous large givers.

In 1950 Chicago had half a million Negroes; it may add another 400,000 in the current census decade, if it continues to increase its Negro population at 8 per cent per year. Like Detroit, therefore, most of Chicago's entire inner city is likely to be predominantly Negro. Whether white or colored, native or foreign-born, there are varying degrees of attractiveness among all peoples. Chicago struggles to discover a formula for congeniality that will make social stratification more Christian, rather than based on racial or nationalistic prejudices.

On Chicago's near northwest side, *Wicker Park United Lutheran Church* affords an example of social change that has involved nationality and language but only recently race. Located in an area commercially developed before "The Fire," this church for the most part serves a section that was also residentially occupied between 1870 and 1900. Here the Poles have been moving west and northwest, and even Polish and Ukrainian displaced persons have been moving away. Now the Puerto Ricans, with their Spanish language and Roman Catholic affiliation, have begun to move in.

This Lutheran parish was made famous a generation ago by its preacher, Simon Peter Long, who seems to have attracted a following rather than a permanent membership and was supported by well-to-do persons. Now this church does well merely to hold its own. Its people come loyally, many of them from great distances. The tendency is of course, for the young people to move out. There are about 300 confirmed members, 340 baptized. Communicants last year numbered 212. In connection with this church's 75th anniversary it entertained the Illinois Synod's 35th meeting.

Two other denominations had tried to plant a church on the same site, Hoyne Avenue and LeMoyne Street. Newcomers to

Wicker Park in 1879 were largely German Lutherans, who bought the original frame building from its unsuccessful owners. A new structure was erected in 1907. In 1909, in its heyday, it had 500 communicants, but the number has dropped to only 100. This is now the oldest Lutheran parish in Chicago still located on its original site.

Rev. Malcolm Shutters reports forty accessions in 1953, many of them from outside the neighborhood. The children served rarely stay in the vicinity long enough to be prospects for church membership. There is a community program; but from its religious aspects the Roman Catholics and Jews, who make up the overwhelming majority of the population, naturally stay away. The church co-operates with the Park district in teen-age square dances (seventy or eighty attend) and has maintained a hobby hour for fifty to sixty younger children. Films are shown two evenings a week in Wicker Park during the summer. In spite of the provision of bus transportation, Sunday-school enrollment has not increased proportionately to the energy expended. Released-time classes reach a somewhat different constituency, averaging 55, as compared with a Sunday-school attendance of 89 last year. There are a number of Neighborhood Houses in the area. At the instigation of Pastor Shutters, a Neighborhood Council has been organized and now includes 45 members and six community organizations.

The problem of language makes communication difficult. A German Catholic church has become Polish; so has an Irish parish. Only a handful of Germans remain, and there are no Irish now.

The church building, a solid structure, seats 400, plus 100 in the balcony and, if a partition is moved, an additional 150 in the chapel. Average attendance from January to Easter was 160. Easter saw an attendance of 475, which dropped to fifty the next Sunday.

As yet there is no financial problem here. Receipts amount to nearly $100 per communing member, not including a $12,000 repair fund this year. The church is foreign-mission-minded; two of its lay members sit on national boards. It has an unusual number of schoolteachers, a lawyer, and two businessmen; but craftsmen and clerks make up most of the membership. Young married couples are few; the number of single people, especially women, is large. Because they have few children, the adult members, who are of high average age, have more money to give to the church, and they give it. The budget, $16,000, includes $3,000 for benevolences; and the anniversary repair fund is extra.

"Outwardly the neighborhood bears little resemblance to a blighted area," wrote Robert L. Nicholas, editor of the Chicago *Tribune*'s financial page, in January, 1952. "The impressive old houses and well-built apartment buildings are still there and the plots of grass are neatly kept. But the interiors bespeak the tremendous change. Chopping up residential units has been going on for years and through conversion and bisecting of apartments and houses the over-all population has been vastly increased." In such a setting Pastor Shutters, formerly a missionary to China, has since 1949 (according to the executive secretary of the Board of American Missions U.L.C.A. "completely revived the spirit of [this] historic congregation . . . and has changed its program to serve its own community which has gone through many transformations. At the same time he has maintained the loyalty of many of the older members who have moved to the outlying districts of the Chicago area. We consider this work a model." [2]

Factors in the success of Wicker Park have been:

1. Sister Grace Boehling, parish deaconess, trained at the Baltimore Motherhouse, whose services are provided by the Board of American Missions. (There has also been a student assistant, and two young people have helped in the DVBS summer program.) Says Sister Grace, "We believe that we are building good foundations in a unified and coordinated program of Christian education and fellowship."

[2] Letter to the writer, November 11, 1953.

2. "The continuing support of a core of the original families of
the parish. They have provided the leadership—spiritual and
financial—to carry on the ministry to newcomers. The Sunday School superintendent drives 25 miles from his suburban
home every Sunday, and the choir director is a granddaugh-
ter of the founder of the church" (1952 Nicholas article).
Not in the Loop, the Wicker Park Church behaves somewhat
as if it were.

In 1948 it almost closed its doors. They are still open. The
pastor is denominationally and interdenominationally active.

Other inner-city situations involving adaptation to new needs
would include the *Community* (Methodist) *Church* in Chicago,
which has survived in an area where the Roman Church
thought itself to be serving adequately, and the whole group of
churches on Buffalo's west side, recently studied by a committee
working with Professor Rasmussen of Colgate-Rochester.

Likewise, in Los Angeles, churches of various denominations
face problems of social change. For example, according to an
article in *The Bible Teacher* by Rev. V. J. Waldron, the *Evangelical United Brethren Community Church*, 66th and San Pedro
streets, "has been sharing a growing interracial fellowship since
1946" in an area that "lends itself to a continuing pattern of segregation and strengthens the tendency to stereotype a people in
an uncomplimentary way. [But] the church should stay and serve,
developing a program adapted to meet the needs of all the people. This we are committed to do. . . . At the present time we
have Negro, Mexican and Latin Americans, Oriental and 'Anglo'
sharing together in all phases and departments of our church's
program and fellowship." The denomination's Department of
Missions makes a grant of $2,500 per year to this work. In all,
Mr. Waldron concludes, there are a hundred E.U.B. churches
"facing problems incident to changing racial and cultural conditions in the community. (See *The Telescope-Messenger* of April
25, 1953.)"

Eight years ago the Episcopal *Church of the Advent* in the West Adams section of Los Angeles was in the midst of a cultural island. Today it finds itself among large numbers of Negroes, Filipinos, mestizos, and Jews. After being a mission for 26 years, its budget has come up from $3,765 in 1944 to $16,325 in 1953; its communicant membership from 169 to 484; the pupils in its church school from 26 to 110.

Another instance of parish adaptation, combining downtown population loss and radical social change, along with high church-manship, is now set forth as

## Case IV—GRACE EPISCOPAL CHURCH, JERSEY CITY

Speaking on Alumni Day, January 21, 1953, at General Theological Seminary, New York City, Rev. Paul Moore, Jr., '48, pictured lower Jersey City, where Grace Church (Van Vorst) is located, as "a place where thousands of people live together in old houses lacking conveniences we take for granted." He added much detail, and concluded one paragraph of his address, "Nothing new, nothing exciting, but day after day after day of dirt, children, noise, fatigue, fear, eviction, dirt, children." In July (1954) Father Moore will have served five years in this parish. How did he happen to go to such a place?

Before attending Seminary he had served five years in the Marine Corps, attaining the rank of captain and winning the Navy Cross and Silver Star for bravery on Guadalcanal. He is now 34 years old. His wife was educated at Vassar and Barnard and is a member of Phi Beta Kappa. In Seminary among his associates were Robert Pegram (now 41), former boys' school teacher, and Kilmer Myers, a Navy chaplain, who saw combat in Europe. In 1948, while still in school, Father Moore as a senior, the others as faculty members, having had some experience in slum work and finding themselves unable to be as effective as they wanted to be among the people of the slums—these three men began to search for a bishop and a church interested in tackling the Church's ministry to the oppressed in depressed areas. "Somehow we had become identified with the plight of these tragic children and their familes," two of them have reported. "We knew we must have a parish of our own," as one of them put it.

Strong encouragement and financial backing came from Bishop Washburn of Newark, who was interested in what a classmate dubbed the "G.T.S. social conscience crowd." He provided "both the church and the tools." [3] The late Dr. H. Paul Douglass, foremost surveyor of urban church life, who had made a survey (see p. 101) of the downtown sections of Jersey City for the diocese, expressed the opinion that "while Grace Church parish might never become strong in numbers he could think of no point on the eastern Atlantic seacoast which stood in more need of such a ministry" as was proposed.

Let us ask in a little more detail, What sort of area does Grace Church serve?

A World Council observer describes the situation thus: "Economically, the surrounding population is sub-marginal, living in overcrowded, largely cold-water tenements, working occasionally but not regularly enough to assure an even minimum adequate living. [Many] are not the trade union members; they are the people who occasionally work at anything and in the meantime suffer from poverty and hunger. They are immigrants and the immediate descendants of immigrants: Irish, Poles, Italians, Germans. With the exception of a few Lutheran Germans, the white population of the area is Roman Catholic. Recently a substantial and increasing number of Negroes have moved into the area, together with a smaller number of Puerto Ricans. Protestant background exists chiefly among the Negroes. Crime, delinquency, drunkenness, prostitution, brutality—the whole gamut of evils attending slum areas are in clear evidence." The pastors can furnish plenty of concrete detail, with names, addresses, and types of human need.

"So far as can be determined, the activities of the Roman

[3] Frederick Sontag in *The Living Church*, June 10, 1951.

Catholic Church are confined to the administration of the sacraments, the conduct of parochial schools, [and referrals to appropriate Roman Catholic institutions]. It is suspected that the
Roman Catholic churches wield a fairly heavy political axe, especially in reference to issues which directly affect the Church.
Aside from the influence of the cult and schools and the supposed political activity of the Church, no [appreciable] impact
[seems] made upon the community.

"The case of the non-Roman churches is told by the history
of Grace Church prior to the start of the present work. It is the
history of a once thriving parish, the beginnings of disintegration
in the face of the immigration of foreign and Roman Catholic
groups, and the final abandonment of the parish by all except a
literal handful. For nine years prior to the start of the present
work [a Church Army layman was in charge of] the church. It
had [very little] impact upon the community. The same is largely
true of the Protestant churches in the community. A large number of store front churches exist. The largest of these has a congregation of from 30 to 50 people. It is to be doubted whether
these churches even in their sum total make any appreciable
impact upon the community."

This is an area which, according to Mr. Sontag, "is one continuous slum right down to the waterfront. Years ago the brown-
stone houses were inhabited by the wealthy. The Episcopal
Church was there, and several parishes flourished. But as the
area changed economically, the Episcopal Church moved out.
Now only Grace Church remains." Says Father Myers, "There
are areas in New York which are more depressed to be sure, but
Jersey City is as a whole the most down-at-the-heel, dismal, depressing city I have ever seen." He adds, with regret, what has
been "the usual story," not only for Episcopalians: "Our Church
follows the prosperous, abandons the poor." To these three priests
it was time to call a halt on this flight to suburbia. Said Father
Myers two years later, "Grace Church itself stood in the shadow
of a Roman basilica. Everyone 'fathered' us as we walked through

the streets. Still, we took heart when we noted the growing Negro population and remembered that half of America is un-churched. . . . It was a risk, a *calculated* risk. We took it and we are not sorry."

Here now is a parish with a $30,000 budget for the year 1954. Of this, $5,000 is to come from the parishioners, $7,500 in response to appeals to friends, $2,000 from endowment income, the balance from the diocese. The summer budget alone now exceeds $5,000, including camp fees. "There is no summer sag in Grace Church," says the *Urban News Letter* of the Episcopal Church.

Grace Church is an old parish. It is now directly responsible to the Bishop and operates like a mission, without a vestry; but, having once been a self-supporting church, it cannot under the canons of the diocese revert to lesser status. Some of the parish statistics for the last decade, as published in the *Diocesan Journal*, are summarized on page 100.

The Rev. C. Kilmer Myers, S.T.B., was a lecturer in pastoral theology at the General Theological Seminary from 1946 to 1949. After graduation from Berkeley Divinity School in 1940 he served successively as a fellow and instructor at Berkeley, rector of a Buffalo parish, chaplain in the U.S. Navy, and priest-in-charge at Grace Church, being the earliest ordained of the three men. For the last two years he has been vicar of St. Augustine's Chapel on Henry Street in Manhattan, one of the mission outposts of Trinity Church. Father Pegram and Father Moore are a Grace Church team, neither of them now designated as the senior priest. Two young people from the parish, a seminary student, and three women workers now assist the two priests. Another clergy associate is to be employed. Three seminarians help in the church school; one comes one night a week to help in the youth work.

The three women are Sisters of St. John the Baptist. They specialize in religious education, which requires special and costly adaptation in such a situation. Their strict rule of prayer contributes great power to the spiritual life of the parish, even if it seems sometimes to reduce their available time.

A lay member of the staff is now a seminary student. "St. Christopher's House, an eight-family tenement down the block, has been taken over to house the Sisters and the Monroe family —he is a lay worker, she is a registered nurse; and to provide much needed classroom, choir room, office, and meeting room space."

In the summer seven college and seminary students have helped in youth and adult group work and in recreational units with area responsibility. There has been some resentment because of alleged "high powered settlement house type of program by outsiders in the summer." It is hoped to avoid this through the development of more indigenous leadership.

This *team* ministry is important and essential. "One man would not be able to endure, emotionally or physically, the strain of the work" in such a church as Grace. "Moreover the mutual stimulation involved in team work is invaluable, especially when the work has no precedent and where counselling problems of such depth and intricacy are involved. A team also permits of a certain administrative efficiency through appropriate divisions of labor" and functional rotation.

These "high church" clergy, serving the remnants of an Episcopal congregation and all comers from the heterogeneous population round about, plus at least one "uptown" Negro lawyer, are seeking to establish *a eucharistic center for a worshiping community.* In general they prefer to develop lay leadership rather than to enlarge the paid staff. They believe in the Continuing Incarnation, and that the Church can give freedom and courage to hard-pressed people. Their concept of the Church pushes them out to serve; it also provides them strength to do so. To them the sacraments furnish symbolic instrumentation of the Grace of God, which it is their high privilege to mediate.

Of 400 people attending Grace Church on Easter Sunday, 1952, three-fourths (300) were non-Episcopalian in their back-

ground. But far more than these "look upon Grace Church as
the one place to which they can turn when trouble comes . . .
any kind of trouble from being burned out to domestic difficulties
and embroilments with the police."

The situation keeps changing. Total population may be shrink-
ing in the neighborhood, but there is still acute need for decent
places to live, in spite of huge projects now unsegregated. Negro
population growth is now less marked, Puerto Rican more rapid.
Of the adults in the parish, 60 per cent are Negro; among the
young people the percentage is higher. Five years ago the church
was all-white, with an attendance ranging from a dozen to thirty
worshipers. The church school averaged twenty or less. Now the
average Sunday attendance is 100 or more adults, and that of
the school 200 or more children. While the proportions have
changed, in terms of absolute numbers the non-Puerto Rican
whites have held their own. This change-over was not accomplished without losses. Quite a few members left before the new
regime began. Fewer than ten children, and fewer than ten adults,
remain from "the old parish." Evidently there was sharp con-
troversy, but that is now only a memory. Grace Church was
pioneering as "the earliest church to move in its specific fashion,"
according to the secretary of Urban Industrial Church Work of
the National Council of the Episcopal Church. Grace Church
seeks to serve "as the parish for almost all non-Roman, non-Or-
thodox people in lower Jersey City."

"Downtown" people in Jersey City are usually the sort of people who aren't leaders. The new clergy arrived in the parish with
"absolutely no plans" for details. The development of lay leadership has been a difficult but important requirement. One method
has been by organizing "Militants," who combine a prayer cell
and lay evangelism program. The Young People's Fellowship includes youth from other churches. Two groups need special attention: youth and young adults. The question is, What activities
best meet their needs? Bus service is provided for little children,
some of whom live as far as thirty blocks away. How to enlist the

support of indifferent parents for the church school serving their children is a problem. On Sundays church school is held at 10 A.M., starting with a children's Eucharist. The Holy Eucharist is celebrated also at 8 and 11 A.M.; and at 9 A.M. a Polish Baptist congregation of forty has used the church. There is a possibility of serving a Spanish-speaking congregation in the near future.

The building ("our beautiful Church, the unknowing gift of the dead to the poor of our parish," Father Myers calls it), erected in 1847, "with simplicity and great dignity," seating 700 easily, is of stone, with a copper roof. It has a square tower and is surrounded by an iron fence, from which the "Keep Out" sign was promptly removed. "From the noise and ugliness of [their] crowded rooms . . . the people come into the silent beauty" of a building that "is coming to life again, filled with new movement and voices."

A bright red bulletin board, saying "Enter into His Gates with Thanksgiving," continues to mark the entrance to the courtyard, at the rear of which is the rectory, a very important nine-room feature of the parish life.

Here the clergy and the Moore family (the children are eight, six, four, and two years old—the third one born soon after the Moores moved in on a 95-degree summer day in 1949) live on the second floor. On the third floor are quarters for the other clergy—Father Pegram is unmarried. Extra rooms are available for guests, including parishioners burned out of their homes, and needy warfarers. The "open rectory" policy is a keystone in this parish. The staff needs only to "come downstairs in the morning" and it is already in the midst of things—if not before. There is occasional stealing but on the whole the rectory is treated like home by those who share it. "Mrs. Moore has the impossible task of trying to keep the house clean, with a constant flow of callers, and open windows bringing in air laden with dirt." "A priest must always be near the rectory, for people come in at any hour with problems that demand immediate attention."

Says Father Moore, "Mrs. Moore [who is very much a member of the team] enjoys having a large and varied family. In the experience of living constantly with others we can, to a very small extent, identify ourselves with the experience of our people with whom privacy of any kind is more often the exception than the rule. Through our door all manner of men, women and children come seeking warmth, food, friendliness. As the church is the symbol of the first commandment, so the rectory provides a symbol for the second commandment—the persons in whom they may find their Lord, the table around which there is fellowship and unity and laughter. The parish is a family, this is their home. Here one is not a teen-ager or young adult, here he is John or Bertha or Mrs. Jones."

This rectory has been "a place where, any time of day or night, persons without homes and having no sense of community can come and be welcomed into both a home and a community. Here they may eat, sleep and be trusted as a friend." The large place of the rectory was hardly anticipated. Says Father Myers, "People . . . just began coming in; we did not stop them . . . they wanted 'community'; they wanted to be with other people; not with other people in the Hudson Tube or in a cheap movie emporium, but in a decent house. Most of them did not have decent houses. . . . The rectory *had* to be open." "Obviously what was needed . . . was a *community of persons,* but a community of persons resting on a supernatural base."

It is reported, "One parishioner remarked recently, 'When I feel down I come to the rectory because it is a happy place.' " This, says Father Moore, "may sound like the advertisement for a bad cigarette, but there is truth in it. We never know for sure who will be at supper."

Let not this report seem to romanticize this Jersey City rectory. To do so would be to be quite unfair. The visitor, especially the journalistic observer, may come away impressed with a "feeling of desperation, violent suffering and squalor, whereas much that goes on—really *most* of what goes on—is not so different from

*Virgil Cheek*

East Harlem Protestant Parish: The hand of fellowship at close of Sunday worship service, Church of the Son of Man, East 104th Street; Rev. George Calvert.

Sunday School children at St. John's United Lutheran Church, The Bronx, where the proportion of Negro pupils varies from one third to one fourth.

Rev. Philip E. Anthes, pastor of St. John's Church (Federated), East Boston, greets parishioner leaving an Italian service conducted by his associate, Gaetano Iorizzo. English-speaking parishioners join in leisurely conversations as they wait for the next service.

Grace Episcopal Church (Van Vorst), Jersey City: Track meet at the annual field day.

Fishing at Milwaukee Christian Center's day camp.

ese children will find it difficult to un-
rstand people with racial prejudice. At
John's United Lutheran Church, The
onx, they learn, worship and play together.

*Marsh Photographers, Inc.*

Mr. T. T. Clement, former Director, with skating enthusiasts, at St.
Barnabas', West Cincinnati.

The chancel choir members procession opening the morning service at
Morgan Memorial Church of All Nations, Boston.

East Harlem Protestant Parish: Church
School Worship begins with lighting
of altar candles, Church of Our Redeemer; Rev. Hugh Hostetler.

St. John's Church (Federated), E
Boston: A communion service sho
ing Italians and Anglo-Saxons p
taking of the Lord's supper.

*Egan Photo Service*

t. John's Church (Federated), East Boston: Boys work at jig saws and sander n woodworking shop in church basement. Equipment was bought with funds earned by the boys of the church.

Watching the swans at Milwaukee Christian Center's day camp.

*Griff Dav*

Grace Episcopal Church (Van Vorst), Jersey City: Boys' choir.

Milwaukee Christian Center Golden Age Club enjoying friendly get-together.

*Egan Photo Service*

t. John's Church (Federated), East Boston: Children celebrate the birthday of Annette de Modena, at the head of the table, during the summer day camp.

*Look Magazine*

East Harlem Protestant Parish: Summer outdoor block party sponsored by 100th Street Church.

"Hanging of the Greens" at St. Barnabas', West Cincinnati.

Playing at Milwaukee Christian Center's day camp.

*Virgil Cheek*

East Harlem Protestant Parish: Church history quiz in junior high school class, Church of the Ascension, East 106th Street; Miss Letty Russell, Educational Director.

*Virgil Cheek*

East Harlem Protestant Parish: Junior high school class, led by Mr. Angel Camacho, full-time member of the staff, Church of Our Redeemer.

East Harlem Protestant Parish: Learning by doing—primary girls' class in Vacation Church School, Church of Our Redeemer ( on 102nd Street).

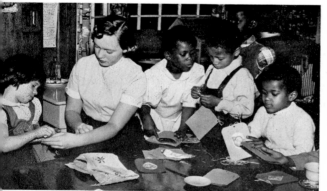

A kindergarten class at the Morgan Memorial Church of All Nations Sunday School, Boston, prepares folders for the minister to take to sick people.

A pupil at St. Barnabas,' West Cincinnati, with instructor in adult education class. He finished the sixth grade, coming only three nights a week, in two years.

*Look Magazine*

East Harlem Protestant Parish: Informal contact on a vacant lot. Rev. Hugh Hostetler in background.

*George Van*

Grace Episcopal Church (Van Vorst), Jersey City: Field Day. The pet contest is about to begin after "blessing the field."

*Virgil Cheek*

East Harlem Protestant Parish: Church council plans for life of a local congregation, Church of Our Redeemer; Miss Dora Martinez, Rev. Hugh Hostetler.

*Look Magazine*

East Harlem Protestant Parish: Boys' lives are touched through street activities. Rev. George Calvert; East 102nd Street block.

Counseling is an important function at Milwaukee Christian Center.

*Marsh Photographers, Inc.*

Miss Helen Lee, Director of Findlay Street Neighborhood House, with a volunteer staff member and a young house member at St. Barnabas', West Cincinnati.

*Look Magazine*

East Harlem Protestant Parish: Rev. Ranson Hammond working with parishioners during annual clean-up campaign.

*Griff Davis from Black St[...]*

Grace Episcopal Church (Va[...] Vorst), Jersey City: Players r[...] hearsing in the Rectory.

St. John's United Lutheran Church, The Bronx: The suggestion that the Lutheran Church is not congenial to the Negro is without foundation.

Taken at a church family night at St. Barnabas', West Cincinnati.

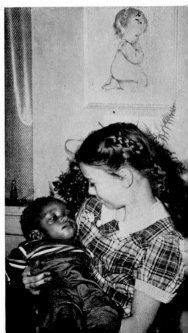

Grace Episcopal Church (Van Vorst), Jersey City: Father Moore instructing acolytes.

*Presbyterian Life*

Jackie Robinson instructs campers on what it takes to be a great athlete at St. Barnabas', West Cincinnati.

Rev. U. S. Fowler teaches adult class at St. Barnabas', West Cincinnati.

parish life anywhere." In all such situations to overestimate the "picturesque" is as bad as to understate how bad some conditions really are. One needs somehow also to convey "the natural, pleasant, and happy [experience] which makes up the majority of the ongoing day-to-day life of the place," according to the testimony of those most immediately immersed in it. They do not think of themselves as "unusual" or "heroic"; still less are they willing to call their attempt to fulfill the age-old mandate of the Church in any sense "experimental." Succeed or fail, in this one parish, they do not regard the Church as in any ordinary sense an "experiment."

In a city politically notorious, community relationships have been unusually important. A nonpolitical Intergroup Council is one agency which Grace Church clergy helped to start. It has already effected integration in all but one public housing project. There has been in the area little or no sense of community, a situation which Grace Church aims to alter for the better. "The factor of racial oppression opens the way for an inclusive community," which may eventually attract nominal Roman Catholics also.

Besides daily and Sunday services of worship, confirmation classes, Sunday and vacation church schools, and group activities ranging from recreation through crafts to discussion, there has been much intensive personal counseling. Other activities include rescuing of drunks, intervention in housing disputes, appearances before police, judicial, and jail authorities, special evangelistic campaigns, and public meetings on social questions—especially race. Work with children and young people has proved to be the most successful avenue of approach to adults. It was found that it took "18 months or more to come full cycle from the introduction to a child to the confirmation of its parents."

There is Holy Communion every weekday, the hour varying from 7:30 to 10 A.M., with Morning Prayer said fifteen minutes before. Evening Prayer is said every day at 5:30 P.M. "We all feel," said Father Myers, "that daily services are an absolute necessity in a situation like our own." A priest is in the church for confessions and counsel from 6 to 6:30 P.M. on Saturdays and by appointment.

At first parishioners may have had only an undefined sense of respect for the Church. As the parish has gathered momentum it was natural "to follow along with one's friends." But more than that, desire for ceremony has produced response to the liturgy of the church. At first this may not have been a conscious desire for worship, but eventually it was discovered that when the desire for worship does arise, at first perhaps quite unconsciously, only the Church can meet it. Other desires include those for decent recreation, for nondiscrimination, for help in problems of housing and rent, or in problems of personal living (marriage, sex, liquor, delinquency, crime, and the like).

As one observer puts it, "The fruitful method and mood of attack upon the total problem, is not the method of reforming a neighborhood, but rather the method of building up a Christian parish community. In the process demands for reforming efforts will appear—faster than they can be met. . . . Such a community is built up most effectively by *acts* of love in helping people." He concludes: "Effective evangelism is the process of living in a Christian community. This process entails instruction, living, Christian practice, and worship. It is the Christian community which makes the evangelistic impact upon the individuals and upon the community surrounding it, and in turn the community deepens those received into it." [4]

To function in this manner in a blighted area, in the midst of "dirty, tumble-down houses; ragged, listless people, and corner gangs of toughs" requires devotion and skill and some new tie that binds people together in the love of Christ. It means helping "two families sharing a common toilet (thirty to a toilet is not unusual) in which there has been no water for two years; a mother and ten children crowded into two basement rooms without a kitchen or toilet of their own; a husband, who works at

[4] This and earlier quotations in this report are from an unpublished paper of the American Study Committee of the World Council of Churches.

night to support his family of eight, spending his days for . . . two months house hunting—his apartment has been condemned and he can find no place to move because he is a Negro and has too many children." (Here, as in East Harlem, this sort of concrete episode can be multiplied endlessly, including true stories of what rats do to children's faces.)

Social action at Grace Church, according to Father Moore, means:

1. The parish, as such, should take action on social issues—especially those affecting the lives of its parishioners.

2. It must avoid political entanglements.

3. When necessary, the clergy must take an active part in committee work. "Why must Christians sit back making pronouncements but be loath to dirty their hands in committee work? How can we live off endowment in cleanliness and comfort while our Christian brothers are on the street?"

Father Moore brings to his task an articulate zeal. "The eyes on the street, the policeman's eyes, see depravity and instability; the eyes gazing over the mask, the doctor's eyes, see disease and death. But from the hill of Calvary, something else can be seen; interlacing the old streets and the unpainted houses, are bright strands of poverty and simplicity. This is perhaps what our Lord sees as he walks among his beloved poor. Once a gibbet became a throne; a slum can become a kingdom of humility and love."

Father Myers in one of the three addresses given in April, 1950, on "The Priest and the Industrial Area" and published by the G.T.S. Missionary Society, mingled much picturesque detail with reflective thought.[5] He endeavored to free himself from the temptation to play up the picturesqueness of the parish in the effort to win interest and support from others. (Cf. the same feeling on the part of the East Harlem staff.) He did not want to "look upon his work in a slum area as a 'project' or as an example in experimental Christianity," or to allow the people of the parish to become " 'objects,' i.e., necessary parts in an experiment; [or]

[5] Earlier quotations were from this address.

worst of all, tools consciously used in the repair of the troubled consciences of middle-class Episcopal persons."

In 1950 Father Myers asked, "Is it possible for a parish of this kind to support itself with the size of the staff we now have?" And he answered his own question, "I do not think so. But we all feel that increasingly the parish can relieve the diocese of some of the financial burden. Unless we succeed in endowing the parish, however, the diocese will always have to help us. Some of our income is received from outside sources, i.e., interested persons. And we have the habit of turning in all our lecturing and speaking fees to the general fund." (Again, compare the East Harlem Protestant Parish.)

GRACE CHURCH (VAN VORST), JERSEY CITY

| | Baptism | | Confirma- | | | Members Bap- | Commu- | Church School | |
| Year | Children | Total | tions | Families | | tized | nicant | Teachers | Pupils |
| --- | --- | --- | --- | --- | --- | --- | --- | --- | --- |
| 1944 | 2 | 2 | — | 290 | | 936 | 503 | 1 | 7 |
| 1945 | 6 | 8 | 10 | 293 | | 944 | 505 | 4 | 41 |
| 1946 | 4 | 4 | — | 75 | | 210 | 170 | 2 | 57 |
| 1947 | 6 | 6 | 7 | 106 | | 348 | 299 | 4 | 46 |
| 1948 | 16 | 17 | 7 | 75 | | 228 | 176 | 4 | 64 |
| 1949 | 9 | 9 | 5 | 75 | | 232 | 228 | 6 | 56 |
| 1950 | 18 | 20 | 1 | 96 | | 169[a] | 70[a] | 6 | 118 |
| 1951 | 12 | 32 | 22 | 108 | | 292 | 93 | 13 | 236 |
| 1952 | 20 | 52 | 57 | | | 350 | 157 | 11 | 231 |
| 1953 | | 75 | 58 | | | 424 | 186 | 18 | 241[b] |

[a] Sharp revision to more realistic figures.
[b] Attendance has climbed faster than enrollment indicates—once-a-month members come steadily now.
(Figures covering disbursements—whether current expense or diocesan assessment—were tabulated for the same period but are omitted because they would require extended interpretation. In general, they indicate that substantial sums have been put into this parish in recent years.)

In 1951 Mr. Sontag wrote, "The work of this Church will probably always have to be subsidized. The priests and their families can always move elsewhere. The people can't. Both know it. The Church can't change the area's economic condition. Both priests and people know this." (Yet these clergy would probably agree with Abbé Michonneau in *Revolution in a City Parish*: "We are not trying to patch up the ills of the world around us; we are trying to rebuild it completely. For that we need real militants who will fill their surroundings with the spirit of Christ, so that men will want to know and follow this Christ. We are not interested in gaining recruits for our church services, but we are passionately interested in gaining recruits for Christ.")

As over against the vast human need of the parish area, Grace Church workers say, like those in many another needy situation, "so great the need, so little done" when we have done all that we can possibly do.

NOTE: From *Jersey City: The Community and Its Churches* (A brief study by H. Paul Douglass for the Hudson County Council of Churches, 1945) with an additional report to the Episcopal Diocese:

"Jersey City is a part of Greater New York and can only be understood and appreciated in its relationships with the metropolitan community." It added a third to its size in fifty years, growing most rapidly between 1900 and 1910, but lost about 15,000 population between 1930 and 1940. (In the last census decade—1940 to 1950—it dropped slightly from 301,173 to 300,447.) "Technically a satellite city rather than a suburb," and primarily "a place for the manufacture and transshipment of goods . . . Jersey City is only incidentally a place for people to live." Its "proportion of home ownership is far below that of the more residential suburbs. . . . This means a proportionately greater instability of population which clearly affects all sorts of social institutions, including the churches." In general, higher income New Jersey suburban people "do not live in Jersey City and . . . as their incomes rise promising and successful young people are continually drafted away into the suburbs." In 1940 approximately two-thirds of the population belonged to stocks of foreign origin. (Note, however, the more recent Negro invasion.)

In 1944 the total membership of 55 churches in eight major denominations was less than 22,000, or slightly over 7 per cent of the population. Sunday school enrollments had dropped to less than 8,000. Public school enrollment had also declined sharply.

Sometimes what was once open country becomes engulfed by an expanding metropolis. First the city explodes; then come radical population changes. A clear example is to be seen in

### Case V—St. John's United Lutheran Church, the Bronx, New York City

In 1860 in Morrisania, now one of many neighborhoods in the Bronx, a borough in the city of New York, 300 German immigrant families lived in rural tranquillity, having escaped as highgrade refugees from the 1848 days in Europe. Of course they organized a church. The present St. John's United Lutheran building was erected at 1343 Fulton Avenue, just north of 169th Street, in 1890. Families still survive who are able to remember when this was essentially a rural parish.

At the turn of the century there came a change. From 1880 to 1890 a new flood of immigration had meant that St. John's Church enjoyed a boom and was able to erect a sturdy stone building, after providing a solid brick parsonage at the rear of the property. (The church now uses two of the basement rooms in a dwelling larger than is needed for a small family under present conditions.) Until 1900 the neighborhood was German and Irish. St. Augustine Roman Catholic Church served both nationalities. Then came the elevated and the subways. The sons of Israel began to move into Morrisania. Grand Concourse ("the Jewish Park Avenue") is only a mile to the west.

Lutherans began now to migrate outward—to Long Island, to Westchester County, and to New Jersey. By 1930 or earlier, Morrisania had become a Jewish community. Loyal members of St. John's enabled the church to stay put, but it meant that some members of the scattered parish came great distances, as measured by time consumed. From Parkchester it is a 45-minute bus trip, from Woodlawn (four miles to the north) it is an hour by bus. Some come by auto. At least half of the membership is still within walking distance. Most of the parishioners live to the westward toward the Grand Concourse. Only a third of the church council live within walking distance. And the membership is no longer exclusively German.

In the early 1940's a second major population change began. The Jews also began a new exodus. The synagogues were up against the loss of their constituents by removal from the neighborhood. As early as 1931, when there were few Negroes in the Bronx, three Negro children had been enrolled in St. John's Sunday school. It happened in this wise: "One Sunday morning a very fine colored Christian mother, who had only recently moved into the neighborhood. . . , dressed her three children and sent them to Sunday School with instructions to go to whichever church would receive them in a friendly spirit. . . . The children decided to try the big, fine church on the hill. . . . They have stayed with St. John's ever since."

In 1938, when the racial change was well under way, two of these children were received as regular and communing members of the church, whose leadership had largely moved out to suburbia. This was in the pastorate of Rev. Henry C. Freimuth. Now "Negroes began coming into the Bronx in numbers from the crowded and oppressing Harlem area of the Borough of Manhattan. The first to come were Negro families with means who bought their own homes, people who were educated and cultured, people who were seeking something better for themselves than Harlem could offer. They were fine neighbors." [6]

On September 24, 1942, a year after Rev. George G. Hackman became pastor, one of the three Negro children, Ashley Bryan, now a church member, was accepted, along with others, as a teacher in the Sunday school, where "he taught faithfully and well, and with the honor and respect and love of the whole staff, up until . . . he left for France for graduate study." By 1943 there were still only 4,000 Negroes in the entire Bronx. A year later there were still relatively few. At this time Ernestine Bryan, another of the three children, became a teacher of an

[6] Unless otherwise noted, quotations are from papers by the present pastor, Rev. Alfred J. Schroder.

all-white class. Pastor Hackman wondered just how she would be received, but again the white girls loved their teacher. She was graduated from Hunter College as an honor student in chemistry but turned to nursing because industry would not accept her as a chemist even during wartime because of her race. "For once the Church showed a better spirit."

In 1946 the number of Bronx Negroes had increased to 75,000, and the number is now estimated at anywhere from 200,000 to 400,000. (The addition of 300,000 people of whatever sort constitutes an enormous problem of assimilation, as Pastor Schroder points out. The basic problem is not one of race but of sheer numbers.) In New York City as a whole in 1950 there were 746,608 Negroes, a number comparable with the nonwhite population of whole Southern states. (E.g., Virginia had 734,174 nonwhites.)

Already older Negroes were beginning to migrate outward from earlier areas of concentration, and some of them now constitute both a high potential for church extension and a new instance of cultural stratification. The facts quite belie the common notion that all Negroes are alike.

In 1941, when the racial problem had begun to be a real one in Morrisania, Pastor Hackman, with denominational backing, adopted an aggressive policy of seeking to win Negro members. The Lutheran Welfare Council of New York City pooled the available resources and employed a group worker for service to several churches.

This was in line with long-time Lutheran policy. The first Negro baptisms in America are said to have taken place in Lutheran churches in New York City. The United Lutheran Church Board of American Missions has lately become newly interested in cities, and consequently in the urban Negro. Likewise, the Division of American Missions of the National Lutheran Council has stimulated work in Negro communities, an emphasis now integrated with the entire urban program. The U.L.C.A. Board of Social Missions and the Women's Missionary Society have also become vitally interested in better churching for the urban Negro. "The Lutheran Church no longer is content with gathering Lutheran immigrants to establish churches, but it is now going out into the highways and byways to preach the Gospel to all people. Many of our newer Lutheran churches have but a very small nucleus of born Lutherans.

"The suggestion that the Lutheran Church is not congenial to the Negro is without foundation. Among the Negroes the Lutheran Church already has a large, sympathetic mission field in the great number of West Indian and Virgin Island Negroes of Lutheran and Episcopal background. Many of these Virgin Islanders are exceedingly well grounded in the Lutheran faith. They are ready to come into the church. In one borough of New York City where there is no Negro Lutheran congregation there are at least 250 known Virgin Island Lutheran families waiting for a church building to become available to them, waiting for pastoral leadership, waiting for many years now.

"Furthermore, there is a large body of educated, well-trained stable Negroes who are quite out of sympathy with the storefront, independent, individualistic churches and the emotional sects with their poorly trained and often self-seeking ministry. They would welcome the establishment of churches in the Negro community by the strong and recognized denominations. And these folk find themselves very much at home in the art and the beauty and the spiritual stability of our Lutheran churches. It must be remembered that one cannot always judge the quality of a Negro's appreciation for fine things by the job he holds. A Pullman porter or waiter may often turn out to be a college graduate."

St. John's accepted the challenge of its new neighbors. Its total membership is now 15 per cent Negro; the active worshiping congregation 25 per cent. A third of the Sunday school enrollment is Negro. No Negroes have as yet accepted membership in the church council, though at least one has been nominated to it.

The membership of St. John's includes a wide economic range.

Some older people are "on welfare"; some parishioners live in Great Neck, Long Island. The higher type of service worker and skilled craftsman are represented, as are insurance and city employees. There is an excess of widows and retired persons, and there is a high turnover in constituency. Preaching to a procession is almost like trying to say grace in a dining car or a popular restaurant. A fourth of the congregation is new within four years. This presents an obvious training problem. How create the requisite loyalties? How maintain the parish tradition and educate newcomers in the Lutheran type of churchmanship?

Now the Puerto Ricans are coming in, even right across the street from the church. (St. John's is again in an area of transition, for the third time in its ninety years of history.) Two Puerto Rican families are attending.

Sunday school meets at 9:15. There is a German service at 9:45, to which come not only older people but also young people in their late teens who are newcomers. There are half a dozen accessions annually from this group. Swedes and some displaced persons of other nations also attend the German service. (As late as 1931, the minutes of the church council were still kept in German.) English service is at 10:45. The church seeks to serve everybody. Naturally its most available constituency springs in large part from Lutheranism, German and other language. These liturgically trained people are now supplemented by Negroes, most of them with a background of less formal worship. For two years a Latvian congregation was housed at St. John's. Their pastor insisted that "the Church is the only place where you will be recognized for what you are." St. John's "seeks to make national, linguistic, and racial minorities feel at home."

In 1953 the church had 27 accessions and lost 24 members, nine of them by transfer. This meant a net gain of three. There are 697 baptized, 409 confirmed members; 250 communing members are a dozen more than a year ago. These last are active, contributing persons, who receive Holy Communion at least once a year.

Other than the pastor, the only staff person available, and that for only one afternoon a week, is the Lutheran Interracial Service group worker. Rev. Alfred J. Schroder came to St. John's in 1949. After high school he had worked for four depression years while attending New York University evenings, then graduated in 1938 from Wagner College, and in 1941 from Philadelphia Seminary. He likes to treat people as individuals; this, he finds, takes time.

St. John's is strategically located. Just north of it is a fine new public school. South of it a public health center is in process of erection.

While St. John's is entirely self-supporting, and it does not need missionary status, Pastor Schroder regrets that for "so large a field so little funds are available." What can be done seems like only the proverbial drop in the bucket. "The little good that we can do and are able and equipped to do is frustrating against the background of what we ought to do. And we all go to bed at night with a bad conscience for our sins of omission and for doing so little of what needs to be done."

Current expenses last year amounted to $12,208. Toward a goal of $2,104 for apportionment benevolences, $1,870 was secured; other benevolences amounted to $2,777. Membership, Sunday school enrollment, total expenditures, and total benevolences were tabulated for each year from 1940 through 1953.

In 1940 the confirmed membership was 950, but roll revision in 1942 and 1945 evidenced the disappearance of former members in large numbers. Since 1951, when the confirmed membership was down to 407, a tighter record has been kept. In 1953 it was 409. Communing membership, which was 522 in the early 1940's, dropped to 228 in 1949 but was up to 250 in 1953. The church school enrollment shrank from 343, was pruned at the beginning of the present pastorate; but with 183 enrolled in 1953 this is still one of the largest Lutheran schools in New York City.

Total expenditures increased from $11,489 to $16,855; some years they were even higher, especially when partial and final mortgage payments were made. The latter, plus the cost of a new sewer line, brought the 1952 total to $31,620. In 1941 total benevolences were only $723 but within the last decade ranged in four different years from $4,392 to $4,720. One of the high points, $4,688 in 1946, was due to a special educational appeal; the best figure to date was in 1952.

Population growth brings congestion. Houses, bought by a corporation which is itself probably only a blind, are converted into small multi-family units. Inferior maintenance is followed by deterioration; thus the slum grows. Further social change seems more or less inevitable. In the event of new large-scale housing, who would live in it?

In any case, St. John's is in Morrisania to stay. The church could have sold and vacated its site in favor of the new school. Its council decided to stay with the community and change as needed. It lived through the Jewish invasion; now, though racially different, the community is again predominantly Protestant. "Be not anxious about tomorrow" is regarded as good counsel for a church like St. John's as well as for its individual members. It is studying persistence and imaginative flexibility, on the theory that, while some individuals and churches ought to move, others ought to stay. It chooses to stay. "We can never tell just when or how this neighborhood where we have been living and working and worshiping may change. But on this the church council, the congregation, and the present pastor are agreed: St. John's Church will continue to serve its community. If the neighborhood remains interracial, so will the church. If the neighborhood becomes predominantly Negro, the church will move in the same direction. There will be Negro members ready to take over full leadership. No matter what population the future may bring, the church will continue its life in service to this community."

Now that Puerto Ricans are coming into the neighborhood, adaptability is needed more than ever. (They have been chiefly to the northeast.) There may be a new opportunity with Spanish-speaking people. An additional staff worker is needed. Costs of maintenance are up, here as elsewhere. The church seats 350 to 400. The pastor asks, Could the denomination make possible some larger use of the church plant? Dreams require cash, dreams require personnel, if they are to become more than dreams. This congregation can carry on as a regular suburban or rural-style church; but for it to become an urban service institution on the scale needed will require resources beyond what it can itself supply.

There are an abundance of people in the immediate vicinity. The church is located in Census Tract 71, east of Third Avenue, where, as compared with 3,834 inhabitants in 1940, there were 5,724 in 1950, an increase of 1,890, or almost one-half. West of Third Avenue, from 151st to 155th streets, Census Tract 65 had 3,454 inhabitants in 1940; in 1950 it had 5,104. This was an increase of 1,650, again nearly one-half. West of Third Avenue, from 146th to 151st streets, Census Tract 67 had 6,412 inhabitants in 1940 and 8,994 in 1950; this was an increase of 2,582, or more than two-fifths.

In the three census tracts as a whole, approximately half of the males employed were operatives or craftsmen; about three-eighths were clerks, service workers, or laborers; about one man in fifteen was in the managerial class. Among women workers, clerks were only a trifle more numerous than operatives; about one woman in seven was a service worker.

Writing in *The City Church* (March-April, 1953) and in *Mission Tidings* (March 18, 1953), William A. Dudde, public relations director of the Lutheran Welfare Council, points out that to a church that has been racially inclusive for over twenty years *the whites keep coming*. White youth have not been scared away. As it has happened, one year Pastor Schroder confirmed a class of one white and six Negro children, the next year as many whites as blacks, and the next year whites outnumbered Negroes five to one. "We are a truly interracial church. A person's color means nothing to us." Roman Catholic Negroes have joined (as well as some Jews), glad for the liturgy and for the freedom from authoritarianism. The women's missionary society, the Luther League, and the Sunday school are all interracial. Of these, the young people of the dating age are the most cagey and circumspect. The Ladies' Aid Society consists of older white women, of an age bracket in which there are few if any Negro women. The church council is open without racial distinction, but no Negro has as yet been willing to accept election to it.

What has happened at St. John's is the slow development of several decades. Pastor Schroder says that his two immediate predecessors "were men of great Christian insight. By their convictions and spirit and by the confidence which the whole congregation had in them, they were able to influence the congregation to do that which should be only normal and natural: to see in every man a child of God, created in the image of God." "The transition to an interracial fellowship," he asserts, "was never officially and consciously planned. No church council ever passed a resolution that now the time had come that we should make this an inclusive congregation." Rather the church felt its way, "seizing and making the best of the present opportunity, a slow and steady growth" resulting.

Moreover, the fact that St. John's is interracial is due solely to population change. "If we had waited for . . . resolutions, I am sure St. John's Church would never have become inclusive. But one Sunday morning [those] three little colored children appeared for Sunday School. They were made welcome and they have come ever since. And from the moment that they came the course of St. John's was clear. There could be no other way." Now "the interracial aspects of St. John's life have become the normal and natural way of Christian life. We do not think of our being an interracial church in terms of its being an experiment at all. Much less do we consider it a problem or a cause. In fact, I personally would not want to belong to any church or association where I would be thought of in terms of a problem or a crusade."

The real issue was: Shall we move and find ourselves in some new area of transition, shall we stay as a white congregation and peter out, or shall we serve all our new neighbors, whoever they are? St. John's has stayed; and it proposes to serve its neighborhood, come what may.

Negroes, Puerto Ricans, or whoever else comes to church will be treated precisely like white visitors, with no more attention, no less. They will be welcomed into an inclusive fellowship and made to feel at home, without having uncomfortable attention showered upon them. And the word will get around. "It is surprising how fast the whole community will have the church sized up." The pattern is established now; and it will be maintained.

## Beginning Again at an Old Location

Sometimes a church with a good building finds its membership living so far away, and its pattern of life so inflexible, that it cannot continue to make effective use of its historic site. In such cases a radical new beginning becomes necessary.

All too often a church which is unwilling or incapable of serving newcomers, who may be a very different sort of people from its traditional constituency, simply sells out to another denomination, perhaps made up of people of another race or language background, predominantly if not wholly. The inner cities of America abound in such instances. In some cases the denomination can shift the property from one of its own congregations to another, with a minimum of lost motion and no lapse of time. The administrative devices by which this can be accomplished are an interesting story in themselves, varying with the polity of the communion.

On the South Side of Milwaukee an interesting inner-city experiment has just been undertaken. This section of the city includes a number of Roman Catholic congregations. A Missouri

Synod and a Wisconsin Synod Lutheran are both widely scattered as to residence and reportedly pay little attention to the immediate neighborhood. An Evangelical and Reformed church is considering a long move to the west, a merger with another church, or both.

An Evangelical (Norwegian) Lutheran Church of 3,500 members (Our Savior) has just moved northwest. The denomination has purchased the former building for the use of a new church, Advent, now being organized by two experienced pastors at the old location, South 9th and Scott streets. It was expected that the 200 applicants for membership in early June would have increased to 250 by the time the charter roll was to be closed on Advent Sunday, November 28. This church is in the northwest corner of Census Tract 116. The immediate area is perhaps half Roman Catholic; that to the south of Greenfield is said to be very much more so. Of one list of fifteen applicants for membership, however, four were of Roman Catholic background. Work began in March, 1954, with 175 attending the first service on April 25.

On arrival, the new pastors were provided with 180 contacts, which they soon increased to 250 in a field 16 x 10 blocks. Their effort represents a new policy on the part of the E.L.C. Home Missions Board. Formerly this Board subsidized churches for years but gave little help as to plant. Now its chief question is merely, Should the neighborhood have a Lutheran Church?— *not* How many Lutherans are there here? If the answer is affirmative to the first question, with the use of tested personnel the Board provides initial funds sufficient for an adequate start.

In this case $60,000 was paid for the old church, organ, and parish house, on a 4 per cent loan basis; and nearly $20,000 was added for the purchase and equipment of a new parsonage. Then an additional grant-in-aid of $22,000 (the figure equals $250 per each $1,000 of loan, plus $2,000) covers salaries for six months and minor equipment. The church is expected to include

an item of 20 per cent of its total budget for synodical benevolences (twice the requirement of another denomination in "high
potential" situations), and to refinance its loan at the end of the
fourth year. New members if Lutherans are expected to attend
three sessions for instruction; non-Lutherans, ten.

Neither of these new pastors is a novice. Rev. Joel Dobbe
served four years at Mason City, Iowa, taking over the leadership
of a 23-year-old congregation still being subsidized and not yet
out of its basement quarters, where the depression had caught
it. In the quadrennium the baptized membership increased from
140 to 460 members, and it now exceeds 500. When Pastor
Dobbe left, 70 per cent of the adult members had not previously
been Lutherans. Of a $12,000 budget, 28 per cent went to benevo-
lences. The Mason City church raised $10,000, borrowed another
$10,000 commercially, and the Board loaned it $15,000 to com-
lete its building. The entire loan is now commercial. (Mr. Dobbe
more recently served three years at Ames, Iowa, where less than
300 members were brought to an $11,000 budget level, with 26
per cent of it going to benevolences. Here a Board loan amounted
to $63,363.)

At Mason City also, for twelve years in a U.L.C.A. church,
worked Rev. M. O. Lee, whom Mr. Dobbe has enlisted to be his
colleague in Milwaukee. They lean on each other, out of long
acquaintance. Mr. Dobbe is the younger. He is on the street, he
preaches, he specializes in publicity. Mr. Lee is a teacher and
administrator, interested in theology and helping a new choir to
start from scratch. A bachelor, his quarters are in the parish
house. Paid good salaries, and equipped to do an urban job, both
men are alert to probable further social changes in the neighborhood.

After considering several other cities, the Board chose Milwaukee for an inner-city experiment. On the South Side there is a
small ministerial association of ten or a dozen men. Milwaukee
as a whole is approximately half Roman Catholic and a fourth

Lutheran. Nearly 90 per cent of the white Christians of Milwaukee are said to belong to one of these major bodies. All the rest, of which the Methodists with 12,000 have the largest number, followed by Presbyterians and the Evangelical and Reformed churches, are hardly more than a third as numerous as the Lutherans of all types.

## Chapter VI

# Making Common Cause, Churches Face
# Social Change Together

For the most part, in the Upper West End, Cincinnati, there has been overwhelming racial change. Northwest of the downtown business district, and a lesser distance northeast of the Union Terminal, are three churches, all of them facing inner-city conditions. We consider first, however, a church in a white island that has been by-passed.

Across Central Parkway (a six-lane highway where once there was a canal) northward, on a steep hillside, *Robertson Memorial Presbyterian Church* is located in the section called "Mohawk," a block and a half up Ravine Street (at No. 2109). This street is the dividing line between Census Tracts 26 and 27, both of which are above flood area, on the northern edge of "The Basin." The pastor, Rev. Raymond Swartzbach, a graduate of McCormick, student under Marshal L. Scott, John L. Mixon, and others, and onetime counselor at the Chicago Y.M.C.A. hotel, now in his first pastorate here, lives two blocks farther up the hill toward Fairview Heights, at 2332 Muriel Court, Cincinnati 19.

Together, the two census tracts appear to have gained in population during the last decade, though less than 2 per cent, as compared with a loss of more than 5 per cent between 1930 and 1940. They now have a smaller number of people than in 1930, but 15.6 per cent more than in 1920. Tract 27 has fewer people by nearly a tenth than in 1920, but Tract 26 increased by 38.6 per cent in thirty years. (The church is located on the west side of Ravine Street in Tract 27.) Female population in these two tracts numbers 112 per 100 males, as compared with 111 in the city as a whole. Only 5 nonwhites, out of a total population of 11,442, were reported in 1950. Five chief nations represented among foreign-born were Germany, Hungary, Italy, Austria, and Rumania. American-born have been largely of German and Italian background, reputedly. The total foreign-born in 1950 constituted less than 6 per cent in this district, less than 4 per cent in the city as a whole.

Median schooling is slightly below that for the city as a whole.

About one family in eight moved into the district from elsewhere in the county during 1949–1950, slightly more than the Cincinnati average rate; but fewer than average moved in from outside the county. A slightly higher percentage than in the city at large lived in the same house in 1950 as in 1949.

Vocational distribution of employed persons is as follows, grouping both sexes and both tracts together:

|  | Per Cent |
|---|---|
| Operatives and kindred workers | 27.8 |
| Craftsmen, foremen, etc. | 18.0 |
| Clerical and kindred workers | 18.0 |
| Service workers, except private household | 9.8 |
| Professional, technical, and kindred workers | 7.5 |
| Managers, officials, and proprietors | 6.6 |
| Sales workers | 6.3 |
| Laborers | 3.7 |
| Not reported | 1.3 |
| Private household workers | 1.0 |
|  | 100.0 |

When age and sex distribution was visualized in a "pyramid," exceptionally high percentages of the total appeared in ages twenty to twenty-nine, in both sexes; and even higher in the under-five-years bracket—4.9 per cent male; 5.3 per cent female. On the other hand, from ages five through nineteen the percentages were abnormally low. Is this the sudden recovery of the birth rate after the depression, the in-migration of more fertile stock, or what?

Median income was $2,575 in Census Tract 26, just east of the church; $3,035 in Census Tract 27, west of Ravine Street, as compared with a city median of $2,644. From the income standpoint these people are better off than the appearance of some of their houses might suggest.

As compared with 37.8 per cent in the city as a whole, 36 per cent of the dwelling units in this area were owner occupied in 1950. Single detached dwelling units were less than one in five; nearly four-fifths of the dwelling units were in multiple housing (two, three, four, five, or more units). More than two out of five of the dwelling units were without private bath or dilapidated; one in twelve was without running water or dilapidated. Nearly 94 per cent of these units were built 35 years or more ago. As compared with 2.7 persons per unit in Cincinnati, there were here only 2.5; but as compared with 14.5 per cent in the city reporting 1.01 or more persons per room, the rate in this district was 20 per cent. As compared with 68.1 per cent of the city houses, there is central heating in 69 per cent of the homes in this area; two-thirds of these plants burned coal. Only 3.4 per cent lacked refrigeration, and more than nine out of ten had mechanical refrigeration, better than the average for the city at large. More than one home in five had television in 1950. Median rents were $27.80 in Census Tract 26, $23.80 in Census Tract 27, as compared with $29.90 in the city as a whole. Median values of one-dwelling unit structures were $7,418 (Census Tract 26) and $8,801 (Census Tract 27), as compared with the city figure of $12,260.

Examination of the block statistics for eleven blocks just east and west of Ravine Street shows that nearly two-thirds of the dwelling units in the immediate neighborhood of the church lacked private bath or were dilapidated in 1950, and that more than one out of five was listed as having no running water or dilapidated. In other words, housing is below average in this neighborhood, though income is not.

In 1947 Dr. H. Paul Douglass ranked the Mohawk section near the top of the lowest quartile, on a group of combined factors: 33rd out of 41 service areas in the city.

On June 1, 1950, the new pastor could find only five active members in a discouraged little Presbyterian mission, which had had a rapid succession of short-term ministers. When larger churches put on a rummage sale in the mission, it received part of the receipts. Mr. Swartzbach made 120 calls per month; he stood on street corners for an hour at a time, making conversation. His parishioners only gradually came to the conclusion that he was there to stay. For a long time he was repeatedly asked, "Have you got a call yet?" Continuity helped. At the end of the first year there were seventeen members. (The 1951 General Assembly membership figure for the mission was 38, as compared with 68 in 1940.) A friendly and alert press helped. So did a rearrangement of the interior of the church, and a general fixing up; e.g., the front exterior is now washable aluminum.

January, 1953, church attendance totaled 251; in the same month in 1954 it was 551, an average of 110 for each of five Sundays, as compared with sixty for each of the four Sundays a year earlier. Denominational statistics had twice shown the Sunday school enrollment to be 29 in earlier years. From January, 1953, to January, 1954, total monthly Sunday school attendance grew from 132 to 331, or an average of 43 per Sunday to 65. Church membership in February, 1954, was 103, mostly young married persons. There were 48 accessions in 1953, of whom 33 were adults coming on profession of faith or baptism. Only four inactive, because nonresident, members have had to be dropped in the last four years.

Of 87 members received between July 30, 1950, and February 14, 1954, 49 came on confession, not having been previously related to any church; 19 on reaffirmation—lapsed church members; 19 by letter of transfer—only two of them Presbyterians.

The youngsters in the church have built a recreation center in the basement. They call it "Bobby's Canteen," a youthful paraphrase of "Robertson Memorial"! Toilets now adjacent to the kitchen sink are to be put in an addition at the rear, thus adding kitchen space. There is sound equipment in the tower, used for community announcements. The minister dreams of buying additional land and of utilizing the roof of a first new unit for recreational purposes. But the present spick-and-span building will have to do until the program and the constituency demand larger and better facilities.

New people are invited but not implored to join this church. "We extend an invitation each Sunday—vocally at least twice each month, twice in the announcement section of the calendar. We want people to make the 'move' of accepting our invitation. This enables us to do a better job of interpreting the responsibilities which come with membership. It has proved successful thus far, for the folks who have joined have remained very active and faithful. . . . Those who join, join because they want to—not because a group of callers have twisted their arms."

Before they are received, new members have to meet certain reading requirements. No boy or girl under fifteen, unless the child of member parents, is admitted. The members live, 90 per cent of them, within half a mile. By 1959 Robertson Memorial hopes to have at least 200 members and to be self-supporting. Now the Board of National Missions puts $4,000 a year into a budget of $7,900 and regards it as a good investment. The old "mission psychosis" is breaking down. The women now give to missions, and the church begins to look forward to independence, when it won't have to report so frequently to overhead offices. Per capita giving for two years is said to have exceeded that of any other Presbyterian church in the city. The church wants to lead, not depend. While the minister continually tries to relate his people to the Church Universal, he finds that their local ties are as yet far stronger than their denominational or world-wide loyalties. He operates on the theory that there must be a real demand for new program items before he favors them. It took more than a year for the men to get him to favor a brotherhood, and it was two years before he was sure that the women were interested to organize with new purposes.

The people of this church are carpenters, butchers, electricians, truck drivers, brewery workers (technically not eligible for membership), a few old-age pensioners, two small store owners. There are no college graduates or managerial or professional people; but for three years the minister has been teaching New Testament at the University of Cincinnati, six blocks away, three hours a week, one semester a year. This means a few hundred dollars in additional income, and contact with 52 students. It means also that some of these, including some future rabbis, are attending their teacher's church. This adds to his neighborhood status. He is likewise an active Presbyter, and chairman of Presbytery's Committee on Christian Education.

What sort of people live in this Mohawk neighborhood?

First of all, north of the Parkway, along which runs a heavily insulating traffic stream, there are practically no Negroes. Probably the Negro population will by-pass this particular hillside, at least in the opinion of informed persons.

Newcomers are now chiefly Kentucky hill people. There is said to be an increasingly large annual population turnover—perhaps nearly a third. Robertson Memorial, the only "old-line" Protestant church in the neighborhood, is winning the more permanent elements. If it featured "hillbilly" music, it might expect to pack the house, but its strategy is long-range. It confessedly does not meet the needs of all types. No other Protestant church in the neighborhood does. Four storefronts meet the needs of some, but these congregations come from all over the city. A Nazarene group is planning on building a few blocks away.

Perhaps half the population is Roman Catholic. At the top of the hill, which serves as a definite sociological barrier, is a strong Roman Catholic church. Not quite so far up is an American Lutheran church of 100 members, who come from all over the city. Eight blocks southeast is St. Phillippus Evangelical and Reformed, a well-equipped city-wide parish.

How has Mr. Swartzbach been able to make such progress? He lists four factors:

1. He has made himself available to the *community*, at all times.

2. He has *preached* faithfully. ("Teaching sermons go over best." Sermon preparation is as careful as if the congregation were made up of college people.)

3. He has *called* faithfully—this might have been rated second a year ago.

4. He has given attention to sound *organization* processes, with emphasis on dignity, responsible pride, and especially missions.

And, as already indicated, he has *stayed*. Obviously he would not have come at all if he had not expected to make a go of it. Three years ago he wasn't quite sure that he could. Now continuity begins to pay off. He has no thought of moving. Perhaps the church can expand, secure the whole corner, grow to be a church of 500 or so, and become a strategic Protestant focal point for a community that would then tend to be more close-knit, in the minister's opinion. One of his deepest wishes is that when he does move, the work will continue in strength.

Meanwhile, says Dr. Harold H. Baldwin of the Presbyterian Department of City and Industrial Work, Board of National Missions, Robertson Memorial "is one of our very bright, shining lights."

## The Transitional Neighborhood

South of Central Parkway, in the Upper West End, the situation is quite different from that of Robertson Memorial Presbyterian Church in the Mohawk district. *The First Reformed* (Evangelical and Reformed) *Church* is located on the southwest corner of Freeman and Hulbert avenues, on the line between Census Tracts 14 and 15. The situation in these two tracts is more fully set forth, census-wise, later in connection with the West Cincinnati-St. Barnabas' study. Here it may be sufficient to point out that the two tracts gained 6.4 per cent in population during the last census decade, instead of losing as might have been expected. By the same token, their Negro population increased from 12.6 per cent of the total to 53.5 per cent. Of the total population in 1950 in the two tracts, 15,874, there were 8,499 nonwhites. The total population increase was greater in Tract 14 to the west of the church, in terms both of absolute gain and of percentages. The loss in white population in Tract 15 amounted to more than half (52.3 per cent) during the decade, in Tract 14 to only a third (33 per cent). Nonwhites in Tract 14 increased from 3.6 per cent of the total population to 41.6 per cent during the decade, in Tract 15 from 19 per cent to 62.6 per cent. Dwelling occupancy by nonwhites in the two blocks nearest this church amounted to 70.4 percent, and 50.3 per cent of the reporting dwelling units lacked bath or were dilapidated. In the block just east of the church (Census Tract 15, block 20) Negro occupancy had reached 82.3 per cent. Tract 15 especially is in the area of Cincinnati's "chief Negro concentration"; and the whole Upper West End was ranked by Dr. Douglass as "next to the lowest of all Cincinnati districts" on a group of combined factors—40th out of 41. The block just northwest of the church has no residents, being occupied wholly by industry or trade.

To the west are a Methodist and a Reformed Presbyterian church, and there are a number of regular Negro churches in this section, together with many storefronts. West Cincinnati-St. Barnabas' is a co-operative interracial, interdenominational neighbor slightly to the southeast. An expressway to be built just west of First Reformed Church may increase its city-wide accessibility. No redevelopment in the immediate neighborhood is in sight.

"Under the pastorates of Dr. Arthur P. Schnatz who first began a modest community program and Rev. Oliver C. Hotz who carried this program to much greater length, the congregation, although largely consisting of members dwelling in suburbs, has given excellent support to a program designed to assist the children and young people as well as families of the neighborhood. . . . The present pastor, Rev. Jacob Wagner, came from a pastorate in the Bronx, New York. . . . The Board of National Missions assists with subsidies to help in carrying on the community program [and has] made it clear that [it] definitely favor[s] complete integration of the races in all activities but [has] also insisted that the decisions must be made freely and fully by the congregation itself." [1]

In 1954 First Church was 109 years old. Several decades ago this was a fine residential neighborhood, but now it is blighted. Floods drove out most of the economically substantial earlier population, and their homes have been divided up into small flats for the new inhabitants, in accordance with an all too frequent succession pattern. Newcomers were at first Southern mountain people—"poor whites" from Kentucky and Tennessee. Recently came an influx of Negroes, which hit hardest in 1949, just when the church had reached a membership peak. During the 1937 flood forty to fifty people lived in this church building for weeks.

Three fine public schools in the area are closed to children and youth in after-school hours. The city provides no neighborhood recreation in this area during the fall and winter. First Church uses the Findlay Street Neighborhood House one Sunday night a month. (See under West Cincinnati-St. Barnabas' below.) The nearest public school (Heberle) is reportedly 75 per cent white, but it is also 75 per cent unchurched. Its pupils are largely from Kentucky and Tennessee hill families. Negro children constitute 90 per cent of the near-by Sand School, to which St. Barnabas is more closely related. In Bloom Junior High School the role of the white pupils—only 20 per cent of the total—is a difficult one, and is influenced by real fear of the Negroes. First Church conducts a limited program of recreation and group and social work.

Some loss of members occurred before the arrival of the present pastor, owing to proposed "integration." Mr. Wagner takes the

[1] Letter from Purd E. Deitz to the author, December 28, 1953.

attitude that whether the local church should be inclusive or not is not within its right to decide. The congregation has sustained him in his view that the church has no option but to serve everybody in its neighborhood and open its membership without racial distinction. Yet he proceeds slowly, not pressing the issue. "There is a long road ahead" in a "city where tensions are very severe." In January, 1954, a committee was commended by the congregation for its study of the problem, but a vote on the main issue was avoided by unanimous consent. [2] Racial inclusiveness is both a major problem and an outstanding opportunity in this church.

At the peak this church had 600 members. By January 1, 1953, the membership had dropped to 411, and a year later to 402. Average attendance figures give a more accurate picture of ups and downs that have been somewhat less violent. In 1931 it was 186; in 1941, 167; in 1950, 207. In January, 1954, average attendance was 167, not counting children attending for part of the service. Ten applicants awaited confirmation, and a nucleus of five were ready for next year's class.

First Church has been able to assimilate a number of white families who were poor during depression days. Some of these have exhibited qualities of leadership, even in an urban situation very different from the rural hill-country culture in which they grew up. Several groups are now interracial; some are still wholly white. The way is now open to receive Negro boys and girls into the Sunday school; and eventually, probably fairly soon, Negroes will be received into church membership.

Perhaps thirty members are over seventy years of age. Obviously death will take its toll, and there are those who, displeased with the changes that have taken place in the neighborhood, have moved out of it into better residential areas. Perhaps a third of these older people, however, live near the church, a number of them in relative squalor, as vestiges of the neighborhood's former

[2] See report of the annual meeting, in the local church *Messenger*, January 24, 1954.

status. A fourth of the church membership resides near the church; four out of five of the boys and girls in the Sunday school live near by. The farthest church member lives ten miles out; in general the church serves a six-mile radius. "Many of the members live more than three miles away; but they continue to worship and assume responsibility at First Reformed Church, feeling a sense of mission in the life and work of the parish."

A sturdy stone edifice, with possibilities of expanded facilities in its basement, is supplemented by a parish house next door, which once served as a huge parsonage. Here too is an apartment for the assistant minister. A courtyard between the two buildings is used for games.

In June, 1954, the staff consisted of the minister, a full-time parish worker, a boys' worker, a part-time choir director, and a custodian. Marriage and the draft had somewhat reduced the number of paid workers. The full-time parish worker combined group work and Christian education abilities, but had more to do than one person can cover. She had a heavy club-work schedule. There was no secretarial help, doubtless an extravagant economy.

This report makes no attempt to review the program of this church in detail (twenty pages of mimeographed annual reports were submitted January 24, 1954). The following is a summary list of parish activities:

For children:

One day and a half of Weekday Church School—a larger load could be carried, were the church more adequately staffed

Rainbow Club—after-school group of 75 children from six to eight years of age

Crusaders—after-school group of 75 children from nine to eleven years of age

Junior Boys' Club, meets after school, fifteen boys from nine to eleven years of age

Intermediate Boys' Club, meets at night, eighteen boys from twelve to fourteen years of age

Senior Boys' Club, meets at night, a dozen boys fifteen years and
older
Girl Scouts, twelve enrolled
Senior Girls' Club, ten girls over fourteen years of age
Knot Hole Baseball, boys up to fourteen years of age

For young people:
Youth Fellowship, Sunday nights, average attendance twenty, over
twelve years of age
Canteen, recreational program, Wednesday nights, average attend-
ance 45 (35 to 60), over twelve and mostly over fifteen years of
age—games, dancing, etc.
Basketball team, boys up to sixteen
Softball team, boys up to twenty
Summer camp period of one week for fifty-five children and young
people

For adults:
Mr. & Mrs. Club, couples, recreation and discussion
Friendship Circle, evening group of women, discussion and volun-
teer assistance
Basketball and softball teams for adults
Bowling teams for adults

In addition, there are Women's Guild, program of worship, discussion, and service; Evening Circle, program similar to Guild;
Sunday school; and various commissions and committees. Worship is in the somewhat formal tradition of the Reformed Church
in the United States.

Besides doing club work, the parish worker and the minister
have a responsibility for counseling and social work, for which
there is a great deal of need.

Sunday school enrollment January 1, 1953, was 191. It
dropped to 149 by November 1, the lowest in years, but was up
to 168 (plus 28 on the cradle roll) at the end of the year. Sunday school attendance averaged 120 in 1953, as compared with
190 in 1949.

There are further possibilities in connection with social work referrals, a supportive or liaison ministry, counseling, and case work. Retirement of the boys' worker, in his sixties, gave the personnel committee an opportunity to rethink the staff situation. The amount invested in the salary of a student minister, added to the boys' worker salary, could be used to employ a full-time director of community activities. If the public schools could be opened up, the demand for church facilities and program would be appreciably lessened.

Besides racial integration and staff reorganization, First Church, of course, faces the problem of finances. It inevitably loses its older, more solid supporters and cannot easily replace them with younger persons able to supply the same financial backing. The pastor is convinced that a church so located cannot serve its neighborhood adequately and at the same time be self-supporting.

In 1953 general account income amounted to $18,527.91, as compared with a budgeted expectation of $18,490. Of this, $3,620.50 was contributed by the Board of National Missions. Total expenses amounted to $18,965.66. The sum of $3,139.36 was disbursed for mission and benevolences, and $557.80 additional for World Service, over and above the general fund. Both of these met or exceeded the apportioned amounts. Three additional funds handled added thousands of dollars. Indebtedness slightly exceeded $12,000. Total budget expenses for 1954 amounted to $18,514.

Evangelism and stewardship emphases were pastoral proposals for 1954.

## Case VI—WEST CINCINNATI-ST. BARNABAS'
### (A Study in Interracial and Interdenominational Integration)

We have considered a Presbyterian church on a Cincinnati hillside, where the population is white, and a Reformed church in an area increasingly Negro. Moving slightly to the east, we come now to an interdenominational (Presbyterian-Episcopal), interracial project in an overwhelmingly Negro neighborhood: *West Cincinnati-St. Barnabas'*.[3]

The church building and parish house are located on the north side of Poplar Street, opposite the end of Dudley Street, east of Freeman Avenue in Census Tract 15, but only a short distance from Tract 14, which begins at Freeman. Approximately 16,000 people are within relatively easy reach of this church building, parish house, and near-by neighborhood house. In 1937 the flood entered the basements on Poplar Street, a fact which helped to change the character of the neighborhood.

Between 1920 and 1930, Tract 14 lost heavily in population, and slightly during the next decade, but gained between 1940 and 1950. Yet it had only a few hundred more white inhabitants in 1950 than in 1930. Tract 15 gained rapidly from 1920 to 1930 and has increased slightly during the last two decades. Together the two tracts show a thirty-year population increase of less than 10 per cent. In 1930 in Tract 14 only 3 per cent of the people were nonwhite; in 1950 there were nearly 42 per cent; and in Tract 15 the percentage rose from 13 to 63—chiefly in the last census decade.

In the eight blocks nearest to the church nonwhite owner occupancy in 1950 ranged from 67.3 to 100 per cent and averaged 82.6 per cent. In these blocks nearly two-thirds of the houses were without private bath or dilapidated, and 7.5 per cent were reported as having no running water or dilapidated. These blocks housed 684 families. Less than 1 per cent of the population was foreign-born. One family in six had moved during the year 1949–1950, most of them (four out of five) from somewhere else in the county.

Median income in Tract 14 was $2,262, in Tract 15 only $1,847, as compared with $2,644 for the city as a whole.

Combining the figures for both tracts and both sexes, vocational distribution of the employed was as follows in 1950:

[3] Maurice F. McCrackin, "Policy Became Practice," *The City Church*, Jan.–Feb., 1954.

|                                                        | Per Cent |
|--------------------------------------------------------|----------|
| Operatives and kindred workers                         | 30.3     |
| Service workers other than private household           | 18.5     |
| Laborers                                               | 17.8     |
| Craftsmen, foremen, and kindred workers                | 9.5      |
| Private household workers                              | 8.2      |
| Clerical and kindred workers                           | 5.9      |
| Managers, officials, and proprietors                   | 4.4      |
| Sales workers                                          | 2.8      |
| Professional, technical, and kindred workers           | 1.7      |
| Not reported                                           | .9       |
|                                                        | 100.0    |

Age and sex distribution for whites and nonwhites in Census Tracts 14 and 15 is shown in the accompanying population table. In each case the base is the total population for the racial group.

| Male | | | Female | |
|------|------|------|------|------|
| *White* | *Nonwhite* | *Age Brackets* | *White* | *Nonwhite* |
| 1.0 | .4 | 75 and over | 1.7 | .4 |
| 1.2 | .6 | 70 to 74 | 1.4 | .5 |
| 1.7 | .8 | 65 to 69 | 2.1 | .9 |
| 2.0 | 1.1 | 60 to 64 | 1.9 | 1.0 |
| 2.7 | 1.5 | 55 to 59 | 2.2 | 1.3 |
| 2.6 | 2.4 | 50 to 54 | 2.4 | 2.3 |
| 3.0 | 3.2 | 45 to 49 | 2.7 | 3.0 |
| 3.0 | 3.5 | 40 to 44 | 3.1 | 3.8 |
| 3.0 | 4.1 | 35 to 39 | 3.0 | 4.9 |
| 3.2 | 4.2 | 30 to 34 | 3.5 | 4.6 |
| 4.4 | 5.0 | 25 to 29 | 4.5 | 5.8 |
| 3.8 | 4.2 | 20 to 24 | 4.2 | 5.6 |
| 3.3 | 2.7 | 15 to 19 | 3.7 | 4.1 |
| 4.4 | 3.5 | 10 to 14 | 4.5 | 3.8 |
| 4.2 | 4.6 | 5 to 9 | 4.3 | 4.6 |
| 5.7 | 5.7 | Less than 5 | 5.6 | 5.8 |
| 49.2 | 47.5 | | 50.8 | 52.4 |

Excess of whites, age 50 and over, both sexes: male, 10 to 19; female, 10 to 14

Excess of nonwhites, age 20 to 49, both sexes: female, 15 to 19; 5 to 9, both sexes; female, less than five

Owner occupancy is slightly greater in Tract 15 than in Tract 14 but averages only 13.3 per cent in the two tracts, as compared with 37.8 per cent throughout the city as a whole. Of the owner-occupied homes, 69 per cent were nonwhite; of the renter-occupied, only 48.7 per cent. Most of these dwellings (84.1 per cent) are two, three, four, five, or more attached units. Three out of four units had no private bath or were dilapidated; one in seven had no running water or were dilapidated. Homes now 35 years old or older constituted 97.1 per cent of the total. Median number of persons per dwelling unit was the same in both districts as in the city at large, 2.7; but 37.7 per cent of the dwellings had 1.01 or more persons per room, as compared with a city-wide average of only 14.5 per cent. Only one in six of these dwellings had central heating, with coal used as fuel in nearly two of these cases out of three. Seven families out of ten had mechanical refrigeration; one in four, iceboxes. (The total, 95.6 per cent, is high; but the proportion using ice is unusual.) Nearly one family in six had a television set.

Median rent in Tract 14 was $14.75; in Tract 15 it was $16.33 —as compared with a $29.90 city median. In Tract 14 there were 24 homes valued at less than $3,000 out of a total of 87 one-dwelling units. Median value of such homes in Tract 15 was $4,524, as compared with a $12,260 city median.

St. Barnabas' was an organized mission of the Diocese of Southern Ohio. In 1944 it reported 200 baptized members, 139 communicants, 70 families. The church school enrolled 163. There had been six baptisms and 24 confirmations the previous year. Total disbursements were $4,244.62, as reported in the diocesan journal. This church was located at 901 Findlay Street, on a corner a block and a half northeast of the present federated church site (West Cincinnati Presbyterian). The Episcopal edifice has since been transformed into a neighborhood house.

West Cincinnati Presbyterian Church, itself a merger of three of the earliest congregations in the city, reported 220 members and a Sunday school enrolling 205, in the 1945 General Assembly statistics.

On August 5, 1945, with the encouragement of Presbytery and the bishop of the diocese, these two enterprises were federated for purposes of worship and work—but they are technically not a federated church.[4] Both congregations concurred in the new arrangement, which was a natural result, in part, of the economic straits in which each was involved.[5]

"Both of these churches were going to seed because the Negro population of that area was growing by leaps and bounds and there weren't enough white persons to support two churches." [6] Rev. Maurice F. McCrackin, a Chicago Presbyterian, was brought to Cincinnati to serve this "area of great crowding and many social needs," where the churches were "failing to serve 60 per cent or more of the population." "It was the original intention to organize (as an intermediate step) a Negro congregation and social service program at what was the Episcopal building, [some] believing that in this border city, 'a northern city with a southern exposure,' extreme care must be exercised in any interracial activity." The leadership soon became convinced, however, that such a move would be wrong, morally and strategically. Integration is not hastened, according to a 1947 memorandum of Mr. McCrackin, by setting up new segregated organizations even though both are under the supervision of an over-all planning and policy-making group. That is, it was contended that churches should break present patterns of segregation, not set up new ones. Since then "the myth has been exploded that Negroes are

[4] See pp. 140–141.
[5] There is a parallel federation under quite different circumstances in the Indian Hills section of the city, a desirable residential area, with the Rev. Luther Tucker as pastor, using a former Methodist building.
[6] Joseph Garretson in the Cincinnati *Enquirer*, August 11, 1948.

crowded outside waiting to associate with white people, and that . . . the church would be 'taken over.' "

Here were all the characteristics of the upper "Basin" and the "West End." This was Cincinnati in its most underprivileged area, although districts nearer to the heart of the city were still more blighted.

Within a 2½ block radius the population was 70 per cent Negro. Probably 90 per cent of the Presbyterians lived in the suburbs. St. Barnabas', a twelve-year-old mission, drew more on the community, but only white people. In 1945 both congregations were seriously considering their future, if any. The Presbyterian pastorate was vacant; there was a lay leader at St. Barnabas'. There were weekday programs, subsidized and slow-going. In 1945 a Negro social worker was employed as director of the program at the Neighborhood House, since 1947 a Community Chest agency. When this man resigned, a Negro woman, employed about the same time, was made director. Co-operative experience made for the "exposure of people to each other, gradually building respect and fellowships. The decision for integration became one of common consent, not one that was urged on a moral and ethical basis. While earlier it might have been accepted on an intellectual basis, at the beginning without exposure there would not have been emotional consent." [7]

A mixed staff was employed, with a Negro secretary and book-keeper at the church office. Nonsegregation began at the Neighborhood House and in the annual summer-camp program.

St. Barnabas' church building was utilized as the *Findlay Street Neighborhood House*, serving all comers. Most of its patronage is within a mile, a large part of it within five or six squares. Yet now some older boys, who grew up in the neighborhood, return from their better homes in the East End to play on teams they had grown to like so well. Some white people from Kentucky, Tennes-

[7] M. F. McCrackin, "The Inclusive Christian Fellowship," at Workshop on Racial Practices of Churches, First Presbyterian Church, Indianapolis, Feb. 26, 1952.

see, and Indiana, but not hill people, are moving in. The Neighborhood House does not have a visiting staff. It is the church visitor who sends newcomers to the Neighborhood House, which is a distinct service enterprise, not used as a bait or tool.

While it is too soon to draw any definite conclusions about the social benefits resulting from the Neighborhood House program, there are strong evidences that community feeling is growing and family life is being strengthened. The old church building is a usable makeshift. "Red Feather" help is transforming the basement into work and club rooms. At least two additional group workers are a primary staff need. When the old steeple was condemned, it was torn down at a cost of $1,200, as against the $1,600 it would have taken to fix it. The Advisory Board of the Neighborhood House is interracial—two-thirds Negro.

"The organization was frankly feeling its way" for the first three years. While the leaders were sure that "White [sic] and Negro children would get along swimming and going on outdoor camps together," adult reaction was unpredictable. But at the end of three years they said: "It does work" (adapted from the *Enquirer* article).

A camp of about 75 acres at Kroger Hills, formerly operated by the St. Barnabas' congregation on a segregated basis, had been idle for years. In 1946 the church "went to the Park Board and said it would like to take [it] over. The Park Board agreed immediately. The camp was opened in 1946 and was named Camp Joy." The Park Board has been helpful about repairs on the buildings, and the city pays the water bills for both swimming pools. On a Sunday afternoon "nearly a dozen boys had ridden their bicycles all the way from the West End (surely a 25-mile round trip) just for the opportunity to swim."

Here then were a Neighborhood House and a new camp program, coming into being as a product of the federation of two churches, in spite of denominational and racial differences. How about the federated church program? What happened there? Not everybody stayed by; a few left. A couple of white youngsters, influenced by their elders, did not attend the interracial camp. But progress was made.

In the February, 1950, *Crisis,* Mrs. Iris V. Owens, an N.A.A.C.P. worker, called this "Cincinnati's proudest example of true community help through church activities . . . in a city where separation is the rule and the tradition." She pointed out: "The national pattern of racial segregation is more evident in our Christian churches than even in our public schools." Before the federation of the churches, "their only mixed activities were in a city health clinic, sponsored by the health department, and a weekday church school which brought the children from a near-by public school where there is complete integration.

"As the community became more and more mixed, and white and colored worked together in school and community projects . . . the inconsistency of welcoming Negroes to every activity but church school and church services . . . became increasingly ridiculous. Negro and white children went to school together. They played together. Their parents faced the same community problems and worked together on community projects. Negroes were coming to Findlay Street Neighborhood House and taking advantage of its recreational advantages. . . . An occasional Negro would come to the worship service, and would be made welcome, [but] Negroes were not asked to join" the church.

"Then one day a little golden haired girl, who had asked her Sunday church school teacher if she could bring her friend to class with her arrived with her playmate, a colored child." The church, face to face with the opportunity, named a special committee to think through an over-all policy as to race relations. As a result, a completely integrated program was established by a vote of 12 to 2 of the Governing Board. On November 30, 1947, three out of eleven adults confirmed were Negro. "Their reception broke the pattern of segregation that had existed for generations in both congregations." Since that time the confirmation classes, at first about equally divided between Negro and white, have become about 70 per cent Negro. Negro members are now completely integrated, as teachers, deacons, members of vestry-session, and governing board.

In 1946 the child-care group for children of working mothers was still all-white. "The children went to school together, but (at first) the parents went nowhere together. There is confusion no longer, since at church they now worship and play together." Said a Negro who visited one Sunday, "Here for once I feel like a whole person."

Mrs. Owens reported: "Interested people, especially schooled in human relations, came from various suburbs to join the church and offer their services. Additional people, Negro and white, joined the church, so that community support increased steadily." She quotes the pastor as saying, "Where church or community leadership is forthright and takes the brotherhood pattern as right, and acts on this premise, there is a minimum of opposition."

By 1950 Mr. McCrackin told Harry Mayo of the Cincinnati *Post* (June 10): "After over four years of worship and work together we know that there are no differences ecclesiastically and no barriers racially that cannot be resolved and broken down. The leaders betray the people when they do not give them the opportunity to express their natural and innate sense of justice and good will." A year later, writing in *Outreach* (the Presbyterian women's monthly missionary magazine) for June–July, 1951, he said: "In areas of transition in our great cities the common practice of the established denominations is to walk out on their new neighbors." This behavior is excused and rationalized; but "a church, if it is a church in the true sense, will welcome, not only verbally but by devising approaches and a program that will appeal, all those moving into the neighborhood, without regard to color or economic status. Apart from the basic responsibility of the church to square practice with creed, the more established denominations, because of greater financial resources, have a responsibility and a privilege to stay and become a church for all the people, ready to serve them in a seven-day-a-week program."

In Indianapolis in 1952, Mr. McCrackin stated the conclusion he had reached after these years of experimenting:

1. The major responsibility in breaking the pattern of segregation rests with the leadership of the church (presbyteries, conferences, dioceses, individual ministers, consistories, sessions, vestries). Where the leadership is forthright and courageous, you can count on the people's support. Too frequently the leadership makes a scapegoat of the people, saying, "They won't accept it," when it is something they don't accept themselves.

2. If the doors of the church are opened, no minority group rushes in to take over. All people do not want to go to church . . . especially is it human nature to stay away from a place where you are not convinced you are welcome. Minorities don't "invade" an area, the majority retreats.

3. Intellectual change is not enough, there has to be an emotional conversion which can only come as people know each other on a basis of social equality and friendship.

4. Growth in individuality and in changing mores of society comes only through conflict, where traditional patterns are challenged. Otherwise the majority says, "There is no problem." Conflict on each specific issue is a healthy experience for everyone.

5. A person is not a whole person unless he is accepted and accepts others, all others, on a basis of full equality. To the minority person wholeness comes as he feels that barriers to complete fellowship are down. Wholeness has come to the white members of our congregation. (Otherwise there is isolation—"How can you live in such a neighborhood? Aren't you afraid?") Now one doesn't bolster his security and show how insecure he really is, by regarding someone else as inferior.

6. Institutions that claim to be democratic, and certainly the church which claims to be Christian, must begin to put into practice its pronouncements and creeds. The time is ripe, both for those suffering the blight of prejudice and discrimination, and for those who take seriously their discipleship.

There is now an entirely mixed staff in church, Neighborhood House, and camp. This did not happen overnight. At the camp for the first two years, while the staff was interracial, the children were segregated. Integration came in 1948. In 1947, when Negroes were first received into the church, "the congregation admitted that there was a contradiction in Christian practice of interracial meetings at the Neighborhood House through the week and segregated church services on Sunday. So segregation was wiped out" (*Enquirer* article cited above).

All young people and most adults are now confirmed. "Confirmation class members are received into both denominations. The Bishop follows the Episcopal Confirmation Service. As a part of the service the pastor of the congregation, following the laying on of hands by the Bishop, asks questions concerning faith and practice and extends the right hand of fellowship and welcome to the new members."

The entire membership is reported to both denominations. According to the 1952 General Assembly statistics, there had been ten infant baptisms, and 34 were received on profession or reaffirmation during the calendar year; 8 were dismissed, 3 died. This resulted in a total membership of 258. The church school numbered 323.

In early 1954 the Sunday school, which is a joint activity, as is the worship, was distributed departmentally and racially as follows:

| Sunday School Department | White | Enrollment Colored | Total |
|---|---|---|---|
| Beginners | 11 | 13 | 24 |
| Primary | 16 | 34 | 50 |
| Junior | 21 | 36 | 57 |
| Junior high | 13 | 30 | 43 |
| Senior high | 2 | 10 | 12 |
| Men's class | 2 | 2 | 4 |
| Adult women | 22 | 5 | 27 |
| | 87 | 130 | 217 |

With the pastor away, church attendance on one February Sunday numbered around 100, including perhaps fifteen children who left after a story by one of a rotating group of volunteers.

The Holy Communion is observed monthly, eight times a year in the Episcopal fashion, quarterly in the Presbyterian manner. All members are free to join in either observance. An Episcopal neighbor officiates in the Episcopal observance.

The church staff includes the pastor, who gives half-time to the Neighborhood House, full-time office service (a treasurer-book-keeper two days a week, a secretary three days), and a full-time custodian. For three out of the six years there was a second staff person, an Episcopalian. Rather than another clergyman, a full-time religious education director would now be most helpful, according to the pastor. A Negro full-time worker (employed five days a week on the staff of the Council of Churches) gives two days a week to weekday religious education classes at St. Barnabas'—on released time. Three days a week a city health doctor holds office hours in the parish house, and two mornings a week there is a Planned Parenthood Clinic. The musical director is part-time. A church visitor works ten to twelve hours a week, and half-time at the Neighborhood House.

The neighborhood postal zone is #14. Within it are 69 addresses of 103 out of 280 present members. Allowing for a higher percentage of inactive members living at a distance, the active membership is approximately one-half resident near by. A third of the total membership is Negro; in the Sunday School the ratio is about three Negroes to two whites.

The affairs of the church are handled by a vestry-session and a governing board, composed thus:

6 members elected by and from the congregation
2 appointed by the Bishop
2 appointed by the Presbytery
2 appointed by the Advisory Board of the Neighborhood House and the Pastor

The worship service is a modified form of Morning Prayer, according to a printed booklet of *United Worship* and a weekly mimeographed bulletin referring to it.

Headings on the church monthly report blank, showing weekly attendance, include:

| | |
|---|---|
| Acolytes | Mothers' Club |
| Adult Discussion Group | Peace and Goodwill Society |
| Children's Choir | Senior-High Young People |
| Deacons' Calls | Senior Choir |
| Devotional Services | Teachers and Officers Meetings |
| Governing Board | Vestry-Session |
| Home Visits | Weekday Church School |
| Junior-High Choir | Woman's Auxiliary |
| Junior G.F.S. | Women's Society |
| Junior-High G.F.S. | Youth Council |
| Junior-High Young People | |

Union Lenten services with the First Reformed Church were undertaken in 1953 because that church had no pastor. In 1954 they were to be heartily repeated, with expected benefits both interracial and interdenominational.

Camp Joy has its own separate board. The Neighborhood House is now open also in the summer. It has no family case worker but uses the referral method. It is a member of the local federation of settlements, but is ineligible to membership in the national organization by reason of its church affiliation, which it has, so far, preferred to keep. Perhaps its self-perpetuating Advisory Board could be made more representative of the neighborhood (a third of its active members are residents of the community) and could to advantage include persons connected with the First Reformed Church. The Advisory Board handles program and public relations and is represented on the Governing Board, which decides policy. There might be a satisfactory way for the Neighborhood House to become eligible to national affiliation, by dissociating it organically from the congregation but not from the co-operating denominations. Its chief needs include two new group workers; case-work training and group-work experience would both be helpful. A nursery school might be added, but only if a thorough analysis of possible program additions confirmed this opinion. If the Neighborhood House continues to serve with Community Chest approval, it is greatly to be hoped that it may eventually acquire an adequate new building, better adapted to its program. Its long-time use for gymnasium purposes has been discouraged by the architect. On the exterior of the Neighborhood House appears a sign: "Your Community Chest gift is at work here."

A projected express highway will displace 6,000 families. Subsidized housing below Liberty Street, in an area 1 1/2 x 3 blocks, might increase the Neighborhood House opportunity; even if it greatly reduced the number of families living in the area, this would certainly be for the good of everyone.

The above was written with frequent direct and indirect quotations from the pastor of these churches, as the responsible head of the total enterprise. The writer knew full well that these churches are in "a very controversial position, as far as the polity of [the Episcopal] Church is concerned." Yet he had no reason to doubt the accuracy of the *Enquirer*'s report that Bishop Henry Wise Hobson, of the Diocese of Southern Ohio, has looked upon these Cincinnati experiments (both St. Barnabas' and Indian Hills) as a "vast success," and has thought "they might well prove a pattern for Protestant unification over the country." Rev. Lowell H. Palmer, executive secretary of Presbytery, was likewise quoted as agreeing, with a hearty "Amen." Circumstances did not permit interviews with either of these men.

Under date of March 3, 1954, Bishop Hobson writes: "It is, indeed, a thrilling adventure which we are carrying on, because it represents the ability of the Churches concerned to work together in close unity and it also gives a demonstration of how the Christian Church can bring together members of different races in united action." But he precedes this hearty word by three statements, seemingly somewhat at variance with the impression given to the writer by the pastor:

. . . There are definitely two congregations involved, each organized in accordance with the regulations of the Church with

which it is affiliated. In other words, we do have an Episcopal congregation organized under our Canons and a Presbyterian congregation organized under the regulations of the Presbyterian Church.
Thus, we have not a federated Church, but two Churches wor-
shipping and working together in a single program.

. . . Our Canons don't really provide for any federated Church
program, and we set up the project with the arrangements which
we are following so as to avoid violation of any of the regulations
of either the Presbyterian or the Episcopal Churches.

. . . There are times when an Episcopal minister ordained in our
Church takes the Communion Service and other services in connection with the program being carried on in this project.

Technically, therefore, from the Episcopal standpoint, this
co-operative activity on the part of two congregations might perhaps better be called a joint *project*, rather than a federated
church. To be sure, these churches use one letterhead, which is
headed *West Cincinnati-St. Barnabas' Church*. Moreover, from
the standpoint of the Sunday morning worshiper, or the weekday
visitor, one must confess that the two churches behave strangely
like one congregation. One says this partly in recognition of what
is an open secret: these two churches could not have come so
far together had it not been for the courage and ecumenical
vision of Bishop Hobson and his willingness to work with Presbyterians and other communions, to the limit of his canonical
privilege. Likewise Presbyterian willingness to join hands with
Episcopalians in meeting a neighborhood situation is to be heartily
recognized.

The actual facts as to this situation, and the varying interpretation of what has happened, have very important bearing on
how reproducible this pattern is elsewhere. In Massachusetts
there appear to be genuine federations of Congregational and
Episcopal churches, and in at least one instance of these two and
a Methodist church; but in each case regular relationships are
maintained within each denomination, and separate ecclesiastical
entities continue, though united in work and worship. The

churches federate, but from the standpoint of "Faith and Order" is there any "federated church," in the sense of a fully united local body?

This distinction is important to maintain, if one is not to assume that more progress has been made toward Christian unity at the grass roots than realistic candor and honest objectivity can admit.

An added factor in the Cincinnati situation is the interest of the pastor in all sorts of phases of social reconstruction. He has been called a radical idealist. His spirit also is like that of Abbé Michonneau, in *Revolution in a City Parish*. He seeks not so much to build up a church out of the community as to reconstruct, so far as possible, all our urban culture. This inevitably brings him praise and censure.

A fair question may well be: What new indigenous lay leadership is being developed? Of course the time has been short. Here and there are glimpses of vocational ambition among young people, aided and abetted by stimulating church life. At a recent meeting of a dozen church-school workers (nine white, three Negro), of whom five live in the neighborhood, the pastor presided. Is responsibility being delegated and lay leadership trained? Any fault here would clearly be one of omission rather than commission. Loyalty, initiative, and competence on the part of volunteer workers were quite evident.

In this situation one sees two or three seeming impossibles actually taking place. Ideally, the achievement acquires genuinely normative value. Obviously it would not be easy to get widespread acceptance of this pattern. Should we slow down the idealists and the experimenters, or should we modify our ecclesiasticism to fit the facts of local achievement? To do the latter would require that canons, disciplines, and other denominational rules of procedure be changed, so far as interdenominationalizing local churches is concerned.

As for inclusiveness, racially, it would seem necessary on the other hand only to remember that the word "white" almost never occurs in any organizational procedures. To achieve "integration" would seem only to require that we reinterpret our commitments, leaving out the racial labels and customs which somehow have been permitted to slip into our church practice.

Any adequate assessment of West Cincinnati-St. Barnabas' must consider its interracial achievement, its interdenominational significance, its social service ministry (both at the Neighborhood House and at the parish house), and the social ideals for which its ministry has stood.

If this situation be a controversial one, it is largely so because it is the scene of so dynamic an enterprise.

Statistically, the situation is ambiguous. There is as yet no clear practice by which one can easily get an accurate picture, from denominational publications, both of the separate churches and of their combined activity. Obviously statistics, though a useful tool, should not become an end in themselves. Statistical difficulties would hardly seem to justify an unfavorable attitude toward local church co-operation.

When the expenditures for the last fiscal years reported are summarized, irrespective of denominational lines, the total enterprise is seen to involve no small sum:

| | |
|---|---|
| Camp Joy | $13,314.50 |
| Findlay Street Neighborhood House | 40,068.82 |
| West Cincinnati-St. Barnabas' churches | 18,041.98 |
| | $71,425.30 |

This is a considerable undertaking.

This study has made no effort to study the Neighborhood House as to the professional adequacy of its staff or as to the social work standards maintained. Backed by two major denominations and the Community Chest, it appears to be rendering a needed and appreciated service. Perhaps a competent and sympathetic survey of its organization and program might throw light on its relationships, and how they could be clarified and strengthened.

If new quarters were ever in sight, the question of location might come up. In an increasingly Negro neighborhood can an interracial program be maintained? If not, should such a settlement move in order to demonstrate interracial possibilities, or should it remain and serve the people living in its neighborhood? The same would apply to the Presbyterian and Episcopal churches.

Is this a racially transitional situation, or will it remain biracial?

FINDLAY STREET NEIGHBORHOOD HOUSE, 1952

| Monthly Average | | Attendance | |
| Total Enrollment | Groups per Month | Sessions | Persons |
|---|---|---|---|
| 498 | 24 | 1,594 | 29,839 |
| 182 | 11 clubs | 537 | 6,735 |
| 198 | 8 classes | 496 | 7,089 |
| 69 | 4 teams | 397 | 9,575 |
| 46 | 1 noon recreation hour | 162 | 6,415 |
| Organized group activities, without definite enrollment | | 131 | 12,963 |
| Individual use of facilities (mass recreation) | | | 31,478 |
| Interviews, etc. | | | 166 |
| Outside groups using facilities—average 2 per month | | 62 total sessions | 1,300 total attendance |

Registrants 12/31/52   359 M, 335 F          Under 18:   325 M, 150 F
Different persons registered:

| | During 1952 | | | January, 1954 | | |
| | Total | Male | Female | Total | Male | Female |
|---|---|---|---|---|---|---|
| Under 18 | 707 | 423 | 284 | 663 | 406 | 257 |
| 18 and over | 254 | 75 | 179 | 247 | 53 | 194 |
| Totals | 961 | 498 | 463 | 910 | 459 | 451 |

Staff:

| | December, 1952 | | January, 1954 | |
| | Full-time | Part-time | Full-time | Part-time |
|---|---|---|---|---|
| Professional and administrative | 2 | 2 | 2 | 1 |
| Clerical | 1 | 1 | 1 | 1 |
| Volunteers | — | 14 | — | 23 |
| Nonprofessionals | — | 8 | — | 9 |
| Totals | 3 | 25 | 3 | 34 |

## Camp Joy, June 29 to August 28, 1953

|  | Total Attendance | From Registration Area Only Total | Male | Female |
|---|---|---|---|---|
| 5 years and under | 6 | 6 | 2 | 4 |
| 6 to 8 years | 90 | 89 | 41 | 48 |
| 9 to 11 years | 149 | 148 | 81 | 67 |
| 12 to 14 years | 104 | 104 | 50 | 54 |
| 15 to 17 years | 10 | 10 | 5 | 5 |
| Totals | 359 | 357 | 179 | 178 |
| 8 through 14 days | 355 | 353 | | |
| 22 through 28 days | 4 | 4 | | |
| Beds: campers, 90; staff, 45 | | | | |
| Camper days | 4,356 | 4,260 | | |

| Staff | Number | Days in Camp |
|---|---|---|
| Administrative | 3 | 217 |
| Program specialists | 6 | 150 |
| Group counselors | 48 | 1,440 |
| 17 and under | 31[a] | 930 |
| 18 to 20 | 12 | 360 |
| 21 and over | 5 | 150 |
| Clerical, food service, and maintenance | 7 | 356 |

[a] Part-time in training.

## Summary of Camp Joy Receipts and Disbursements for the Year Ended October 13, 1953

| | | |
|---|---|---|
| Cash on Deposit, October 16, 1952 | | $1,254.82 |
| RECEIPTS | | |
| Episcopal | $ 733.00 | |
| Presbyterian | 2,100.81 | |
| Businesses | 1,719.00 | |
| Individuals | 5,103.04 | |
| Organizations | 767.00 | |
| Anonymous | 43.00 | |
| Fees | 2,191.12 | |
| Four miscellaneous items | 249.79 | |
| | | 12,906.76 |
| | | 14,161.58 |
| | | |
| DISBURSEMENTS | | |
| Food (cost per person per day, 71 cents) | 4,617.72 | |
| Staff salaries | 4,322.39 | |
| Maintenance help and cooks | 1,684.25 | |
| 25 miscellaneous items | 2,690.14 | |
| | | 13,314.50 |
| Cash on Deposit, October 13, 1953 | | $ 847.08 |

*Racial Change Succeeds Language Shifts*

*Two Methodist Churches Team Up*

East Baltimore is a section of Maryland's metropolis where, as often, language and nationality changes have been followed by racial succession. Traffic changes have meant that trucks have been diverted from East Baltimore Street, and a considerable area has been rezoned for residence. This has bettered the outlook of the East Baltimore Station, one of the oldest Methodist churches in the land, founded in 1772, with Francis Asbury as its first preacher.

This church now occupies its third location in the Fells Point area, the oldest section of the city, where there has been much shipping and market activity. In 1887 the present church site was in an up-and-coming neighborhood, predominantly Protestant. Within thirty years the area became almost entirely Jewish; then came Negroes, and with World War II white defense workers from the Southern mountains looking for high wages.

Seventy years ago churches weren't built to serve the kind of people who live in East Baltimore now in the manner in which they need to be served. Yet Southern mountain folk like pulpit-centered churches better than those with chancels. Here have lived Italians, Poles, and Negroes, in an area of blight and slums. (The church was burglarized three times in a year.) Perhaps a tenth of the population is Jewish, the rest about equally divided between Roman Catholic and Protestant sympathies, with almost a fourth really unchurched.

Houses are overcrowded. Structures built for a single family now shelter nine or ten, a family to a room, with quite inadequate toilet or bathing facilities. "No place to go" is a common complaint after school. Playground facilities are totally inadequate.

A few blocks to the west is Broadway Methodist Church, long affiliated with the Goodwill Industries under the able leadership of Dr. John S. German. Here, since 1953, Rev. Edwin Schell has served as pastor and as Goodwill chaplain. A former Transit

Company employee, but trained for the ministry at Drew, he has faced the East Baltimore situation with imagination. "Along lower Broadway large numbers of single adults reside in the rooming houses."

To the East Baltimore Station came, two years ago, a man with a quite unusual background, Clifford C. Ham. Member of a Congregational church in a Boston suburb, he had graduated from M.I.T. after specializing in city planning. He could have had a good salary in that field, but he found himself more interested in people than in buildings and streets. So he attended Andover-Newton. On graduation, not finding an inner-city task in Boston Congregationalism, which was still closing up churches, and offered the East Baltimore Station by the Methodist district superintendent, at a salary far below what he could have secured three years earlier, he took it. Having learned something about the study of the city, Ham teamed up with Edwin Schell on his arrival at Broadway, and together they studied their area. The results are interesting.

First, this allegedly solidly Roman Catholic section of the city turned out to be 48 per cent Protestant. Moreover, the older Poles, whose children had married and moved out, naturally had fewer babies than the in-migrant Protestant mountaineers. "There is one child for each two adults among Roman Catholics, but one child for *each* adult among Protestants" in this area. Spot maps of residences showed that the two churches were foci of two different groups, with little overlapping. So the two men did not force a merger but joined hands and staffs. Each preaches for the other once a month; in the summer they have union services. Women's and youth fellowships are combined. There is boys' work and girls' work; and there are choirs. There is a seminary student helper, a music director (one day a week in each church), and a woman worker at each church. All are listed by both churches.

In the vicinity of the East Baltimore Station 2,800 unchurched were discovered; near Broadway there were 1,700.

There is an annual turnover as high as 100 per cent, especially among the unchurched. To the east a few blocks, where the Hams live, things are quite different—better houses, more permanent residents. And a surprising number of the more solid, older residents want to stay in East Baltimore. While there is mobility even among church families, a large proportion of Protestants— 83 families out of 105 who answered queries—wish to remain in the neighborhood.

Redevelopment and slum clearance may quite change the nature of this whole section of the city. Some day, when projected housing developments are completed, the two congregations might unite on a new site.

Meanwhile East Broadway Station has the only Scout troop in the whole area. Why is the panel in the basement door broken? Why is choir rehearsal interrupted? Answer: The children want to get in to play.

"Children of the neighborhood look upon both churches as being community centers. Children of all denominations frequent the activities, though even Protestant parents are reluctant to take part. Negro children enter some of our clubs; one boys' club has been established as an interracial club; but no Negro adults attend. 'Goodwill,' for many years, has been operated on an interracial basis." While Negroes have long been present and are slowly increasing in number, "the opportunity for work among white persons may be expected to continue unabated," according to competent counsel.

Sunday mornings last year, attendance at church at East Baltimore Station averaged eighty, at Sunday school half again as much; at Broadway the figures were about the same. March, 1954, figures were higher: 170 at church, 270 at Sunday school, on the average. Into these two churches goes $7,000 of mission money a year. The 400 members in the two congregations raise $10,000, and stewardship education can be expected to up this amount. (Previous to last year no concerted every-member canvass had been made for years.) The Goodwill, for services rendered, adds $2,000. Total 1953–1954 budget, $19,000; and this has probably increased during the present year. The two comrades play a team game, fighting side by side in the changing city. Last year the two churches secured 42 new members.

The last two paragraphs in the January 30, 1954, *News of Broadway* tell of a religious survey conducted in December, 1953. "More than 500 families (every 15th one) were canvassed. . . . The religious affiliation and activity of each person was sought. The most significant finding was that there are 6,023 persons in the area (out of an estimated 30,000 total population) who are either Protestant but don't now attend church, or else are unchurched. This number of persons, far beyond our expectations, can and must furnish us with opportunity for doing the Lord's work. The Catholic population will decline shortly. Our area will become either *more Protestant or more pagan.*"

In other words, population change is not always to the disadvantage of Protestantism. Sometimes it increases Protestant opportunity.

Methodist strategy in East Baltimore is based on careful analysis. A strong study committee, resulting from the joint action of the two official boards on November 2, 1953, was chaired by the district superintendent and included leading lay persons in the district. Four meetings were held, and a committee on ways and means held two later sessions. As of April 21, 1954, a careful memorandum reviewed the work of the study committee, which had been instructed "to study means to marshal existing forces to do a more effective job . . . with no idea of leaving the neighborhood." It was interested in history, but regarded the future as more important than the past. Acting on the data carefully tabulated and mapped by the two pastors, and awaiting possible neighborhood redevelopment, the committee called meanwhile for "demonstrating through a combined staff operating at both sites how much an intelligent, enlarged program in Christian fellowship can mean to a downtown area."

A solid basis for progress has been laid by a total of 1,500 calls through staff visitation in nine months. Immediate needs include some thousands of dollars for repairs and renovation. A full-time boys' worker was to come in June. The denomination has been competently committed to backing these two churches in the light of the "unsuspected opportunities" revealed by "existing conditions and future trends." Here survey leads to action and to long-range planning.

### Two Denominations Team Up

Also in East Baltimore, but a little nearer the heart of the city, stands McKim Community Center at Aisquith and East Baltimore streets. The building housed the first free school in the city. It was willed to the care of Stony Run Friends Meeting (Hicksite, formerly Park Avenue) for educational purposes. In it the Friends conducted a day nursery until 1947. In former years it also housed an Italian Presbyterian church. With the death of the Italian minister, this group had run its course. Since then, under a new pastor the Church of the Savior has been conducting a holding operation, with the hearty approval of Presbytery, awaiting the new potential community which seems likely to be erected almost at its doorstep. Several new housing developments are at various stages of completion in this section of the city.

At present this is an area of rapid turnover, of old housing occupied by highly transient families and individuals. Most of the newer whites are hill people from the South, relatively uneducated. The church does not have a staff large enough to render adequate pastoral service. Other activities have seemed more important than calling on people who are here today and likely to be gone tomorrow.

In 1930 this church, then Italian, had 77 members and a Sunday school enrolling 129. In 1935 church membership had increased to 84; from 1940 to 1945 it held steady at 92, nominally at least. Then came the change-over. Church membership in 1950 was only a dozen; Sunday-school enrollment, forty. Both figures increased slowly, so that the last General Assembly statistics show 25 church members and 59 enrolled in Sunday school. Pretty much the same group comes first for Sunday school at 10 A.M. and remains for church at 11—35 to 40 children plus perhaps an average of ten adults. Two Sundays a month there is an evening service.

But this is the smallest part of the McKim story, a part that may loom larger when better housing provides a more rewarding field from the standpoint of church activities. The McKim Community Association is an organization with a Board of Directors a third of whom are Friends and two-thirds Presbyterians.

The objects of this Association are:

"1. To conduct activities for the betterment of the spirit, mind, and body of young people and children, especially in areas of Baltimore City where there is special need of Christian help and leadership.

"2. To coordinate the work of the McKim Community Center and of the Boys' Haven and to organize the participation in this work by members of the Society of Friends and by the members of the Presbytery of Baltimore.

"3. To direct the activities centered in the McKim School Building at Baltimore and Aisquith and the activities centered in the Boys' Haven, at Lombard and Pennsylvania Streets, Baltimore, Md., owned by the Presbytery of Baltimore, and in any other property either may use for the purposes of the Association, this direction of activities having the consent of the owners of the properties so used."

The work of the Boys' Haven, which is located eighteen blocks away in West Baltimore, will be taken up later. For the moment, let us consider the Community House program. In the first place, there is the Day Nursery, or Morning Play School, conducted by a mature woman, from 10 A.M. to noon, Tuesday through Friday. An average of seven children attend. Ten would be the maximum permitted by the health authorities, unless children's toilets and a second stairway were added; and with more children, more personnel would be needed.

Other activities, Monday to Friday, are as follows:

| Day | Afternoons | Evenings |
|---|---|---|
| Monday | Boys' activities (60 to 70 attending) | Scouts (Haven Troop to be merged) |
| Tuesday | Interracial sports (70 to 80 Negroes, 4 or 5 whites) | Open house, teen-agers (attendance 50 to 100) |
| Wednesday | Elves (attendance 12 to 18) (younger girls) | Junior Optimists (15 to 20 members) (crafts and sports) |
| Thursday | Girls' activities (attendance 15 to 20) | Open house (attendance 50 to 100 juniors) |
| Friday | Lincoln Club (attendance 25 Negroes, 10 to 13 years) | Movies (45 to 60 attending) |

Trips on Saturdays, after sleeping Friday night at the Center
Also swimming at the "Y"
Camping activities, and athletic teams in all major sports

The area served stretches six to eight blocks in each direction. Perhaps 600 different persons are reached, half of them in any average week. (Total attendance figures for 1953 were 22,327.) Some activities are biracial, but when Negroes attend, whites tend to stay away. It is reported that the Negro boys who attend are for the most part better disciplined than and both intellectually and physically superior to their white neighbors. "During the year 1953 more than two hundred Negro boys took part in experimental groups which were so successful that they have been made permanent," said the director in his annual report. These boys are said to have made a "warm, affectionate response."

Last year more than 70 per cent of the membership "moved from the neighborhood as their homes were torn down by the city to make room for two vast housing projects. . . . Most of the area south and north . . . was converted into . . . rubble by the demolition squads, and thousands of people moved away." Nevertheless the Center felt "the constant pressure of more children who wanted to come than" could be absorbed. "In about two more years a minimum of three thousand new children will come into [the] vicinity almost over night." Obviously this may present the need for more adequate facilities.

The 1954 budget of the Center includes three major items:

| | |
|---|---|
| Operating | $1,300 |
| Program | 1,500 |
| Salaries | 7,200 [a] |
| | $10,000 |

[a] Not including that of the director.

The Boys' Haven cost $11,770 in 1953, and the 1954 cost was to be larger. It is operated in a 27-room house, which once belonged to a sea captain, located at 700 West Lombard Street, donated by Friends. Here lives the remarkable Rev. Robert Meyer, who is pastor of the church and director of the Center and of Boys' Haven. He is a markedly effective speaker and spends perhaps a fourth of his evenings in financing this varied enterprise.

Living with him is a Mennonite service unit of four persons: a housekeeper, a cook, and two young men who are rendering "alternate service" as conscientious objectors to military conscription. They help gather rummage, the sale of which now provides income amounting to $100 a week; they help in maintenance at the Haven and the Center, and in the care of the boys at the Haven. As "the only private home for delinquent boys in the state," the Haven has its "capacity of eight constantly filled." It is hoped "to increase the quota to twelve as soon as possible. The boys at the Haven are those who have the most difficult problems that society can produce." A psychiatric social worker spends one day a week here. Mrs. Dorothy Curtis Melby, director of the Baltimore Department of Welfare, and a Presbyterian laywoman, helped get the necessary legal sanctions for the Haven.

This report has no technical competence to evaluate the work of the Haven, which is regarded by Dr. Harold H. Baldwin, chairman of the Department of the Urban Church of the National Council of Churches, and secretary of the Department of City and Industrial Work of the Presbyterian Board of National Missions, as "a unique and outstanding ministry which should have national recognition." These are boys whose cases nobody else wants to tackle. "Stealing, drunkenness, running away, truancy, shootings, knifings, etc., have been the normal patterns of their lives." What sort of man Mr. Meyer is, is indicated by his statement that last year "work with the delinquent and problem children continued as our special interest." (James W. Hoffman, writing on "Boys Wanted," in *Presbyterian Life* for January 7, 1950, says that Bob Meyer, Princeton Seminary '47, was "looking for a job with a lot of boys in it—preferably 'tough' boys." Later the same writer described "A Houseful of Boys" in the same journal for February 21, 1953, with well-deserved recognition of Betty [his wife] as well as Bob.)

During 1953–1954 Mr. Meyer was assisted at the McKim Center by John Sexton, a part-time teacher at Friends School, who lives just across the street from the Center and was to be employed there full-time effective the summer of 1954.

Into these combined enterprises the Presbyterian Board of National Missions, working through Presbytery, puts $6,800 a year, the local Friends $1,000. At least $9,000, over and above public payments for the boys at the Haven, is needed to make up the balance.

It will be noted that this very considerable threefold enterprise is at present marking time in several particulars. Because of an inadequate number of paid personnel, home visitation is necessarily limited, and high transiency makes it difficult to establish a sense either of neighborhood or of Christian fellowship. The Boys' Haven would appear to be performing a difficult function, impossible without skill and devotion, which in the long run might perhaps be a responsibility of Co-operative Protestantism as a whole.

Relationships in this threefold enterprise are a bit ambiguous. A printed announcement and financial appeal says that "McKim," which is termed "your only local Quaker charity," conducts Sunday school, church, and Bible study groups. But the church is Presbyterian! Is this to be regarded as a happy indication of the fact that denominational distinctions are being increasingly outmoded, or as evidence of structural vagueness?

More systematic reporting, by the Association itself, not so much for promotional or public relations purposes but as a sober accounting in terms of program and finance and of social work functions performed, would help the objective student. A chief center of interest, from the standpoint of this study, is the Church of the Savior. Will it be helped to embrace the new spiritual opportunity which seems to lie ahead of it? Will it be adequately staffed and housed? Will it become a fellowship of Christian persons, thoroughly committed to building the Kingdom in East Baltimore?

# Chapter VII

# Language and Nationality Changes

Sometimes social changes involve not race but language or nationality background. Often in such cases, where non-Protestants are on the increase, and for one reason or another total population may be decreasing, more or less radical readjustment of Protestant forces is required. An exceptionally well-documented instance of this sort has progressively developed in East Boston, Massachusetts.

A quite separate section of the larger city, East Boston was the scene of a significant piece of "action research" (*Protestantism in East Boston, 1920–1946*), completed by the Massachusetts Council of Churches' Department of Research and Strategy in 1947. Its then director, Dr. William J. Villaume, sought not to prescribe solutions to the manifest problems inherent in the over-churching of a decreasingly Protestant area but to provide a factual basis for action by the parties at interest.

(In 1950 East Boston had 51,112 inhabitants, as compared with 790,863 in the city as a whole—a sixteenth, or 6.4 per cent, of the total. Details of population trends and certain other social data will be presented later in this chapter.)

After his two-year study of the area, Dr. Villaume gave it as his judgment (p. 128) that "Protestants in East Boston are an unchurched minority in an overchurched community. There is nothing unique or especially disgraceful about it; it can be duplicated in almost any metropolis in the country. The churches in East Boston have the opportunity to point the way to competent rear guard action and an appropriate offensive. Survival can be

won only at the price of adaptation of attitudes, edifices, personnel, programs, and all the other aspects of an urban church, so
that Protestantism in East Boston may be capable of serving
tomorrow rather than yesterday." To Dr. Villaume it seemed evident that "larger units are the price of survival" (p. 130).

Gradually certain practical consequences of this 1946 study
emerged.[1]

The Baptists decided not to spend a proposed $75,000 on reno-
vating their old building; as an Italian Club, it now presents
certain problems to the neighborhood. The Universalists sold
their building to the Baptists.

A number of churches proceeded on their independent courses,
but two groups of congregations decided to federate. One of these
federations, "effected in 1948 by vote of the congregations," involved three centrally located churches: St. Paul's Italian Methodist, East Boston Congregational (Italian), and St. John's
Episcopal. The two Italian missions "were the major Italian
congregations in East Boston." The other federation was in
Orient Heights, at the eastern end of East Boston, and consisted
of St. Andrew's Episcopal Church and the combined Baker-Maverick Congregational organization. We consider first the three-way
federation now housed at St. John's.

## Case VII—St. John's Church, Federated, East Boston, Mass.

An Italian congregation was organized at Maverick Congregational Church in 1929. When the Baker-Maverick merger occurred in 1933, the Italian group moved to St. Mary's Episcopal
Church; then in 1942 to Union Methodist Church, and in 1944
to the Presbyterian building. Thus it is now in its fifth building
in 25 years, St. John's. All this is a part of the consolidation of
Protestant forces in the light of population change.

Rev. John J. Romolo was pastor of the Congregational Italians

---

[1] See Rev. Philip E. Anthes, "Facts and Faith in East Boston," in *The
City Church*, Sept.–Oct., 1952.

from 1929 to 1946. In later years this church had no youth program.

St. Paul's Italian Methodist Church was organized in 1920, as the sole heir to the Saratoga Street Methodist Church, which was organized in 1842. St. Paul's once reported 35 young people. Rev. Frank L. Pizzuto served this congregation for more than twenty years; he also taught at Suffolk University. (His daughter now sings in the choir at the Italian services at St. John's, Federated.) In the autumn of 1946, in a church seating 800, average attendance was 72. Church expenses for the year 1945–1946 amounted to $615. Of this, $120 was added to the $1,500 denominational salary subsidy. (In 1934 the Methodist Church had abolished its bilingual conference, an event which in that denomination brought to a head the transition from bilingual to normal connectional status.)

The total membership of these two churches and a Lutheran congregation in 1946 was reported to be 488, but active membership, even as optimistically claimed, was a different story:

| Italian Churches in East Boston | 1930 | Active Members 1940 | 1946 |
|---|---|---|---|
| Congregational | — | 58 | 77 |
| Lutheran | — | 50 | 50 |
| Methodist | 173 | 228 | 140 |
| Total, as reported | 173 | 336 | 267 |

The total Sunday school enrollment showed the same rise and fall: From 125 in 1930, to 204 in 1940, and down to 91 in 1946.

A third of the active Italian Congregational members were said to live outside of East Boston in 1946, but less than a tenth of the active Methodist Italians. (Of 54 addresses now on the Italian membership list, only four are outside of East Boston—in Chelsea, Everett, Hyde Park, and Revere—involving ten persons. Only two East Boston Italian member families live east of Day Square, but Grace Church has at least one additional Italian family.)

Neither of the Italian congregations had a suitable building. The Congregationalists were housed by the Presbyterians. The Methodist edifice was ill suited to the use of a small congregation. One argument favoring the use of St. John's was the consequent reduction in maintenance costs. When the federation was effected, the Methodist Church sold its property, and under the new ownership the building was demolished down to the ground level. The site is now occupied by a bowling alley. The proceeds of this sale were used in behalf of Negro Methodist work in Boston's South End, an episode which was unfortunately the cause of some unhappiness on the part of the East Boston Italian Methodists. There was also some resentment because the East Boston study seemed to treat East Boston Italians as "guinea pigs." They felt "pushed around," even where there had been the most resolute effort to avoid ground for any such feeling.

It was not easy for the two Italian congregations to shift their loyalty to a new setting. The arrangement was accepted by them as the best possible at the moment, under the guidance of their denominational leaders, but without enthusiasm. No alternative course seemed open to them. They thought of the federation as a temporary makeshift, or saw in it a hope that has not yet been realized. They have never given up the hope of "our own church." Attendance was never up to expectations. The English congregation intended to welcome them heartily. "Equipment, facilities, and programs for young people were the best to be had in East Boston." However, the Italian and English congregations, after six years, do not yet constitute a unit of Christian fellowship, as was intended.

While in their original articles of agreement (March, 1948) the three churches agreed "to form and act as one congregation for all purposes of work and worship," it was also early agreed (May, 1948) that "in order to prepare the two congregations of Italian people to worship together and to become accustomed to new surroundings, the Italian churches worship separately in St. John's Church . . . until Sept. 19, 1948." At the time agreed upon, the two Italian congregations began to worship together in the Italian language. It had been contemplated that the entire federated church would sponsor two services; one in English and the other in Italian. The latter was a concession to the older Italian people, but young people of all three churches were expected to attend the chief service, which was in English. There has not been a noticeable influx of Congregationalists or Methodists at the English service. Is this because the service is basically Episcopal in its form? The fact remains that for purposes of work and worship the number of congregations has been reduced from three to two, but not to one as originally contemplated. The English service remains largely a service for Episcopalians.

Another argument in favor of federation was economy of other budget costs. In 1940 Congregational and Methodist treasuries each subsidized their respective Italian missions by $1,500 annually. (The Methodist total subsidy had been $3,450 in 1920; and in 1930, four years before the bilingual conference was given up, it was $2,000.) The amount received in 1953 by the federated enterprise for Italian work included $1,200 Congregational aid and $300 Methodist. A gift of $100 was received from an Episcopalian. These three items provided the Italian minister's salary and the organist's small stipend.

As compared with the $500 which the Italian members had hoped to pay toward salary, contributions in 1950 amounted to only $265.23, a decrease of $144.31 from 1949. However, benevolences were up from $8.50 in 1949 to $82.42 in 1950. Total Italian giving for the last three years is listed on page 161.

Counting the 1953 membership of the Italian congregation as 66, the contribution per member amounted to $5.60. In 1945–1946 the contribution per member was $3.90 for the Congregationalists and $7.73 for the Methodists. Unfortunately the present arrangement makes no adequate appeal to the loyalty or generosity of the Italian congregation. They report that they do not feel they are supporting their own church. The $221.84 given to the federation in 1953 seems too much like rent, and from the stand-

|  | *1951* | *1952* | *1953* |
|---|---|---|---|
| Current Expenses |  |  |  |
| Pledges | $150.26 | $ 38.00 | *a* |
| Loose offerings | 63.04 | 158.34 | $221.84 |
| Total | $213.30 | $196.34 | $221.84 |
| Benevolences |  |  |  |
| Pledges | $ 32.30 | *a* | *a* |
| Loose offerings | 38.71 | $101.75 *b* | $147.78 *c* |
| Total | $ 71.01 | $101.75 | $147.78 |
| Grand total | $284.31 | $297.09 | $369.62 |

*a* Pledge system discontinued.
*b* Congregational $51.10; Methodist $50.65.
*c* Congregational $73.89; Methodist $73.89.
(Figures taken from the annual reports of the church treasurer.)

point of the host congregation no doubt such an amount is inevitably thought of as a rather modest sum that hardly more than pays for the added expense. The Italian people have never given generously, and the federation has not inspired them in this regard. The decrease in subsidies is related solely to lowering the expenditures for "overhead."

There were formerly two part-time Italian pastors; since 1949 there has been one full-time minister for both Italian groups, which have worshiped together at 9 A.M. in St. John's Church. Rev. Gaetano Iorizzo, who does not live in the community, but at 185 Summer Street, Lynn, is a man in his late sixties. Born near Naples, he spent three high-school years in Italy, later studying at Bloomfield Seminary, Colgate-Rochester, and Biblical Seminary.

In May 1954, Mr. Iorizzo listed 68 active members: 53 of Methodist background, 15 of Congregational. However, the figures are still ambiguous. Of 113 total members, including inactive, 23 may be called Congregational in background, but not all the others would call themselves Methodist. Several families have been for a while associated with a Lutheran church. In 1952 a total of 80 active members were reported to the Methodist Conference, along with 146 inactive; and 34 members (of whom six were "absent") were reported to the Congregational year book. Combined Methodist and Congregational attendance now ranges from 35 to 40, largely older people. On Easter Sunday, 1954, there were 66 persons present.

The Methodist name (St. Paul's) dropped out of use. It was planned at the time of federation to use the name of St. John's because of its prestige value in the community, and to speak of the Episcopal, Methodist and Congregational "rolls." Yet, in the Congregational year book there has as yet been no reference to "St. John's, Federated," but only to "East Boston, Italian Federated."

The maintenance of adequate denominational contacts has not been easy. In the 1952 Congregational year book no contributions to the Congregational Christian World Mission were recorded. There appear to have been no Congregational accessions for several years, and reported Congregational membership in the church decreased more than half (59.5 per cent) in five years. One does not know how much of this loss was due to "cleaning the roll." The Boston City Missionary Society formerly supplied a lady missionary.

During Lent, 1954, two new members were received, the first since the reception of two others in June, 1953.

As a matter of convenience, money received from the Italian congregation is by agreement distributed thus: 20 per cent to the Methodist Church, 20 per cent to the Congregational, both for benevolences; and 60 per cent to St. John's Church, Federated, for local expenses. The treasurer of St. John's Episcopal Church is also treasurer of the federation.

For business purposes the Congregational membership is supposed to meet monthly; the Methodist district superintendent attends the fourth quarterly conference of the Methodist membership.

Denominational lines seem decreasingly significant. Italians are interested chiefly in "the church," not *which* church. "Where do you want to join?" puzzles them. Recently hopeful experimentation with bilingual services has given some evidence that the 9 A.M. worship can be more than a rear-guard action in behalf of elderly Italians who speak English haltingly and worship most congenially in their native tongue. The younger members of the Italian congregation are largely Americanized, and desire to be thought of as English-speaking Americans.

There is one Sunday school for all three of the federated churches. It meets at nine-thirty, which theoretically means that boys and girls, and young people, of the Italian families must choose between it and the overlapping worship service for Italians. Actually, however, only one or two are involved in this schedule conflict, and it has been assumed they would prefer to attend the English service at eleven o'clock. It also means that Italian children are being integrated into the experience of the federated parish. Further, it should be remembered that St. John's gave up the use of its church by its school, using basement rooms instead, so that the church could be available for the Italian worship. It must be added that when the churches federated, there was no longer any Italian Sunday school or youth work. Obviously it would be possible for boys and girls to attend the first half of the Italian service and the whole Sunday-school hour, provided their parents would linger half an hour after service or join in the closing portion of the church school.

The formalism, even of the Low Church Morning Prayer at 11 A.M., seems not to appeal to the older Italians who have been brought up in nonliturgical worship patterns; yet they appreciate being able to hold their own service in the church. They rejoice in the beauty of the edifice, but they are not too sure of their welcome.

We turn now to *St. John's Episcopal Church*, considered in its own right. In 1946 "the Episcopal Church was the largest and most active in East Boston. Its youth program was more extensive than any other in the Protestant churches of the area." This is still true. From 1946 to 1953 St. John's communicant membership dropped from 215 to 187; and church school enrollment from a high of 150 in 1950 to 105 in 1953, or 56.1 per 100 communicants, but only 41.5 if 66 Italian members (the number before the most recent accessions) are included. This Sunday school loss reflects both the removal of 25 children in families that have recently left the area and also the death of a church visitor. Over against constant losses by migration outward and by death, confirmations have averaged nearly seventeen per year for the last five years, which gives a creditable evangelistic index of nine per 100 communicant members.

Confirmations for the last five calendar years and for early 1954 have been as follows:

| Year | Confirmations |
|------|---------------|
| 1949 | 26 |
| 1950 | 18 |
| 1951 | 13 |
| 1952 | 10 |
| 1953 | 17 (total, 5 years, 84; average 17) |
| 1954 (to May 1) | 11 |

Of these persons, six have themselves been Italian or Portuguese, or one or both of their parents have been. Immediately after Easter of each year a new group begins instruction. A year's previous attendance is required for confirmation. These look like the figures of a healthy, if somewhat leaner, church.

In addition to an occasional Italian confirmation, several young people of Italian background are now taking hold in the youth work and church school and are proving to be faithful and competent workers. Is an increasing number of requests for weddings, sometimes of mixed faith, an evidence of a growing respect for St. John's place in the community life?

Missionary giving increased from $1,082 in 1946 to $1,200 last year, or from $5.03 to $6.42 per member. Total expenditures were $11,109 in 1946; in 1953 they had risen to $12,620. This latter figure includes the salary of the Italian minister, but not the diocesan contribution (approximately $1,600) to the rector's stipend. There is an investment income of $800 per year from an endowment of about $26,000. A major recent expense item was the cost of new guttering. This is one of a number of projected property improvements, some of which will make the church more attractive as well as improve its physical condition. A new outside light, and some paint on a couple of doors, will help quite out of proportion to the cost.

(It is not always easy to distinguish between St. John's Episcopal Church with 188 communicants, and St. John's Church, Federated, with 256 members. The former has so large a proportion of the membership and the financial responsibility of the federation that the two are readily confused. Seemingly, the federated budget amounts to about $14,220, but $3,000 of this is subsidy, the cost of student help not being included in either figure. Deduct endowment income, and the three congregations would seem to be giving or raising for all purposes approximately $10,420, or $41.19 per member of the federation excluding two recently added. There is also $11.37 per member in subsidy, and $3.14 per member from endowment income, thus making a total, including benevolences, of $56.21 per active member, an amount significantly large. Even if all Episcopal constituents (624) [2] and

[2] On examination, Mr. Anthes' constituency list is found to contain 624 different persons' names, including parents of interested children, but not all of the girls in the Girl Scout troop. It would probably be conservative to say that St. John's serves nearly 650 people.

As to their relationship to the parish, the 624 persons, all of whose names and addresses have been carefully checked, are distributed thus:

| | | |
|---|---|---|
| Communicants last year | | 211 |
| Episcopal | 188 | |
| Other | 23 | |
| Other confirmed Episcopalians | | 86 |
| Other baptized Episcopalians | | 153 |
| Of confirmation age | 31 | |
| Under confirmation age | 122 | |
| Other baptized adults | | 87 |
| Other baptized children | | 22 |
| Other constituents | | 65 |
| | | 624 |

113 active and inactive Italian members are considered, the per person expenditure was $19.29. The total Italian work expendi-

These individuals are distributed as to family grouping thus:

|  | In East Boston | | In 15 Other Places | |
|  | Families | Persons | Families | Persons |
|---|---|---|---|---|
| Individuals |  | 112 |  | 16 |
| Families of |  |  |  |  |
| 2 persons | 56 | 112 | 6 | 12 |
| 3 persons | 35 | 105 | 3 | 9 |
| 4 persons | 30 | 120 | 1 | 4 |
| 5 persons | 13 | 65 | 2 ᵃ | 10 |
| 6 persons | 5 | 30 |  |  |
| 7 persons | 3 | 21 |  |  |
| 8 persons | 1 | 8 |  |  |
| Totals | 143 | 573 | 12 | 51 |
|  |  |  | 155 | 624 |
|  |  |  | 283 addresses |  |

ᵃ Includes State Hospital, Mattapan.

Approximately a tenth of the members resident in East Boston live east of Day Square, and another tenth on Maverick Street or southwest of it. These latter are the faithful remnant of old St. Mary's parish, who formerly worshiped at Cottage and Marginal Streets. There is no Protestant church in that entire area now. Special pick-up transportation is provided for these loyal members.

Practically the entire membership is within attending distance. Of the 573 constituents in East Boston, almost all live within a mile of the church, probably the great majority of them within walking distance—at least according to pre-automobile standards.

The degree of what the sociologists call acculturation already accomplished by St. John's is shown by the following 43 surnames, lifted by inspection from the constituency list:

| | | |
|---|---|---|
| Abric | Gonzales | Nazzaro |
| Amarena | Gozzi | Pappas |
| Amirault | Hansjohn | Paquin |
| Bentilla | Heino | Patz |
| Boehner | Ivany | St. Croix |
| Cerrato | Korvek | Silva |
| Chamness | LaCortiglia | Sodergren |
| Charotas | Lapolito | Surette |
| Corauna | LeGallo | Tackach |
| Damelgo | Loche | Tascha |
| Dedeo | Lupo | Vasce |
| Diaz | MacLean | Veje |
| Doucette | MacNiel | Volpini |
| Fortier | McShane | |
| Gomes | Mello | |

ture seems now to be about $1,870, or $28.33 per active member, as compared with $5.60 per member received from the Italian group, as previously noted. That is, of the total amount spent by and for the Italian members, they provide 20 cents on the dollar.

(Incidentally, the basis of the subsidies may well be examined. Some individuals and organizations believe it wise to support persons; some denominations are increasingly clear that it is their privilege and duty to "subsidize a *program*—not a *person*." Have the supporting denominations given sufficient thought to program at St. John's Church, Federated, and their responsibility for periodic program review?)

The rector of the Episcopal church and pastor of the federated enterprise, Rev. Philip E. Anthes, who lives opposite the church at 85 Lexington Street, now has the help of two theological students, one of them for only a small fraction of his time. Earlier a third student helped to shift the boys' work program, which perhaps had been too rapidly expanded, to Boy Scout work. There is also a Girl Scout troop.

Migration outward and competition of other community activities have sometimes crippled the men's work of the parish. As the older generation dies off, the younger people tend to leave East Boston, especially this older section of it. Often it is problem families who move in, and this affects Sunday school discipline. Yet the continuing housing shortage means that there are occasionally promising church prospects among the newcomers, especially among temporary residents near the airport.

During the last five nationally reported years the neighboring East Boston Presbyterian Church has dropped from 192 to 131 members, and its Sunday school at the end of 1953 enrolled only 60, or 45.8 per 100 church members—a better ratio than St. John's presents if its Italian members are included. Current expenses for the four years ending in 1952 averaged $5,781 per year. Last year local expenses were $5,600, or $42.75 per member; benevolences were $225, or $9.20 per member. St. John's and the Presbyterians co-operate in weekday religious education, and the Presbyterian pastor's wife has been a worker in this activity. The present Presbyterian pastor, Rev. A. E. Drake, 59 Monmouth Street, has been in East Boston three years; he says the church is able to enlist children from the housing project. Several Italians sing in the Presbyterian choir. The original Scotch members of the church keep moving out, but Mr. Drake is hopeful about the future of the church. There seems to have been some recent step-up in this work.

The recent nonresident Baptist minister, who moved elsewhere, has been succeeded by a busy Boston City Hospital chaplain, unmarried, formerly a missionary in China. A Tuesday evening Holy Week service was held at this church. The revamped building (formerly belonging to the Universalists) is said now to need additional repairs.

There are now only three resident Protestant ministers in East Boston: (1) Mr. Anthes, who has been there for twenty years; (2) the Presbyterian pastor; and (3) the Orient Heights minister, who lives in a distinct section of the area. The Unitarians, however, have reportedly purchased a parsonage for their new minister, under whose leadership they have recently shown some signs of renewed vigor.

Half a dozen men, or less, attend the ministerial association. A student serves an Augustana Lutheran church, and a retired minister a scattered Norwegian parish. There are also a small Salvation Army unit, which has recently sold its commercially desirable property and will probably seek a new site, and a Gospel Hall. In spite of mergers, there is still some overchurching; further consolidation of Protestant forces, if possible, might strengthen the witness of Protestantism, as compared with the present competitive effort of a number of small enterprises.

The rector of Sacred Heart Roman Catholic Church has recently been made a monsignor. There is also a Roman Catholic Portuguese Mission. Archbishop Cushing has been aggressive. The city sold the Roman Catholics a building, at a reputed bargain, which helps to provide better facilities. The C.Y.O. is in-

creasingly active. In 1946 indifference was reported. Perhaps
one result of the research study was to stimulate all the churches
to greater community service. The Italian Club is largely Roman
Catholic; yet reputedly many Italians lack enthusiasm for this
Church.

Part of the Protestant problem is how to serve Italians who
move out of East Boston. On the other hand, some people have
moved back.

The success so far of St. John's Church, Federated, has been
attributed to three factors: (1) a solid basis of fact, in the research study, "which reviewed every aspect of the community
and church life in East Boston," (2) unique ministerial personnel, and (3) co-operative relationships among the denominations. There appears to be no annual summation of facts and
figures for the three churches in the federation. The vestry and
the Joint Committee have met together, and there is a Parish
Council; but the work of the federation as a whole has not yet
been regularly and convincingly documented. However, it is only
fair to add that while denominations have a habit of expecting
annual reports, interdenominational structures have as yet rarely
evolved to the place where an accounting of federated effort is
regularly requested.

St. John's is already one long step farther along than the situation which often obtains elsewhere. For example, more than one
strong church has built a mission for a language group. Parent
church and mission may have been geographically only a few
blocks apart, but their separation in terms of "social distance"
has been very great, even within the same denomination. The
result is that, confronted with the possibility of being deeded the
property in which they have long worshiped, the mission congregation is unwilling to accept the gift, knowing its inability to
maintain the building. At the same time, in such cases, it would
often require long, patient mutual education to enable the parent
church successfully to welcome the members of the mission congregation into an integrated fellowship. At St. John's the differ-

ent constituencies have for years worshiped under one roof and have maintained a Joint Committee. In spite of certain real surface differences, they may now be far closer together than has yet been realized.

## Orient Heights

Earlier reference has been made to a second and similar federation, in Orient Heights. Day Square is the line between the older portion of East Boston and Orient Heights, to which the East Boston tunnel line of the M.T.A. has been extended. We turn now to this interesting by-product of the East Boston study.

In the Orient Heights section of East Boston, *Grace Federated Church* has since 1949 combined the work of Baker-Maverick Congregational Church (itself a merger of two congregations, one of them located in the older section of East Boston) and St. Andrew's Episcopal. Both had been served only by students since the early 1930's and had been steadily declining in membership and Sunday school enrollment until the federation enabled the churches to call a resident pastor.

The unchurchly Congregational building is used in winter. It is quite inadequate. Its boiler is not long for this world, its roof is a problem, it has only one toilet. The church owns some extra land. St. Andrew's small fine building was the gift of a millionaire rector. It is used in summer, and frequently for weddings. It is likewise too small for the needs of the combined churches. Its site is valuable. The Congregational building is midway between Day Square and the Orient Heights station, the Episcopal not far from the Orient Heights station.

The pastor since 1949, Rev. Roger P. Cleveland, a Congregational minister, has been confirmed in the Episcopal Church. The rector of St. John's administers the Holy Communion for him monthly.

The St. Andrew's members (96) have more financial resources, including some endowment; but they are fewer than the Congregationalists, and their number is practically static. Some of them attend only the services held in their own building. Congregationalists are numerically stronger (163 members). However, no effort to balance the elected personnel is longer necessary; and even missionary distinctions tend to drop out, with all members giving to the missionary causes of both denominations. Although there had been some friction between the two congregations at the time of federation, it seems entirely to have disappeared or to amount to "even less than in any average congregation." Owing to some increase in available housing, more Protestants are moving in; but they are often problem families. Four families important to the church have recently moved away. One of the functions of Grace Church, located as it is in a neighborhood from which people migrate outward, is to train people for other parishes. It thus serves as a sort of "transmission belt to suburbia." There are some accessions from Roman Catholic families.

As compared with five years ago, the combined membership (259) has increased 38.1 per cent, as a result of consistent growth. Average attendance for 10 months in 1953 was 92, or 35.5 per cent of the total membership, as compared with a total of 60 in the two churches in 1948. Last year at the 10 A.M. service on Easter 210 attended; 31 had come at 6:30 A.M., and 24 were at the 9 A.M. Holy Communion; 95 were present in the evening. Easter, 1954, morning services were almost as well attended, in spite of contagious illness in a number of homes. Confirmations have averaged a little more than eight per year, and the evangelistic index has been 5.9 for the last seven years. Of 225 constituent families, at least four-fifths live in East Boston. A dozen or fifteen were once connected with old Maverick Church.

Sunday school attending enrollment (97 in 1953) is approximately two for each five church members (37.4 per cent). The school increased 41.3 per cent in enrollment in five years, 54 per cent in six. There is a large cradle roll, and the primary department is the largest of the attending departments. There could be a nursery if there were room. These facts promise well for the future. Young married couples are now tending to stay in Orient Heights. Confirmed young people drop out of Sunday school.

A Boy Scout troop (#1, East Boston), sponsored by the church, is only a third Protestant boys. Weekday religious education reaches ten out of the 100 Protestant children in the grades affected in the Heights school.

There are three Roman Catholic parishes in the Heights, and a small group of Jehovah's Witnesses. Roman Catholics help with Scouting. Neighbors proposed a raffle as a means of buying Mr. Cleveland a car. He is chaplain of Kiwanis and a member of the board of the Family Service Association, and is assigned Protestant court cases.

A former "Joint" Committee, now called "United," consists of three groups of two members from each of the two churches, elected for terms of three years, plus certain co-opted officers.

The Massachusetts Congregational Conference has helped with the insurance, and the City Missionary Society formerly supplied a visitor; a student assistant has been paid by the diocese. No cash subsidy is received toward the regular budget. (The Congregational church had been receiving $1,500 before the federation.) In 1952 local costs appeared to average $21.25 per member, but this was on a total of only $5,505 as compared with $9,000 three years earlier when the membership was smaller. (There is some inevitable ambiguity in figures reported to two denominations by federated churches.) Denominational benevolence giving to Congregational agencies amounted to $1.79 per member in 1952. The people, even those who "have nothing," are reportedly "always willing to give."

Outstanding needs include a parsonage or rectory and an adequate church building, to seat perhaps 150, with educational and recreational rooms. The situation would be strengthened if the pastor could receive Episcopal orders.

## Social Determinism in East Boston

In East Boston, as elsewhere, the fortunes of the churches must be considered in the light of population changes, both for the area as a whole, and in the particular neighborhoods involved.

Writing in *Christian Social Relations* for November 15, 1948, Mr. Anthes summarized the situation thus: "East Boston, as an area, has exhibited lowered income level, high juvenile delinquency, poor health standards, and inadequate social resources. The thirteen Protestant churches, suffering from decreased membership and high overhead, have been unable to contribute to its moral and social improvement. Faced with this serious situation, several of the churches united their efforts to find a constructive solution."

The figures for the last four federal censuses show that population loss has been sharply accelerated in recent years. During the decade 1940–1950, while the city of Boston as a whole gained 4 per cent, as contrasted with a slight loss (1.3 per cent) in the previous decade, the East Boston shrinkage increased to 10.1 per cent, almost three times that of the previous decade.

| Year | Population East Boston | Percentage of Gain or Loss for Decade East Boston | Boston |
|------|-----------------------|---------------------------------------------------|--------|
| 1920 | 60,778 | — | — |
| 1930 | 59,242 | −2.5 | — |
| 1940 | 56,928 | −3.9 | −1.3 |
| 1950 | 51,112 | −10.1 | +4.0 |

According to the East Boston *Times'* report of the annual police count, there are now 31,456 persons over twenty years of age in East Boston, a drop of 282 in 1953 and a loss of 8,000 in a decade.

Of course such population losses are not equally distributed. In the Orient Heights census tract (A-1), where St. Andrew's Church is located, the population loss during the last decade was only 5.6 per cent. In the tract where Baker-Maverick is located

(A-2) the shrinkage amounted to 9.6 per cent. On the other hand, the St. John's neighborhood (A-5) showed only 6.2 per cent loss, while the business district to the south (B-1 and B-2) lost more than three times as much or 22.2 per cent.

Tunnels and bridges, and particularly their exact location, affect many such redistributions of metropolitan population.

Of the 51,112 total population in East Boston in 1950, those born in Italy numbered 7,121, as compared with a total of 25,315 in Boston as a whole. In East Boston approximately one inhabitant in seven was Italian-born, or 13.9 per cent as compared with only 3.2 per cent city-wide. As early as 1940 "six out of ten from Italian stock in America had been born in this country and one of the other four had been here since childhood." [3] "Eventual assimilation" seems inevitable, and a large extent is already accomplished. Other indices of social conditions vary similarly.

Owner occupancy in 1950 was as follows in the four neighborhoods just mentioned.

*Per Cent of Dwellings Owner Occupied*

| | |
|---|---|
| Business district | 19.4 |
| St. John's district | 23.4 |
| Baker-Maverick district | 37.2 |
| St. Andrew's district | 39.9 |
| Boston | 24.4 |

Dilapidation, including lack of private bath or running water, varies likewise.

| | *Per Cent with No Private Bath* | *Per Cent with No Running Water* |
|---|---|---|
| Business district | 48.6 | 11.8 |
| St. John's district | 25.9 | 3.0 |
| Baker-Maverick district | 9.1 | 2.6 |
| St. Andrew's district | 3.1 | .3 |
| Boston | 15.4 | 6.1 |

[3] William J. Villaume, *Protestant Ministry to Italian People in Massachusetts*, p. 32. Monograph published by the Department of Research and Strategy, Massachusetts Council of Churches, Boston, Mass., Feb., 1951.

Overcrowding shows a similar picture—as measured by percentage of dwellings with more than 1.51 persons per room:

|  | Per Cent |
|---|---|
| Business district | 3.6 |
| St. John's district | 3.6 |
| Baker-Maverick district | 1.5 |
| St. Andrew's district | .1 |
| Boston | 3.2 |

Average monthly rent for dwellings varies in similar fashion:

|  |  |
|---|---|
| Business district, B–1 | $21.44 |
| Business district, B–2 | 24.26 |
| St. John's district | 26.03 |
| Baker-Maverick district | 28.75 |
| St. Andrew's district | 35.64 |
| Boston | $38.39 |

In like manner, East Boston median monthly rents indicate that the people of this section of the city live economically so far as housing costs are concerned:

| East Boston | | Boston | |
|---|---|---|---|
| 1940 | 1950 | 1940 | 1950 |
| $20.04 | $28.03 | $28.41 | $35.40 |

Median family income in 1950 was $2,811 in East Boston as compared with $2,643 for the city as a whole.

Block-by-block statistics show that the situation in the immediate vicinity of St. John's Church also varies greatly from block to block. In the following tabulation the block in which the church is located is labeled NE, the one to the south SE, the one diagonally across the corner SW, and the one to the west NW.

|  | Owner Occupied (Per Cent) | Dilapidation No Private Bath | (Per Cent) No Running Water | Over-crowding (Per Cent) | Average Rent |
|---|---|---|---|---|---|
| NW | 26.4 | 28.3 | 26.6 | 1.9 | $23.63 |
| NE | 36.6 | 21.9 | 3.7 | 1.3 | 28.08 |
| SE | 31.5 | 18.5 | 1.9 | 3.7 | 29.95 |
| SW | 12.9 | 46.6 | 3.1 | 9.5 | 27.96 |
| 4 blocks | 23.6 | 32.7 | 5.8 | 5.6 | — |
| Boston | 24.4 | 15.4 | 6.1 | 3.2 | $38.39 |

Such figures throw a new light on church statistics. They go far to explain why five major Protestant denominations have only 911 members in East Boston, or less than 2 per cent of the population.

A major question facing both these federations of churches is, Can and will East Boston be redeveloped? Obviously the churches should make the most of the Mayor's interest in this, and should develop their city-planning contacts.

### Next Steps

#### At St. John's

The problem of St. John's Church, Federated, lies partly in the "social distance" between the non-Episcopal members of Italian background and the Episcopal members with their chiefly Anglo-Saxon traditions. Here are three churches worshiping in two congregations, using different languages, under the same roof. Yet psychologically they are not yet a federated unit. One hears talk about "they"; "we" and "ours" are not yet used by either group with reference to the total enterprise. Is the federation getting anywhere?

There are at least a few straws to show that the wind has been blowing in the right direction.

In the first place, Congregational and Methodist Italians have dropped both labels and are now a unified congregation, with the Italian language regarded as a spiritual asset, though less and less a necessity. Moreover, from the standpoint of faithful, bona fide worshipers, rather than year-book statistics, the Italian congregation has recently increased. In spite of the grave difficulties he has faced, Mr. Iorizzo's leadership has brought the situation into a period of new opportunity.

In the second place, while they would very much like to have their own home, the Italians are realistically aware that they could neither secure nor maintain a church building on their own resources; and the same goes for the employment of a full-time minister, resident in the community. Accordingly, the survival of Protestantism among the Italians in East Boston is squarely up to the denominations which began these missions.

Third, it is great gain to recognize the actual facts. In two instances there has been serious misunderstanding.

1. The Joint Committee on Organization, on May 23, 1948, recommended "that both congregations call the Rev. Philip E. Anthes as chief pastor of the federated congregation." It had been presumed that the Italian congregation had taken this action. Their unanimous testimony is quite to the contrary. They seemingly understood that during the period when the former pastors of the two Italian churches were withdrawing and a new Italian minister was being sought, the rector was to serve as pastor of all three congregations; but once they had their own pastor, the Italians did not think of the rector as their pastor also. To be sure, in the May, 1954, mimeographed bulletin of St. John's Church (Federated), Mr. Iorizzo is listed as associate to its rector, but such a listing does not make a team out of two men, both of whom speak of each other with appreciation and respect.

2. It was agreed, by the members of the three churches and their denominational officials, in March, 1948, that "the members of the several churches shall be enrolled as members of the

federated congregation." This has never been fully implemented. It would be easy to complete such an enrollment as of May 1, 1954. This would enable all persons involved to see the federation as a co-operative unit and to understand the relative strength of its constituent congregations more clearly, and the residential distribution of the total membership.

Fourth, the co-operating denominations need to see that to bridge the gap between two languages and cultures, and three ecclesiastical entities, requires imagination, patience, and exceptional give-and-take, plus the utmost candor withal, if this bilingual, three-way fellowship is to be solidly representative of the Church Universal.

Fifth, while in the long run future Italian-Americans are going to be just Americans, and Italian Protestants already prefer just to be called Christians, even the younger members of the Italian congregation are strongly in favor of maintaining a separate church for East Boston Protestants of Italian background. They regard this as an essential witness in a non-Protestant environment. Clearly the present arrangement is not commanding the all-out enthusiasm of the Italian membership or exhausting anything like the full potential of its support or loyalty.

Sixth, the Methodist and Congregational denominations clearly owe it to the people whom they have invited into their fellowships, and to their Episcopal partners, to continue their support of an Italian service as long as it may be meaningful. Eventually such an Italian service may not need to be held weekly and might be scheduled less frequently; but the continuity of the cultural group is a different matter. A church of people of Italian background would eventually face the problem of becoming a more inclusive group, with non-Italians welcome; but for the moment the Italians themselves feel the need of their own fellowship in Christ. They need some arrangement which can be publicized in the name of the supporting denominations with enthusiasm; e.g., an attractive printed folder about Protestant Italian work in East Boston could be of very great value as a tract for distribution. It would need to be both honest and expectant, constructive, winsome. Have we perhaps wishfully sought too rapidly to accelerate the process of assimilation in the field of organized religion, where church fellowship is a chief means of conserving an ancestral culture?

Seventh, this study has provided the occasion for much plain speaking. Some people have discovered, for the first time seemingly, attitudes on the part of other people of which they had been unaware or to which they had been inadequately alert. At first blush, some vociferous talk was a bit disconcerting. On second thought, however, one is grateful even for the tension; it could be a sort of growing pain, a sign of progress, a clearing of the ground for new constructive action.

Eighth, one does not fairly look for perfection in a deteriorating community. All involved in this enterprise can rejoice that St. John's, even though not perfectly adapted to the increased demands of the federated churches, does make available quite adequate facilities. It is also a matter for gratitude that the ministers of these churches and their denominational administrative officers have so long been able to see eye to eye. It would be easy to blueprint a theoretically more perfect setup, but in an old area like East Boston nobody starts from scratch. Everybody has to do the best he can with what he has, and remember that loyalties and sentiments built up through the years are as precious assets as some of the more tangible and material necessities of church life. Here at the very least is an experiment in which three communions have sought to make common cause under circumstances of admitted and increasing difficulty. It is a time when all concerned may well hold steady. Earlier agreements need to be reassessed and if found valid then implemented more solemnly. Surely they were made in good faith.

It is quite possible, however, that this federation faced a more difficult task than was at first realized, and attempted too much. Doubtless also the human assets were at first too optimistically appraised. In 1948 it was said that "the combined membership exceeds 1,000"—but that was a generously inclusive figure, which has hardly stood up. While it is still true, as in 1948, that "the potentialities for developing intercultural and interdenominational understanding through this project are obvious," it is quite possible that the federation has now accomplished all that under the circumstances it can hope to achieve. Perhaps its largest success may be registered in terms of some new venture, which would not have been possible six years ago. In any case, the co-operative spirit among the communions must be maintained, at all hazards. The sole question is, How can these three communions now best help one another to build the Church in East Boston?

Ninth, the maker of this study had the immense advantage of repeated opportunities to confer with the members of an interdenominational East Boston Committee, made up of the ministers of the five federated churches (including those in Orient Heights), administrators from the denominations involved, and the staff of the Department of Research and Strategy of the Massachusetts Council of Churches. This chapter was repeatedly submitted to the members of this committee for constructive criticism and revised in the light of its counsel. It is earnestly to be hoped that this committee can establish the habit of regular meetings, at least semiannual, for open-minded consideration of the sort of co-operative action from time to time required by East Boston's ecumenical experimentation.

*Finally*, this study was brought face to face with an unavoidable alternative. Either this federated enterprise must be much more intimately cemented into an integrated Christian fellowship of a sort not yet here attained, or it must be regarded as a successful interim process preparatory to an unscrambling and a new, bold Protestant witness among the Italians of East Boston. These alternative courses would seem to include certain obvious requirements:

1. If the federation is continued, it would seem essential that the three congregations should do what was originally intended, choose one senior pastor; that other members of the staff be recognized as his associates; and that all employed personnel should constitute a team. All three congregations should federate, not simply the Italian groups. The holding of occasional united services between the English and Italian congregations should be approached not hesitantly and timidly but with eager expectation as an adventure in Christian fellowship,and as an ecumenical, democratic opportunity. The present relation of host-and-visitor must give way as rapidly as possible to a feeling, "This is *our* church. It belongs to us all." However great the difference in numbers and resources between the two language groups, or in churchmanship, nothing short of this will accomplish the original intent of the federation. The pastor of St. John's Church, Federated, must be the leader in this integration.

2. It may well be that one or both of the two denominations which have supported the Italian congregation should now ask:

Can and should we provide some satisfactory place of worship which the Italian congregation can think of as its own?

Can and should we provide the necessary personnel?

If it be a conservative hope that the present Italian membership can be doubled, and that it can give or secure $1,000 a year, and can serve from 500 to 800 constituents in East Boston, can we make up the balance of the necessary budget?

Can and should we influence especially the younger Americans of Italian background in East Boston so that as they move out into more favored sections of the metropolitan area they will be conditioned for partnership in the evangelical enterprise wherever they may live?

We set out to do a job. Do we propose to see it through?

Ought not the East Boston Committee to face squarely the

choice between these suggested alternatives, perhaps devising a better procedure than either of the two? [4]

### In Orient Heights

The situation in Orient Heights is one of such gratifying progress that only a few suggestions need here be noted.

1. A parsonage or rectory, owned by the parish, would be of great assistance to its ministry.

2. Of far more importance would be an adequate church building more centrally located, to seat perhaps 150 and provided with educational and recreational rooms, to replace the present two widely separated structures. Such an edifice would furnish a year-round base, a new sense of "our" church, and much better facilities. Processes already under way looking toward such a possibility were at first properly only investigative. (When certain parish and denominational officials met recently to consider the building needs of the program, they were forced to do so in the minister's home—Baker-Maverick Church was too fully occupied to permit such an additional meeting.)

3. There seems now to be no reason why the minister should not apply for and receive Episcopal orders. Such a step would enable the members of St. Andrew's Church to receive the Holy Communion at the hands of their own rector.

4. Here, too, added staff personnel might well be provided, as may prove possible and agreeable, perhaps through the use of an additional theological student.

*In sum,* one dares believe that East Boston Protestantism has now begun to look forward rather than back. One is confident that new lay leadership can be discovered among younger Italians as well as among older American Protestants. Let everything possible be done to encourage a spirit of outgoing expectancy. The shift from frustration to courage may be easier than many

[4] On May 26, 1954, the East Boston Committee's judgment was clearly in favor of the first alternative. Continued support of the federation was voted, "with continued study and re-study of program."

have dared to believe. Yesterday was a time of subsidized competitive denominationalism. Perhaps tomorrow has already begun to be a time of self-reliant Christian community leadership. The Protestant problem in places like East Boston would seem to be to learn how to play the role of an effective, well-integrated minority in an area of population change and loss. Have not both of the federations made a significant contribution toward the solution of this problem?

# Chapter VIII

# Radical Experimentation

Sometimes situations require radical treatment. This can be initiated in a variety of ways. In the most metropolitan centers there are denominational, undenominational, and interdenominational agencies which, by reason of their resources, imagination, and long experience, are equipped to meet sudden new opportunity. Occasionally the phrase "Here today, gone tomorrow" operates in reverse. Sometimes an old church finds itself surrounded by new apartment houses, or a whole new parish is created by public housing or redevelopment in a churchless area in the changing city. There is mounting evidence that this may become a widespread condition. In New York City alone a million people live in recent large-scale housing projects.

The old nondenominational *DeWitt Memorial Church* of the New York City Mission Society nestles in the Baruch Houses planned for nearly 10,000 people in 1,900 units on the lower East Side. Through a system of "block captains," this church had already served residents of the sixteen buildings of the Lillian Wald Houses, an earlier low-income city housing project. Out of 1,857 families in these buildings, 420 Protestant families were discovered, as compared with 532 Jewish and 693 Roman Catholic. The church gained 150 new members, while Sunday-school enrollment increased from 275 to 400. According to the New York *Herald Tribune* for March 10, 1953, this church has held services in German, Chinese, Hebrew, Italian, Russian, Ukrainian, and Spanish. Half those then attending the Sunday school were Negroes, more than a quarter were Puerto Rican, and the

rest included Italians, Germans, Russians, Chinese, and Indone-
sians.

When Rev. Donald J. Walton began his famous pastorate
here in 1923, virtually all the tenements, now demolished, housed
Jewish families. Built as a memorial in 1881, for a pre-Civil War
congregation, the donor planned it to be "the most attractive
spot visited by the people who came here." (Large and fine
churches had been moving uptown.) From 1884 to 1893, this
church's banner period, attendance at three services averaged
515; at Sunday school, 570. But the 1953 record at English,
Russian, and Spanish services, and at the church school, was en-
couraging; e.g., in December total church attendance averaged
208; Sunday school, 331.

*The Church of the Open Door*, in Brooklyn, has the distinction
of being the first new church to be built within the bounds of
any New York City housing project. Erected by seven denominations, the Brooklyn Division of the Protestant Council, and the
New York City Mission Society, by April, 1953, it had a membership of 276.[1]

Another form of pioneering in the changing city is through
personnel employed by some central agency and contributed to
local churches for the increasing of their effectiveness. Metropolitan city-wide missionary agencies, or denominational units, are
able to strengthen the hands of individual congregations repeatedly. The Harlem Unit of the New York City Mission Society
was begun in 1920 as an extension of the Society's program of
bringing the church to the unchurched. "From the outset the
Society has proceeded in Harlem on the conviction that the greatest help it could give to the area was to strengthen the work of
the churches with children and youth." Accordingly it has made
available the services of eighteen full-time, well-trained leaders,
and as many as twenty part-time workers. These persons have
assisted seventeen Negro churches, of at least seven denominations, in Manhattan, the Bronx, and Brooklyn.

[1] See "Skyscraper Parishes," in *The City Church*, Jan.–Feb., 1953.

In 1930 a camp was opened in the mountains near High Point, nine miles from Port Jervis, New York. The camp area now comprises 600 acres. Campers come from the churches in which the Harlem Unit is at work. Each year the camp is swamped with applications. In a typical year there were 267 campers at each period, with 44 leaders. The activities of the staff during the rest of the year integrate the ideals taught at camp into the entire religious education program.

Besides released-time classes for religious instruction, Sunday school, and Bible classes, this unit also conducts activities in crafts (carpentry, weaving, leather work, sewing, and cooking), music, and leadership training. Total enrollment in a recent month was 6,810, with an aggregate attendance of 20,947.

Likewise the primary work of the Boston City Missionary Society "is done by its 'city missionaries.' Each of these seventeen persons is employed to work in a Health and Welfare Area in cooperation with a local church (usually but not always Congregational). The staff includes Chinese, Negro, and Armenian workers serving on a nonsectarian basis. Though the missionaries' weekly round of duties may include some group work or religious education, their 'major' is calling in the district, serving the aged, the indigent, the transient, the lonely, ill, or confused people of the city. They utilize social work resources available through the Society's membership in the Greater Boston Community Council and its participation in local area-planning groups."

Other instances of this sort of supplementary local church service could be cited. Sometimes complications arise. There can be divided loyalties—between phases of the work of a local church, or between the employing agency and the church served. In some instances the added work is ably done but inadequately integrated into the local church program. Nevertheless, this sort of relationship holds great possibilities. One society has discovered that the work of theological students, secured on a scholarship fund basis, may be less effective than the full-time service of more experienced workers.

Some of the most fruitful experimentation in the changing city has been student and seminary led. Stemming first from Union Theological Seminary in New York, this new approach has now spread to Yale and New Haven, to Chicago, and to Cleveland. Before examining the East Harlem experiment in greater detail, these other outreaches may be briefly cited.

In the November 26, 1953, issue of *The Friend*, Ruth B. Ferguson, a student at Yale Divinity School, had an article entitled "The Church of Christ on Oak Street" (in *New Haven*). This church "carries on 'Operation Rat' to curb the rat menace, shows films on health, gets signatures for a petition to the city government for a housing code, operates a weekend work camp to paint and repair people's houses, gets the city to build a much-needed playground, and helps alcoholics to get clinical help where it can." It has attracted favorable editorial comment from the local press and the Council of Churches' *Newsletter*.

One of the reported difficulties in New Haven has been the failure on the part of some to realize that a city of less than 200,000 can have slum conditions that need radical adaptation of church programs. Another problem has been one of securing a budget adequate for a permanent full-time staff. Competent evaluation of Oak Street, and its relation to Yale Divinity School, awaits further objective study.

On West Roosevelt Road, Chicago, is located the *West Side Christian Parish*, another adaptation of the East Harlem idea. Here, operating in an ample storefront, nondenominationally but supported almost wholly as yet by the Congregational City Missionary Society, three ministers (one white, two Negro; all Baptist), one or more religious education or group workers, and a minister of music, utilizing the group-ministry principles, are seeking to establish the relevance of Christianity to slum conditions. During the early months of this enterprise, now three years old, Don Benedict, of the East Harlem Protestant Parish staff in New York, was on the ground to help organize the Parish.

Tenements do not rise as high here as in East Harlem, but

tenants are similarly evicted to make way for new housing. Meanwhile the water may be shut off, and the plight of these householders may be regarded as an appropriate subject for prayer at church on Sunday morning.

The area served is the southern portion of the near West Side running from the river to about 2600 west, and from the Congress Street Expressway to 15th Street, but most of the Parish work has been concentrated in the smaller neighborhood from 1400 to 1800 west, and from 1000 to 1300 south. Four large nationality groups—Negro, Mexican, Italian, and Puerto Rican—live here in close proximity but with few contacts. Every depressing factor normally associated with slum living is present. Many of the people have become so immersed in the bare necessity of making a living, and their lives are so determined by what happens in an economic society beyond their control and understanding, that there is little opportunity for personality development. Bad housing and overcrowding have long been among the major problems. Migrant groups seek this area as a haven, leaving it as soon as a sense of urban responsibility has developed.[2]

From this section of Chicago many people migrate westward into North Lawndale, where the more regular churches have grown discouraged, and some have quit. The Parish has recently thought that perhaps it could make available its leadership and insights, so that new groups could take over one or more church edifices, as a measure preventive of further disintegration and community disorganization in this newly occupied area. Meanwhile redevelopment near the original location of the Parish means transition upward, and a more stable kind of people will be attracted to the neighborhood.

From the standpoint of the City Missionary Society, this Parish is "out on Protestantism's frontier in the city"; but it is only one of a number of projected experiments in establishing new ways of evangelizing the changing city and helping to work out a

[2] Adapted from a statement by Archie Hargraves. See also Beverly Dean, "Trail Blazing in City Jungles," in *The City Church*, May–June, 1953.

Protestant strategy for the entire West Side and other inner-city areas. The Church Federation of Chicago likewise, after long years of intensive and extensive study, is coming to grips with the whole problem of an inner-city strategy that will conserve present denominational assets and look toward the possibility of an ultimate offensive on a broad scale. Meanwhile the West Side Parish has already taken the offensive, "without tarrying for any."

With a membership that now exceeds 100, this Parish keeps Archie Hargraves, one of the original East Harlem leaders, and his associates more than busy. Each of the three ordained men has a territorial assignment within the neighborhood. They have been persuaded to avoid running for office but have been active in practical politics in the interest of their parishioners. They believe in the non-equipment approach to community problems, and in a personnel policy flexible enough to meet shifting requirements; but they begin to feel that traditional church buildings would appeal to some who look with suspicion on store-front religion. Their dignified but hearty worship has to face the criticism both of those who find it too formal and of those who wish it were still more enthusiastic. Here, as in East Harlem, one is impressed with the interesting combination of intimacy and liturgical dignity, as shown by hearty prayers for the sick, the needy, and the rejoicing, and in the union responses, spoken and sung. As developed in the East Harlem tradition, ritual achieves human warmth and symbolizes group friendliness rather than evidencing stereotyped formalism.

Present costs approach $40,000 a year. Of this, the national Board of Home Missions of the Congregational Christian Churches appropriated $3,000 for its current fiscal year, in addition to the contribution of the City Missionary Society. As yet no very active liaison with the numerous theological seminaries of Greater Chicago seems to have been established.

When these studies were being made, the most recent outgrowth of this movement was just getting under way as the *Inner*

*City Protestant Parish* of Cleveland. Here, as in Chicago, Don Benedict of the East Harlem staff pioneered the new work. This latest experiment in "ecumenical Christianity at the local level" was undertaken after opportunity in two other major cities had been explored, and Cleveland's welcome seemed the most hearty. Cleveland developments are a somewhat unexpected but generously supported outcome of a conference called by a former member of the Church Federation staff to stimulate church interest in the inner city. Two Presbyterian churches are interested (one provides $1,000; the other, $5,000); the Cleveland Congregational Union has pledged the income from a fund being established through the liquidation of an inner-city church, and the national Board of Home Missions of the Congregational Christian Churches has made an appropriation to help initiate the work; the American Baptist Home Mission Society and the Evangelical and Reformed Board of National Missions have both promised support. Two other denominations have expressed interest. Details of location, relationships, etc., remain to be worked out, but in May, 1954, Mr. Benedict was already on the ground. He was to be assisted by two seminarians. An initial seven months' budget of $10,000 was to be provided.

Cleveland too is very much awake to its inner-city problem, which has been underscored by the publication, now in process, of data showing the distribution of churches and their members by census tracts, denomination by denomination. Here again experimentation and the laying of sound foundations for long-range strategy occur simultaneously.

Looming largest among frankly experimental programs, growing out of seminary student imagination and devotion, both in size of budget and in number of staff persons employed, as well as persons served, is the bold venture now presented as

## Case VIII—THE EAST HARLEM PROTESTANT PARISH

Denominational city church administrators and other readers of this report will have read or heard repeatedly about this outstanding experimental Parish. Limitations of time have prevented any thorough sociological study of the area, or any long-continued observation of the Parish. All that is here attempted is an analysis of (a) the objectives sought by its organizers, (b) the area served, (c) the nature and structure of the work carried on, and (d) some of the resulting achievements and unsolved problems.

a. *The Objectives Sought by the Parish Organizers*

The originators of the Parish were students of Union Theological Seminary. They declared, "We desire to be a pioneering fellowship under God drawing our power from His decisive act." They had been influenced by Tillich's *Protestant Era* and the study of forces later described by Hoekendijk in "The Evangelization of Man in Modern Mass Society" (*Ecumenical Review*, Winter, 1950). Instead of trying to revive the work of any established church, they were convinced that church buildings built in earlier days for pulpit-centered programs were more of a liability than an asset. They believed that a fresh start, made by a "group ministry" resident in a needy area, unencumbered at the outset by expensive "facilities," would be rewarding. Like the first social settlement workers, they proposed to grow their own methodology as they went along; but they felt that the Larger Parish plan, already tested in rural America, was applicable also to city life.

By 1947 they had begun to formulate their thinking and their planning. They had a general idea of serving neglected segments of the population, where the workers live; East Harlem was an afterthought, and a quite unexpected opportunity. That year a report by the Pathfinding Service of the New York City Mission Society found East Harlem "a challenge to Protestantism of the first magnitude." A large proportion of nominal Catholics were found to have no vital connection with any church. Negroes were not attending the more traditional churches. Visits to thirty storefronts suggested that the primary need in East Harlem was leadership rather than facilities. This 1947 study asserted that here "the Protestant church cannot depend upon the conventional church program." At the same time there was work to be done that in the nature of the case could not be done by the Union Settlement, located squarely in the heart of a section least adequately served from the Protestant standpoint. The study urged the denominations to "move forward concertedly"; it held that we "cannot be content with little plans and little programs." It was convinced that real progress would "require considerable expenditure of funds." Such a situation provided precisely the opportunity the Union Seminary students were looking for. While busy denominational leaders hesitated, failing adequately to implement the findings of the Pathfinding study, the Union students went into action. Here, almost under their noses, only a little way across town, was their chance.

Informal personal contact at the January, 1948, Buck Hill Falls meeting of the Home Missions Council helped them to get under way. Support now began to accumulate, plans to definitize. Disturbed at the social stratification evidenced by our middle-class churches, and wanting to do something about the apparent failure of our churches to meet the needs of people in congested areas, they evolved a statement of purpose of the East Harlem Project (1948):

"1. To bring the basic Christian gospel to those underprivileged groups of the deteriorated sections of the city among whom for various reasons the conventional church approach has been unsuccessful.

"2. To explore methods of personal evangelism and small fellowship groups which may provide new techniques for Christian ministry in underprivileged areas.

"3. To provide a training center for seminary students who feel called to missionary service in the disorganized areas of the inner city."

Again, like the founders of the social settlements, they were eager to remake the community. As a first step they sought to establish neighborhood solidarity. Later they found that this involved working with single blocks in heavily congested territory. Their minds and hearts moved out too into strong hopes for the reconstruction of the whole urban social order. They proposed to take hold on a more or less catch-as-catch-can basis, and by becoming acquainted with people and their problems to find out how to rebuild our entire society.

When a World Council representative studied East Harlem, he concluded that "the aim of the Parish [was] to proclaim that Jesus Christ is Lord of every area of life, to relate this proclamation to the various areas of life in this community (family, vocation, housing, health, recreation, education, etc.), and to create a group of people, a community, which is witnessing to this Lordship at every point, but especially at points of tension and crucial decision in the area."

So much for purpose and attitudes. What was the scene of the experiment?

## b. *The East Harlem Area*

Whatever else the East Harlem Protestant Parish is, or is not, it is a clearly definable area of operation.

The four squares, bounded on the north by 106th Street, on the south by 104th Street, on the east by First Avenue, on the west by Third Avenue, are in Census Tract 170; the eight squares to the south, between 100th and 104th streets constitute most of Census Tract 164. (The East River Housing is east of First Avenue, and many blocks stretch away to the west of Third Avenue, to Lexington Avenue and beyond.)

The population of these two census tracts in 1950 was 27,693, including eight squares in addition to the twelve just bounded, or a total of twenty squares between 99th and 109th streets. Census Tract 164 increased 67.2 per cent in total population from 1940 to 1950; Tract 170, 50.4 per cent.

Tract 164, including two squares south of 100th Street, was 41.5 per cent nonwhite in 1950. Of its total population, 34 per cent had been born in Puerto Rico, as had the parents of an additional 7.4 per cent, making a total of 41.4 per cent, or more than two out five, of Puerto Rican background. The special significance of these figures is that "the Puerto Rican in New York City finds himself at the bottom of every ladder he tries to climb." (There is an even heavier Puerto Rican concentration west of Third Avenue.) North of 104th Street, in Tract 170, the proportion of Puerto Ricans was less than one in five; but nearly one in five inhabitants had been born in Italy. In several of these squares there is heavy Italian population. "Members of the Jewish community had begun to move away during the thirties."

Eight of the twelve squares show serious overcrowding, ranging from 9.7 to 20.4 per cent of dwellings having 1.51 or more persons per room, as compared with an average of 4.6 for Manhattan. Per dwelling, Manhattan averaged 2.4 persons; Census Tract 170 averaged 3.1; Tract 164 averaged 3. Owner occupation in Tract 164 was less than 1 per cent; among nonwhites it was infinitesimal. In Tract 170 owner occupation was less than 1.2 per cent. The great bulk of the housing is of course multifamily structures. Median rents per housing unit in 1950 were $23.21 in Tract 164 and $24.26 in Tract 170.

In Tract 164, either no private bath or dilapidation was reported in 36.2 per cent of the dwelling units, and almost as many had no running water. The situation was slightly better in Tract 170. In Tract 164 less than 1 per cent of the houses had been built since 1920. Such facts show why there has been considerable demolition since 1950. These were "tired and worn-out buildings."

In Tract 164 more than one in five units lacked central heating, and the situation was worse in Tract 170. In Tract 164 mechanical refrigeration was available in only two homes out of five (41.3 per cent), but in Tract 170 in nearly seven out of ten. One home in ten in Tract 164 had television; in Tract 170 nearly a fifth were so equipped.

Median schooling was 7.8 years in Tract 164, and 8.1 in Tract 170, as compared with 9.6 in Manhattan as a whole. Median income in Tract 164 was $1,714; in Tract 170 it was $2,496.[3]

This "poorly served area" had been studied as a possible scene for "block organization" before the East Harlem Parish was organized. In *Group Work in Community Life* [4] we now have competent, objective testimony from social workers, supplementing the Parish promotional materials. Chapter II (pp. 13 to 67) of this volume, "An Experiment in Self-Help at the Neighborhood Level," reports (p. 17): "The needs mentioned first by most of the representative persons consulted were: better housing and more adequate police protection. . . . People responded favorably to suggestions for fixing up empty lots, clearing the alleyways, having more play streets, but in general did not initiate these." Recognition (p. 19) that "the 'only neighborhoods in East Harlem are the blocks extending from one avenue to another on both sides of the streets' " was to become basic in the work of the Parish. Population per block, ten years ago, varied from 1,800 to 3,000; in some cases it is said to be 4,000 now.

The area became too famous. "The low income (averaging $28 per week), the physical deterioration, and the congestion were attended by the concomitant problems of disease, unemployment, delinquency, and social disorganization. The public press and popular periodicals publicized the problems and maligned the people; the entire nation came to know East Harlem as a 'crime-infested slum area' " (pp. 16, 17).

Its residents were "overwhelmed by problems. There were the ever present worries of inadequate wages or lack of income; long waiting lists to obtain day care for children; vermin; no hot water. A routine visit might also disclose the desertion of a husband, or that sudden illness or violent death had struck down the main wage earner of a family. Behind the more obvious difficulties were personality problems" (p. 21).

The effort to help the people of the area to improve their phys-

[3] 1950 U. S. Census of Population, New York, N.Y. by Census Tracts, Publication No. P–D37, p. 514.
[4] Murray, Bowens, and Hogrefe, New York, Association Press, 1954.

ical habitat faced many difficulties. It was not easy to find "key people." Meeting places were lacking. "Some of the most important 'meetings' were held on the curb, a doorstep, or around a kitchen table." Here was social work precedent for what the Parish did a little later.

Have the Parish leaders been too critical of the city? Here is the testimony of these social workers regarding the very situation in which the Parish was organized:

"Municipal government in a large city is remote, complex, and impersonal. It operates slowly; it is highly specialized. Duplication of administrative units and areas of responsibility almost prohibit citizen interest and action. For example, a tenant may have to contact eleven different agencies in reporting housing violations. He reports a leak in the gas stove to the Department of Housing and Buildings; a leak in the gas refrigerator, to the Department of Health. The problem is made more difficult in New York City because of the confusion created by the lack of uniform boundaries, [by] overlapping precincts, districts, areas, and zones, used by both private and public agencies" (p. 58).

"These conditions create a bewildering array of city services at many confusing levels. The citizen is left with no direct access to 'it'—the government. He is left in a tangled maze of legal complications. Discouragement comes easily and naturally."

Have some observers, perhaps including the writer of this report, tended to romanticize the work of the Parish staff? Consider the testimony of those who sought to organize these "blocks": "All agreed that it was a grueling job: climbing dark stairs, standing in oven-like streets in August. Under other circumstances, the same sights, sounds, and smell might have been termed 'unpleasant.' Naturally, we were often disheartened. Had we expected too much of ourselves? Nevertheless, all agreed that it was an unusual, stimulating, and maturing experience. Some real beginnings were made although the period [October, 1945, to April, 1949] was too short to determine the validity of the

project. Five years or more might have provided a more definitive answer" (p. 46).

The East Harlem Parish has now had five years in the midst
of these same difficulties and is in a position to give "a more
definitive answer."

In East Harlem are epitomized all the ills to which metropolitan districts are heirs. Here are all the disproportionate needs—
in welfare, education, and religion—that go with the lowest economic and social resources. Facing so many problems, the organizers of the Parish said:

"The greatest tragedy in East Harlem is not the lack of pos-
sessions, but the absence of hope and vision which would challenge the people to fight against environmental conditions. The
problems in the area grow greater each year. Some of them are:

> poverty, low paying jobs, unemployment
> abominable housing, often dishonest landlords
> a bad health picture, with the highest rate in the city for
> tuberculosis; venereal disease; infant mortality; rat bites;
> malnutrition
> inadequate trash and garbage disposal service
> lack of recreation facilities for all ages
> overcrowded classrooms and too few teachers
> crime, gangs, juvenile delinquency
> use of dope by young boys and girls
> unmarried mothers trying to support their children and them-
> selves
> families broken by divorce or desertion."

Soon the Parish staff began to accumulate their own more detailed data. An April 12, 1950, report on "Housing Problems in
East Harlem" stated: "In ten blocks over 1,200 violations of a
major nature were found and turned in to the Department of
Housing and Buildings."

In the winter of 1951–1952 a broad "Parish Attack on the

Housing Problem" met with "the most wholehearted and enthusiastic response . . . evoked for any project thus far undertaken." In their January, 1952, report to the Advisory Board the staff included four long, close-packed paragraphs showing the sort of conditions and neighborly reactions that roused 100 parishioners to visit over 3,000 homes on three Saturday afternoons, and to secure 1,000 blanks documenting actual conditions, and "continued to keep the ministers and the parish lawyers very busy." Details need not here be included, but are easily available as part of the Parish documentation.

c. *The Parish Work and Structure*

The area served by the Parish extends eastward from Lexington Avenue to the East River, between 96th and 106th streets. This larger area includes about 40,000 people. In it from south to north there are four main Parish centers:

*The 100th Street Church*, at 322 East 100th Street, with a Church Family Center at 317 and a Parish-wide medical clinic in Apt. 4, 311 East 100th Street.

*The Church of Our Redeemer*, with community rooms at 340 East 102nd Street, and an adjoining Children's Work Center at 324.

*The Church of the Son of Man*,[5] at 227 East 104th Street. The

[5] The name "Son of Man" was originally that of a Union Settlement congregation, which for ten years (1897–1907) met in the Settlement itself, then in the adjoining property, until some time in the thirties when population shifts and changes in administrative policy resulted in its discontinuance. Unfortunately the Parish seems hardly to have recognized its debt to the Settlement, or to have shown adequate appreciation of the Settlement's assistance and experience.

The same observation applies to the Parish attitude toward all the constructive social resources of the community. People and agencies are less likely to be willing to be used if they are ungraciously dubbed really not too competent or successful. At this point the Parish has made some errors in public relations which Christian courtesy ought to avoid. Furthermore, those long at work in East Harlem are glad to see the Parish leaders in their publicity increasingly seeking to soft-pedal the faults of their parishioners, and to play up the wholesomeness of those who struggle valiantly against all the heavy odds of crowded urban living.

local church office is located at 247½, and the increasingly important Parish office at 247; a storefront at 202 is used for youth work and as a center for the Parish-wide employment clinic. When forced to vacate this center, the congregation rented new quarters at 225 East 104th Street, right next to the church. "The monthly rental ($100) is being divided between the church and the Militants. A month of work on the part of the men and young people . . . produced a very attractive meeting place."

*The Church of the Ascension*, a Presbyterian affiliate, at 340 East 106th Street, recently received into full partnership in the Parish.

Ascension has a substantial brick building, formerly serving an Italian mission congregation. The other three Parish churches are in various stages of evolution from basement storefronts into more churchly but modest worship rooms. The Church of the Son of Man now occupies a chapel owned by the Union Settlement. The Church of the Redeemer, largely by volunteer labor, recently transformed its new quarters within a fortnight from an abandoned double storefront to an attractive center for worship and recreation. Over a dozen men helped to get the new quarters ready. This is perhaps typical of periods of concentrated progress, when accumulated strength suddenly becomes visible.

In addition there is a wooded *Parish Farm, or Retreat Center,* where for four summers the Parish has operated its own summer program on a 133-acre parcel of land, isolated in the woodlands northeast of Peekskill. Work camps and week-end retreats are a story in themselves; e.g., March 26–28, 1954, there were nineteen adults from Marble Collegiate Church and eleven Parish workers at work there. They included two skilled carpenters and contributed 300 hours of work. Both men and women worked. A roofer and a plumber were also to help. A main house can sleep and feed about thirty people, and it is planned to convert two other buildings into dormitories. There is a small library. An outdoor chapel has been built. A Spanish-speaking farm manager joined the staff in June.

The 1947 study found Ascension to be the only Protestant church in a church building in the area from 96th to 111th streets, east of Park Avenue. Within the immediate Parish area nine storefronts were reported. One of these, the Church of God in Christ, No. 4, a Negro enterprise, is still located at 103rd Street and Third Avenue. Three blocks south, the Firstborn Church of the Living God now bears the title, "New Jerusalem Holiness Church of the Lord Jesus." Here was announced in January, 1954, "A Great Revival conducted by the Holy Ghost through Elder H—— and Mother B——."

Other churches included

> Spanish Pentecostal Assembly of God
> St. Paul's C.M.E. Church
> Church of God of the New Creation in Christ (Negro)
> Universal Hagar Spiritual Church, No. 10 (Negro)
> Star Baptist (Negro)
> Holy Ghost Christian Church (Spanish)
> Power House Church of God in Christ

There seems to be no accurate up-to-date list available. Merely to let the eye run down these names reveals something of the problem of church co-operation in the area.

And of course there are strong Roman Catholic parishes:

*St. Cecilia,* 106th Street and Lexington Avenue, which has a very large parochial school with three branches and has sought to minister to Puerto Ricans with a bilingual ministry.

*St. Lucy's,* 344 East 104th Street, which is primarily Italian and tends not to welcome Negroes and Puerto Ricans. It holds a giant street festival on 106th Street between First and Second avenues on Labor Day week end. In 1953 it set up the statue of its saint directly in front of the Church of the Ascension bulletin board.

*Holy Agony,* 101st Street and Third Avenue, newly built

directly across the street from the site of the George Washington Houses. It has been staffed with young priests and is definitely aimed at Puerto Ricans.

The whole Parish area is now undergoing radical change. Between Second and Third avenues the entire district from 97th to 104th streets is in process of shift from old to new housing. As far north as 100th Street new public housing is under construction. North of 100th, the inhabitants of a four-block area were notified to vacate by April 1, 1954. All this will affect the Church of the Son of Man, 104th Street, mightily. Its present congregation will be increasingly scattered; a whole new constituency, perhaps of a quite different sort, will be located just to the south of it. Meanwhile the blocks between First and Second avenues, where the other three churches are located, will remain "as is," save for the possible development, in the undetermined future, of middle-income housing. On February 17, 1954, a new site, 106th to 108th streets, was approved by the City Housing Commission; but in September, 1954, the city council had not yet acted.

"In 1948 a group of Protestant ministers (chiefly connected with Union Theological Seminary) founded the East Harlem Protestant Parish. With a small group of people from the community, they started a first storefront church to testify to their conviction that there is in the Christian faith a dynamic that can transform society and a strength that can turn even the weak into champions in the fight for justice." Earlier they had conducted vacation church schools in storefront churches already established in the area but soon found that they needed their own base of operations. This they found first in a converted butcher shop on the corner of 102nd Street and Third Avenue. Visibility, accessibility, and availability were all underscored by placing staff desks behind storefront windows at the sidewalk level.

The staff is made up of two types of full-time members: full members of the "Group Ministry," all of whom are under a serious "discipline," and probationers, who must serve a year before being fully inducted into the Group, even though they are ordained seminary graduates.

This discipline consists of four elements:

1. Economic: "No person on the staff is paid on the basis of seniority or status, or longevity in the Parish" but on the basis of need.
2. Political: The staff acts as a unit; a clear majority is not to be blocked by a dissenting minority. The staff does not directly involve the congregations, except as their support for policies agreed upon by the staff may be sought.
3. Religious: Including weekly communion and other practices of personal and group observance.
4. Vocational: Individual opportunities for professional service elsewhere are reviewed by the Group as a whole. Mutual counsel has proved invaluable as new decisions have become imperative. Members of the Group Ministry are particularly grateful for the "encouragement, evaluation, and criticism of one another's work at their weekly meetings."

January 1, 1954, full-time staff members included five ministers, four educational directors, an administrative secretary and co-ordinator of activities (with a stenographic assistant), a nurse, and one lay pastor and translator. In addition there were three part-time lawyers and a part-time doctor, and a varying number of seminary students serving the Parish as part of their field-work program.

It would be difficult to exaggerate the centrality of the staff in the work of the Parish. The fact that all the full-time workers live in the area is of course of the utmost signficance both to their parishioners and as evidence of the depth of staff consecration.

The Parish is said to have snowballed in its contacts in the last eighteen months or two years. As a rapidly expanded enterprise it presents a Group Ministry containing new blood, some of which is additional, some of which takes the place of older personnel that has been utilized as transfusion material elsewhere. All this meant necessary adjustments.

The original motivation for the use of storefronts was to make the pastors visible and accessible. As their duties have increased, it has not always been easy to arrange for at least one staff person to be available at each location. On the other hand, the recent development of a Parish office has offset this difficulty and greatly contributed to the unity of the enterprise.

After a little more than five years, during which there has been deliberate effort not to high-pressure people into membership, the membership in each of the four churches as of January, 1954, was as follows:

| Church | Active Members (Jan., 1954) |
|---|---|
| 100th St. | 44 |
| 102nd St. (Redeemer) | 20 [a] (attendance ranged from 24 to 36) |
| 104th St. (Son of Man) | 75 |
| 106th St. (Ascension) | 60 [b] |
| | 199 |

[a] Had increased to 30 in September.
[b] Had increased to 85 in September.

"There is no set 'covenant' now in use in all of the churches. In general, the covenants used by the different churches cover these areas:

1. Acceptance of Jesus Christ as Lord and Savior and the desire to become a member of His Church
2. Regular attendance at church services
3. Personal devotional life
4. Regular financial support
5. Work for social justice and evangelism through Parish activities or by participating in other groups in the community

These are not strictly enforced on the whole but represent the ideal kind of church membership which we are seeking to develop. Our general practice is to accept people at the point where they are in their Christian development and to train them from there through membership class and participation in the life of the church."

Constituency figures would be far larger than membership— perhaps ten times as large.

Elected persons from each of the four churches, plus the staff, now make up the Parish Council. It meets every other Monday night, following an afternoon session of the full Parish staff and a supper session of the Group Ministry. The alternative meetings of the Council consist of Council committee sessions, which are increasingly replacing staff committees. The Council chairman-ship has been rotated each month among its lay members.

Full agenda enable the lay representatives of the churches to share increasingly in all sorts of administrative decisions, program leadership, and matters of policy; but major items, such as an-nual budget in particular, were not subject to Council review.

A Board made up of representatives of eleven bodies, denom-inational, interdenominational, and undenominational, all of them interested in the Parish, and most of them contributing to its budget, receives carefully prepared monthly mimeographed reports concerning the work of each of the four churches and of the Parish as a whole. With the help of the Parish staff, this Board fixes and administers the budget. It appears to take its cue in major matters of policy from the staff, but legally the corporate reality of the Parish inheres in its Board.

The Parish was incorporated in 1951 "to encourage and assist the development among the people of East Harlem of a sense of belonging to a community group working together in the Chris-tian tradition for the common good. . . ." The explicit intent was to set up an orderly and efficient procedure that would be "simple, informal, and democratic so that all members of the Parish may play a role in strategic policy formulation." Yet it was speedily agreed that "the legislative and policy-making func-tions . . . are to be concentrated" in what is now termed the Parish Council, with reports to the Administrative Board on property matters and affairs which concern the utilization of personnel, funds, and materials which are provided by outside sources. The present By-Laws and Rules of Procedure were adopted May 11, 1954.

The evidence that many members of the Board have first-hand knowledge of what actually goes on in the four churches of the Parish, on the basis of their own personal observations, is not impressive.

This report makes no effort to set forth in adequate detail all the program activities conducted by the Parish, many of them of great human interest. One of the first techniques emphasized in the effort to get acquainted with the people and their needs was the instituting of Agape Meal Groups in tenement dwellings. These were of very great significance as evangelistic contacts, leading to later opportunities for instruction in the meaning of the Church and the Faith. As outlined in a recent printed folder, the general program includes, besides worship and religious education, counseling, legal advice; medical clinic and health education; employment clinic; some economic help; fighting the use of narcotics; clubs and Bible classes; planning for community-action projects such as better housing, satisfactory trash and garbage disposal, adequate educational and recreational facilities.

Services for children and young people include "just plain friendship at all times," Sunday school, choir, religious instruction and discussion groups, released-time activities, hikes and trips, preschool play group, teen-age canteen, clearing lots for playgrounds, friendly guidance, clubs, and parties.

Summer activities include vacation church school, Long Trail hiking program, work camp at the Parish Farm, Friendly Town program (in co-operation with the *Herald Tribune* Fresh Air Fund), youth conferences, retreats for adults and youth, outings for adults, Parish Farm for adults.

Certain details will strike the attention of the outsider. For example, Sunday services are announced at noon, and a children's service, a choir recital, and a Passion play were scheduled for the Playlot on East 101st Street, as part of the Holy Week activities.

The financial commitments of the nine cooperating denominations for 1953 and their actual payment (in some cases in advance on 1954) were as follows (various boards and local church treasuries being involved):

| | *1953 Receipts* | |
| | *Budget* | |
| *Denominations and Agencies* | *Estimates* | *Actual* |
|---|---|---|
| American Baptist | $ 2,400 | $ 2,725.00 |
| Congregational Christian | 8,300 | 10,266.32 |
| Evangelical and Reformed | 2,000 | 2,000.00 |
| Evangelical United Brethren | 2,000 | 2,000.00 |
| Mennonite, General Conference | 2,700 | 2,064.60 |
| Methodist (New York City Society) | 1,200 | 1,200.00 |
| Presbyterian, U.S.A. | 8,100 | 6,040.00 |
| Protestant Episcopal churches [a] | 800 | 2,971.00 |
| Reformed in America | 8,000 | 8,050.00 |
| | $35,500 | $37,316.92 |
| Home Missions Division, N.C.C. (Consultant) | | |
| Union Theological Seminary | | |
| New York City Mission Society | | |
| Individuals | $12,000 | |
| Speeches, writing | 3,000 | |
| Miscellaneous organizations | 3,000 | |
| Foundations | 2,000 | |
| New Sources | 9,300 | |
| | $29,300 | $34,692.71 |
| Summer program designations | 6,000 | 4,843.50 |
| | $70,800 | $76,853.13 |

[a] Voluntary contributions—no representation on the Board.

Of these total receipts $10,271.94 was not applicable to 1953 operations, because of donor or Board restrictions. Some of it was advanced for 1954, some was an operating balance for the new year.

While the New York City Mission Society does not appear as a cash contributor to the Parish, it provides thousands of dollars' worth of competent, specialized service on the part of its comptroller. The Society handles and accounts for all Parish finances. From the corporate standpoint this safeguard is invaluable, and from the analyst's the clarity of the accounts is of great help.

Main items of actual *expense* for 1953 included:

| | |
|---|---:|
| Staff (salaries, $29,485.67) | $45,608.50 |
| Program | 10,202.11 |
| Office expenses | 3,900.62 |
| Cost of centers | 7,432.06 |
| Total budgeted expenses | $67,143.29 |

Non-budget receipts amounted to $6,325 additional, and expenses to $5,303.04. Gross expenses amounted to $72,446.35, as compared with $83,178.13 gross receipts. Such figures are impressive as a whole and instructive in detail. However, they do not tell the complete story.

First of all, there is the worry about items not yet assured. In April, 1954, it had to be said, "We cannot commit ourselves to students willing to help in the summer program—we have only half of the money in sight." Receipts in December, 1953, which exceeded $8,000, made it possible to reimburse members of the Group Ministry for salary cuts taken in the early fall. "The Parish is able to proceed with program only as funds become available."

Second, there is the need for a $10,000 capital fund for the Retreat Center.

But third, there is the story of what the four local churches have done, outside the budget, which is another impressive set of figures (See table, top of page 208).

Deducting the Presbyterian contribution, and a few other items, "The four churches raised *in the community* a total of $9,232.09, the bulk of which was used towards the renting and maintenance of the churches and recreation centers," over and above the gen-

| Local Church | 1953 Receipts | Expenditures | Balance |
|---|---|---|---|
| 100th Street | | | |
| Family Center | $ 1,398.02 | $ 1,371.60 | $ 26.42 |
| Church | 1,899.74 | 1,532.12 | 367.62 |
| | $3,297.76 | $ 2,903.72 | |
| Duplicate item | 179.66 | 179.66 | |
| | $ 3,118.10 | $ 2,724.06 | $ 394.04 |
| Son of Man | 1,989.23 | 1,766.08 | 223.15 |
| 102nd Street | 1,706.24 | 1,698.88 | 7.36 |
| Ascension | | 9,394.74 [b] | 868.39 |
| Outside | 6,941.40 [a] | | |
| Local church | 3,321.73 | | |
| | $17,076.70 | $15,583.76 | $1,492.94 |

[a] Chiefly from Presbyterian Board of National Missions.
[b] Not including E.H.P.P. worker.

eral Parish expense. In other words, "Practically the entire responsibility for financing and planning the maintenance of the local church facilities is done by the (local church) councils." Moreover, in 1953 the four churches raised $229 for the Retreat Center, $170 for Parish bus operation, and $700 for the summer program. This makes a total of $10,331, of which more than $600 was spent for program and worship supplies. This amounts to the surprising figure of $51.91 per active member.

In addition to the organizations listed above as represented on the Administrative Board, many individuals, churches, and other groups have become interested in the Parish. A plan for the enlistment of Associates, not only as contributors but as sharers in a discipline, is now being implemented. To the extent that this effort is successful, a body of genuinely interested persons will be far more than "sold" on the Parish; they will be committed as partners in the enterprise. The Group Ministry hopes "that in the Associates there will develop a community of individuals committed to the Christian Witness to the victims of our technical civilization." The staff feels that it needs "the active, informed support and criticism of those who can see our work in a wider perspective; only with this kind of a relation to individuals can we maintain our interdenominational character and witness."

In May, 1954, it was reported that 84 persons had signed as Associates, that contributions during a five-month period, November 1, 1953, to March 31, 1954, had amounted to $1,443, and that $1,138 had been pledged for payment during the balance of 1954.

An additional unofficial but exceedingly valuable part of the Parish structure is the somewhat informal Advisory Council, representing 25 supporting churches. This working group has held a number of sessions. It originated at an Evaluation Conference, April 15, 1953, and shared in an annual conference of Associates, Parish Council, and Group Ministry, May 15, 1954. At the latter session one pertinent question raised was: "Protestant denominations are ready and eager to invest large amounts of money in 'high potential' suburban areas. Should there not be a similar plan of invesment for low-income city areas?"

The structure of the Parish is one of concentric circles. At the center is the staff. Members and others served as constituents resident in the neighborhood are as yet more recipients of noble missionary effort than masters of their own church life. Slow beginnings of indigenous democracy are being made through the Parish Council. Undergirding all are the sponsoring agencies, represented in the Administrative Board, and a widening circle of financial supporters and friends, even partners in the Parish disciplines. The staff feel that "the Parish is more than a ministry of ministers to people. It is a movement." The staff have averaged 25 to 30 speaking appointments a month, thus spreading the knowledge of the Parish among ever widening circles.

As yet there seem to have developed only occasional carefully co-ordinated church reports for a Parish summary, based on schedules of comparable items; there has been very little of the traditional type of Parish statistics that are routine requirements in the average denominational church. Attendance figures were reported for the first quarter of 1950; also a total of 1,893 calls. Four years later the number of calls had increased to nearly a thousand a month.

Something of the present scope of the children's program in the Parish is indicated by the following early 1954 enrollment figures:

| Church | Sunday School | Play School | Afternoon Groups | Released Time |
|---|---|---|---|---|
| 100th Street | 80 | 10 | 80 | |
| 102nd Street | 65 | 9 | 75 | 49 |
| 104th Street | 60 | 12 | 58 | 18 |
| 106th Street | 179 | 10 | 100 | 125 |
| | 384 | 41 | 313 | 192 |

If these figures are compared with church-membership figures noted earlier, it will be observed that there is a ratio of 199 enrolled in Sunday school per 100 active church members. This situation holds real promise for the future, in spite of all handicaps of out-migration, adolescent falling away, and the like. Most urban churches have relatively small schools.

Early 1954 youth figures showed the following distribution:

| Church | Active | Occasional |
|---|---|---|
| 100th Street | 80 | 30 |
| 102nd Street | 25 Junior high<br>50 Senior youth | |
| 104th Street | 80 | 70 |
| 106th Street | 75 | |
| | 310 | 100 |

So, the Parish was reaching 410 different youth at least occasionally, in regular program features, or twice as many as its active church membership.

*The 100th Street Church* has tried "by constant experimentation to discover that body of curriculum material which could readily be duplicated by the people themselves in other cities or in other points in New York." It has its own council of a dozen elected members, a third of whom are men; three of the twelve are under 25 years of age, a majority under 30. Here "the Negro and Puerto Rican groups are now so well integrated that it is no longer a subject of comment or discussion." The small salary for a student choir director is paid by the congregation. Two church members were officers in the P.T.A. of the local public school. Agape groups have now given way to a dedicated church membership and to "intimate gatherings in the church and family center" for "service to the church and neighborhood." The men's group had a nucleus of ten men.

It has already been noted that toward the end of 1953, *The Church of Our Redeemer,* 102nd Street, occupied a new worship center, seating nearly 100, with adjoining hall for social activities —both on the ground floor. It is believed that these better facilities will accelerate church progress. They have also increased local church expenses. While the church still had an active membership of only 28, twelve adults were enrolled in a seven-session membership class. They were to be received into full membership on June 16, 1954. Play school for preschool children meets two mornings a week; the mothers, monthly. There are fifteen active members at the heart of the Women's Fellowship. "More adults than ever are coming into an active role in the total life of the church."

*The Church of the Son of Man,* on 104th Street, has experienced a very high turnover, partly owing to the fact that it is the one church in the Parish west of Second Avenue. A number of its early members lived in houses since involved in the demolition area. The 103rd Street block is said to have been unusually suspicious of the Church. Alleged factors involved include racial suspicion, Communist infiltration, and earlier attempts at block organization. This church has experimented with separate services in Spanish and in English, and in a unified bilingual service;

there are problems both ways, as well as advantages. Five people in a membership class were to be received on July 4, 1954. "Relocation from the George Washington housing site continues to drain potential members away from the church." On the other hand, "a number of families who were on the edge of the church program have become more active."

At *The Church of the Ascension*, originally a Presbyterian Italian mission, less than fifty persons of the old constituency were found to be still in the neighborhood and actively interested. Most of them appeared to have a very different outlook and orientation from those reached in the storefront churches. A new constituency, made up chiefly of parents of children in the rapidly growing Sunday school (Italian, Negro, and Puerto Rican), was very much akin to the other Parish groups. Full Parish membership for this church, deliberately achieved, seems to demonstrate that "a denominational church can work effectively within the interdenominational framework of the Parish," and vice versa. When membership was 75, average attendance was 65. In two years there had been a complete turnover in the Session. Five seminary students help in the work with 200 children and youth, and in home visitation.

The local celebration of the fifth anniversary of the Parish in October, 1953, revealed both the increasing unity of the Parish and the fact that many still did not feel a part of anything beyond their own block. It also made clear to the staff that "there is a central core of lay leadership which is ready and able to carry out certain major projects on a level of equality with the staff." The development of this lay leadership was accelerated by a 1953–1954 training course for deacons, enrolling eight; only one of them had completed high school.

A later anniversary dinner for friends of the Parish at Riverside Church on November 9, 1953, presented an impressive program, with two lay representatives of the Parish making in some ways the most significant remarks.

### d. *Achievements and Problems*

The East Harlem Parish has been an experiment; it is now an established achievement. Yet the student of the urban church, its structure, function, and relationships, finds the experience of this Parish confronting him with many serious issues for churchmanship: What are the implicit meanings of this experiment in terms of polity, theology, cultus, finances, and ecumenical mechanisms? For example, what are the connotations of the Group Ministry and its discipline in terms of personnel placement, church connectionalism, ministerial standing, and the like? Can a minister be under two disciplines?

The Parish has given long-needed and quite exceptional visibility for the experimental spirit in meeting urban neighborhood needs. It has deliberately refused to force statistical growth or membership demonstration. As in some "foreign" missionary fields, it has relied on growth from within, expansion on demand.

Parishes like East Harlem serve to remind our too suburban Protestantism of the desperate problems of the inner city. If we are to think of metropolitan areas as a whole, persons of higher income living in more comfortable neighborhoods need to see what life is like at the city's heart. A direct, dynamic, imaginative break with tradition challenges some of the ablest among seminary students. They are willing to tackle "a tough and demanding" job, perhaps sensing, as does David W. Barry, that "when we fail to speak to basic human needs, our failure comes back to us in the form of ignorance, bitterness, bigotry, and hostility striking at the very roots of the Church."

To win their largest success, however, such parishes need not only the financial support of great central churches and of suburbia but also to be joined in the fight for better housing and other forms of human betterment. Only as the causes of our East Harlems are eliminated will the need for supporting such parishes grow less.

Here ecumenicity does battle in the front-line trenches. On the other hand, the interdenominational character of such work is still vague. Multi-denominational financial support is by no means the equivalent of interdenominational commitment. A major problem of the Parish is how to relate its members with the Church at large in any normal pattern of Christian fellowship. There have been as yet very few transfers either in or out. (The fact that the Parish is inclusive makes it inevitable that some of its members, moving into more exclusive situations, may not be welcome by some other churches.)

Is the time here when this experimental type of churchmanship should seek to make its own thinking more articulate? How can the contacts of the lay members with organized Protestantism be increased? And of members of the more traditional churches with the Parish? What safeguards are essential in the latter case? One friendly theological student, a member of one of the more connectional denominations in another city, on hearing of the East Harlem Parish, inquired, "Just what do they join?" Have the supporting denominational bodies faced up squarely to the implications of that question?

One wonders too whether these front-line troops, in the thick of the fight, have been quite aware of their dependence on their supply lines. Some day when the terrain has been more adequately described and the battle plan more competently sketched it will doubtless be observed that the interest in this warfare was more sympathetic, intelligent, and helpful, both in the Church and outside, than could always be realized in the heat of the struggle.

The staff have been quick to note that secular agencies have increasingly looked to the Parish for information, support, guidance, and resource in their various enterprises. Similarly the staff is coming to understand the difficulties connected with underpaid, rapidly changing welfare field-work personnel. Might it not be good public relations if the Parish became more appreciative of other forces for good, even of fossilized or quite inadequate churches, and less critical of their inadequacy? The original using of what was available in storefronts for a vacation-school program had in it a generosity of attitude which might well be maintained. (One reads with a bit of nostalgic admiration the announcement of a 1948 vacation school sponsored by the East Harlem Larger Parish, the Star Baptist Church, the Power House Church of God in Christ, and the Holy Ghost Christian Church —in co-operation with the Protestant Council of Greater New York. That may have been difficult, and some of its relationships may have been rightly discontinued; but it certainly had its admirable side.)

On the other hand, it is a far cry from that first summer (1949) to 1954's "large and full program of work with the children," of whom 542 were enrolled, and attendance averaged 305. The Vacation Church School met three days a week plus Sunday during July, and an additional day each week in August. Almost 300 of these children spent at least one week (most of them more) out of the city. If this study could have included the 1954 summer and autumn program, it would have marked significant growth along a number of lines of suggested progress.

Along with this, might not a certain humble seeking to find what older hands have learned in long decades of wrestling with the urban octopus be both becoming and rewarding? Many Christian scholars and ecumenical ecclesiasts are grappling earnestly with the problems posed by East Harlem, so keenly alive in the hearts of the Group Ministry. Questing and experimenting go on all round the world. It would be a pity if these consecrated young leaders were to weaken their witness by becoming unconscious victims of a Messiah complex. It would be far more becoming and actually more effective if they approached certain competent and sympathetic leaders with questions like these:

How, in our exceptional laboratory, in a situation recognized as one of maximum urgency, can we best help to implement the established ideals of social work, education, and organized religion? Where do we best lend a hand? Should we do more of what we are doing? What else should we do? Of what we seek to do, what functions are most unmistakably ours? What can we learn from the mistakes and successes of others, at home and abroad? How can we better carry on our work in our needy world-in-miniature?

If, in a teachable spirit, the Group Ministry could inspire the Administrative Board to call together even a one-day conference of resource people (in education, social work, and religion), might not some clear and acceptable guidance come out of such mutual counseling? Of course the Parish would sign no blank agreements in advance, as to policy changes or altered methods or emphases; but it would be free to accept whatever wisdom might commend itself, growing out of a pooling of knowledge, experience, and skills, thus offered in friendliness and sympathetic response to an invitation for counsel. Quite possibly the East Harlem Council, a well-established and experienced body, of which the Parish has been a member for nearly six years, would be willing and able to help in convening such a conference.

One congratulates the leaders of the Parish on having sought once more to implement the vision of all great servants of the city, some of whom have served under other banners but with similar devotion. Quite possibly the Lord has more faithful ones in Israel than lonely Elijahs sometimes realize.

Two other observations are pertinent. First, the staff now has wide and varied social work contacts; its opportunity to co-operate with other churches is strictly limited. Four Parish ministers are reported to have dealt with 100 different public and private agencies in referral and other relationships regarding their parishioners. Second, even with the best of good will, a church-centered program necessarily and properly concerns itself with all of life, and finds itself inevitably involved in tension with secular agencies specializing in particular phases of social work and deliberately trying to keep aloof from religious partisanship. Constructive public relations in such a situation are admittedly difficult. The gospel always was in some sense an offense. Its heralds do well to avoid being themselves offensive, but one must sympathetically avoid all counsels of perfection. Nonchurch forces are also sometimes inadequate and faulty. Sometimes social workers are reportedly "confused by the multiplicity of concerns" which the Parish has for "the whole person in all his life." The gap between "a witnessing Christian Community" and the case-work approach to "clients" is one that has been widely and quite unfortunately broadened in recent years. A better understanding between Protestant and social work forces, so that each can more adequately utilize the resources of the other, is long overdue. In this respect the Parish has felt the effects of a national situation now for perhaps the first time being adequately appraised.

It is the Group Ministry which has made it possible for young couples, some of them with little children, to "take" what otherwise might have been too much for any one of them. Under their own discipline they have developed a sense of mutual responsibility and camaraderie quite different from the isolation of many a discouraged urban pastor, where the whole situation has tended to drag down both church and people and muffle the lilt of the gospel. Acting as a group, the members of the staff have also been "in a better position than an individual to resist the tendency of all our churches to pay their home missionaries starvation wages." They have clearly demonstrated the validity of the pattern.

It could be that theirs has been a twentieth-century equivalent of that haystack experience out of which grew the American foreign missionary movement. On the other hand, one remembers that in 1812, when the first missionaries set sail from Salem, they were memorably addressed by those who had commissioned them. One wishes that American Protestantism were imaginative enough and articulate enough to give some counsel of acceptable wisdom to the Group Ministry.

Ought a fifth element, administrative, be added to the discipline? [6] The staff reports regularly *to* the Administrative Board;

[6] The administrative processes of the Parish have shown cumulative improvement as the organization has matured. Reporting is better; there is more to report. The fruit of slow, patient effort begins to ripen. The May, 1954, monthly report (14 mimeographed pages, single space) in-

cluded many interesting items which have been woven into this chapter. Six full pages were given to statistical analysis of the period January 10 to February 10, 1954. This month happened to cover five Sundays. Counting worship, Sunday school, and similar normal activities, the number of groups or events for each of three major age brackets, per church, was as follows:

| Adult | Number | Enrollment | Sessions | Total Attendance |
|---|---|---|---|---|
| 100th Street | 8 | 131 | 27 | 523 [a] |
| Redeemer (102nd) | 4 | 83 | 15 | 297 |
| Son of Man (104th) | 5 | 172 | 23 | 578 |
| Ascension (106th) | 2 | 105 | 9 | 387 |
| | 19 | 491 | 74 | 1,785 |
| *Youth* | | | | |
| 100th Street | 7 | 123 | 28 | 454 |
| Redeemer | 8 | 131 | 33 | 473 |
| Son of Man | 7 | 192 | 32 | 694 |
| Ascension | 4 | 78 | 31 | 345 |
| | 26 | 524 | 124 | 1,966 |
| *Children* | | | | |
| 100th Street | 7 | 123 | 28 | 569 |
| Redeemer | 8 | 202 | 37 | 650 |
| Son of Man | 5 | 130 | 22 | 474 |
| Ascension | 8 | 443 | 37 | 962 |
| | 28 | 898 | 124 | 2,655 |

[a] In May eight groups enrolling 167 persons showed an average weekly attendance of 95 individuals.

This means a total of 73 groups or events, with 1,913 enrolled, holding 322 sessions during the month, and a gross attendance of 6,406; or an average or more than ten meetings a day, straight through the month, with an average daily attendance of 207.

Additional Parish-wide activities included a youth rally, with 225 attending; the Parish Council, enrolling 24, with half of them attending; and 32 attending seven different committee meetings.

The following is an analysis of the number of families involved in the calling and counseling work of the staff during the month:

| | Church Families | Others in the Area | Not Related to Church or Area | Total | Per Day |
|---|---|---|---|---|---|
| 100th Street | 273 | 113 | 7 | 393 | 13 |
| 102nd Street | 108 | 46 | 2 | 156 | 5 |
| 104th Street | 145 | 31 | 7 | 183 | 6 |
| 106th Street | 192 | 52 | 9 | 253 | 9 |
| | 718 | 242 | 25 | 985 | 33 |

The last few pages of this May report were given over to a careful analysis and statistical summary of the way twelve staff members (six ministers, three directors, and three administrators) spent their time.

does the Board itself from time to time make its own report to its constituents? Is the approach of the staff as a team to the problems of the inner city the equivalent of a genuinely interdenominational mechanism?

Does the staff do well to rotate its leadership? Is the group developing a Quaker-like substitute for that whip-cracking technique utilized by even the most urbane administrator in social, educational, or religious work? In the settlement movement "only gradually did the head worker emerge as leader." [7]

Will there be a parallel development in the Group Ministry? If not, by what process of self-discipline can promptness, economy of time and energy, and unhurried but speedier decisions be achieved in matters of administrative detail? How can lost motion, the fatigue of unduly long staff sessions, and the interruption of individual labors by unproductive group processes be avoided, without impairment of the sense of fellowship so important to the morale of the Group?

Does the Administrative Board do well to put as much confidence in a group as it would in a trusted employed leader? It seems now to be the "policy that the selection and discipline of the staff shall be the responsibility of the Group Ministry, and that any decision involving appropriations must be ratified by the Board." Has the Board fully thought through the implications of this policy? Could the Group Ministry tend to become a new "order" in American Protestantism? It is not quite clear to what extent the "disciplines" are or ought to be subject to Board action.

Is the application of the principle of rotation in the chairmanship of the Parish Council too vigorously pressed? Can lay leadership be developed without continuous responsibility? Could there be still larger use of volunteers? (The Baptist Christian Centers suggest "a minimum of five trained volunteer leaders for each professional staff member.") Obviously this would involve

[7] Woods and Kennedy, *The Settlement Horizon*, New York, Russell Sage, 1922, p. 54.

considerable effort in enlistment, training, and supervision. The present staff and Parish Council committee structures, just getting well under way, are a promising step in the direction of spreading responsibility.

What sort of routine reporting will involve least drudgery and produce an annual summary of facts that will provide bench marks by which progress can be measured and effectiveness evaluated? How can such data be most effectively used in terms of public relationships? What sort of mention of the Parish should be made in the year books of the supporting denominations? How can Co-operative Protestantism best deal with new facts like this Parish, from a reporting standpoint? Does a recent publication mean that there is to be a regular Parish bulletin, to acquaint the members of all four churches, and their friends, with the entire program?

All those engaged in this experiment have found it an experience that has profoundly affected their deepest attitudes. Even suburban churches have discovered that their money gifts to it have brought back to them a new sense of Christian solidarity, *noblesse oblige*, the need of better equalization of spiritual opportunities, and the significance of the Church as an "inclusive" Christian fellowship. Students have come to understand their ministry, their Christ, their call, and the gospel with new vividness. In fact, one of the outstanding by-products of the Parish has been its value to a large but unrecorded number of students, as observers, participants, and probationers.

Detailed personnel appraisal is quite beyond the purpose and capacity of this study. The quality of the staff leadership, as well as the number of persons available, has been outstanding. Perhaps four individuals may be merely mentioned, without any invidious comparisons.

George W. Webber, now dean of students at Union Theological Seminary, has been at the heart of the experiment from the outset.

Donald Benedict, formerly pastor of the Church of the Son

of Man, has been the pioneer in extending the idea to other cities.

Archie Hargraves, now of Chicago, brought to the work the psychological advantage of being himself a Negro. (The recent employment of Carlos Rios as a full-time member of the staff helps slightly to restore the racial balance and greatly to increase the linguistic competence of the Group Ministry.)

These three men were the pioneers, but the staff seems quite able to continue in strength, even if some of its first leaders are no longer available.

On September 22, 1950, a Board committee reported its feeling that "it is necessary to engage the services of someone who can give more time to the Parish than is possible for an executive of one of our missionary or denominational agencies." This led to the employment of Dr. Edward A. Odell. As part-time adviser, and liaison between Board and staff, interpreting each to the other, he has been trusted by both. Formerly a missionary in Latin America and more recently an executive of the Presbyterian U.S.A. Board of National Missions, his mature abilities, and his confidence in the caliber and devotion of the staff, have been invaluable assets.

There have been staff losses. Not everybody has stayed by. One went to important work elsewhere, one attempted to start a new church but came to doubt the theory of the enterprise, and the whole extension effort in that particular direction proved abortive. Several educational directors have moved on to other tasks. (The problem of the unmarried woman is clearly not the same as that of the married man, so far as long-range commitments are concerned.)

On the whole, however, the staff has grown not only in size but in representativeness (it now includes members of seven denominations) and in technical versatility, as well as in group solidarity. Any parish or group of churches anywhere would be fortunate to command the services of so able and so consecrated and self-disciplined a group of religious workers.

Would the staff be strengthened by the employment, when opportunity affords, of a worker trained in group work, another trained in case work, and by provision for the training of one or more staff members in field research methods and in urban sociology and the urban church? Would it be a wise expenditure of effort if case-work records of families, and card records of individuals, particularly children and youth, were maintained? Is "case-work evangelism" still a fruitful concept?

The political discipline is not wholly convincing. Doubtless the staff would agree with Chandran that "a Christian who understands the nature of man in the light of the death of Christ will not expect any party to be perfect." It would appear to be a moot question whether the Church, as Church, as distinguished from the free action of its members, should enter into the partisan political struggle; but there would seem to be no question that the Parish should seek the most effective means of helping to make the municipality itself an agent of a "responsible society." [8]

Further, the resolute determination of the Group Ministry to educate the Parish members and constituency into a sense of political responsibility and an active share in the practical politics of the city deserves all praise. On the other hand, is it not possi-

---

[8] It is doubtful whether the decision of one member of the Group Ministry to run for political office was approved by the Administrative Board. There are bound to be differences of opinion as to the effectiveness and wisdom of such political effort. Among the consequences of this campaign are said to have been a new awareness of voter attitudes even on the part of machine politicians, some new insight into the techniques of public address whether political or evangelistic, when undertaken from a truck in a crowded city street, and new searchings of mind and heart as to the function of the church in a political and economic order that falls so far short of decency, not to say of the Kingdom of God. The freedom of this leader to be a political candidate is itself significant of the generosity and broadmindedness of constituents and sponsors. The utilization of church elections (officers of the congregation, and representatives on the Parish Council) for familiarizing the people with a formal ballot is to be warmly commended as sound adult education, at once in churchmanship and in citizenship.

ble that even within the Group Ministry an honest difference of
political opinion will yield as effective educational influence as
agreement? Does not the principle of free enterprise possess a
certain political validity also? Is it possible or desirable to equate
Christian commitment with any political partisan loyalty or the
support of any particular candidate? Granted that the need for
a Christian opposition may sometimes be crystal clear, is the
Church as Church competent to organize an effective political
bloc? Is there not elequent historical testimony that suggests that
the Church has a somewhat different function to perform? However, there can be no manner of doubt that church members
should be encouraged to accept "the responsibility of political
involvement," and the East Harlem movement is to be congratu-
lated on its "strong emphasis on participation in the machinery
of political life."

It would be entirely logical for the Board to pursue tactfully
but firmly the trend already begun, by which it seeks helpfully
and constructively to review not only the finances of the Parish
but other major phases of its work, such as personnel decisions,
extension, capital investment, and matters involving public relations. The freedom of the Group Ministry is a most precious
asset; conceivably, however, a certain restraint, in terms of experienced counsel, might avoid chronic pitfalls well known to re-
ponsible administrators. These are especially likely to occur in
fields where prophetic courage inevitably faces issues dubbed
controversial by the unconvinced.

How rapidly and by what steps is the shift being made *from
mission to church*? Is the pace fast enough? Have the financial
and evangelistic capacities of the members of the Parish been
adequately appraised? In Chester Bowles' *Ambassador's Report*,
p.155, he asks, "Is it not time to revise our pessimistic, and somewhat arrogant, assumption that *democracy* is practical only for
a highly developed, educated people? . . . How does any nation prepare itself for self-government except by self-government?

The only way to learn to swim is to swim." From first-hand observation this writer ventures to testify that in his judgment the members of the East Harlem Protestant Parish may be more ready to swim than has sometimes been supposed. This does not mean that they could raise and administer a budget of $100,000. It does mean that they deserve steadily increasing authority. Perhaps they themselves would be best able to tap the latent financial resources of their own community.

Is this Parish as yet too largely the extension of an outstretched helping hand rather than genuine "church extension"? When and how does "My Lady Bountiful" withdraw subsidy? To what extent is the principle of the priesthood of all believers being invoked? How largely is the Parish ministerially and professionally dominated? Does such an environment necessarily sharpen the distinction between laity and clergy?[9] In any case, under these conditions, how can the democracy of the Kingdom be increasingly realized?

One of the most gratifying aspects of the Parish life is the articulate sense of responsibility for others elsewhere, repeatedly emphasized by prayer and deed; of mission to the entire world. Does this find adequate expression in terms of gifts for the millions in other lands who are even more tragically depressed? Is it effectively related to the idealism and generosity of churches in areas of greater privilege? (Benevolences at Ascension amounted in 1953 to less than 1.5 per cent of total income; were there any "missionary" gifts in any of the other three churches?)

Probably every one of the questions so far raised has occurred to the Parish staff itself. Transition from the initial domination of two or three key spirits, whose responsibilities have broadened

[9] According to the May, 1954, report, "Our churches will probably never become indigenous. The scene presented by these inner city areas is too complex, too swiftly changing, too huge for that to happen. On the other hand, we intend to develop real lay leadership as fast as possible. The men, and women who comprise the training class are real evidence of God's power to call workers for His Kingdom."

as they have themselves grown in personal and vocational stature, into a more mature group process seems now to be well under way. The members of the Group Ministry are experiencing anew the opportunity of Christ's servants to mediate God's grace to needy men. After visiting the Parish, one executive remarked, "I doubt if the staff have very much uninterrupted home life." Nevertheless they "proceed . . . certain that . . . richer chapters lie before" them.

One cannot avoid the feeling that work like that of the East Harlem Parish is of God. This being true, it has much to teach the Church at large; but its permanent lessons will be taught only as it moves on out of the experiences of its childhood, so to speak, through adolescent strivings into seasoned maturity.

It may well be that the recent setting aside of one staff member as a researcher, charged with keeping the Parish informed as to legislative and administrative matters of vital concern to its people, may serve also as a means by which the Parish and its busy staff can continuously engage in that sort of time-consuming self-survey, of church and community, which is so essential to sound long-range planning and accurate seasonal appraisal of achievement and responsibility. The whole Church would be enriched by such findings.

Already a complex fact, the Parish has now begun to think in terms of its second five years. Its pattern evolves. One ventures the guess that it will increasingly discover the importance of emphasis on the Christian fellowship itself, as distinct from any church activity, however desirable. New housing may mean new constituents, and new programs.

Nearly seven years have elapsed since on March 11, 1948, the use of both a chapel and a residence was referred to the Union Settlement officers by its Board, with power. Work began that October on 100th Street, and on 102nd. In early 1950 the latter unit moved to the Chapel of the Son of Man, on 104th Street.

From a $10,000 budget the first year, the work has expanded until it was handling nine times that amount and employing sixteen full-time workers and thirty part-time volunteers. Staff meetings and Parish-wide occasions of all sorts have become important points of contact among workers who could easily be lost in the separate blocks and churches.

At the outset the staff were convinced that "the traditional trappings of the church must be forgotten" until people became interested enough to ask for facilities. So they took the non-equipment approach. Has it justified itself? Seemingly it was the only one possible. But others have utilized church buildings with good results elsewhere, and one is inclined to believe that the Church of the Ascension may make one of its most important contributions to the Parish through its building. In any case, others also have succeeded in the inner city, and the event may prove that the historic development of "churches" in the sense of buildings has been abundantly justified.

Are the Associates of the East Harlem Parish to be matched by Associates of other similar parishes? In a late 1953 letter the Group Ministry said: "For quite a while now, we have felt the need to move beyond the formal relations of denominational ties and the informal bonds of speaking engagements—beyond these to a living fellowship with others who share our concern for the urbanized, industrialized masses of the inner city." Are "associates" to be supporting members of all such parishes? How are the parishes to be related?

It would seem more or less self-evident that prerequisites for the wide development of this sort of work include (1) able and consecrated leadership, (2) adequate financial support, (3) responsible sponsorship, (4) *time* to get acquainted with and develop the leadership resources and group response of the resident population.

Sooner or later, too, any such Parish may arrive at a familiar fork in the road, where it will have to choose between closer affiliation with the denominations, perhaps in some new interdenominational pattern, and less affiiliation with them. If it should ever seek to be *un*denominational, how would it avoid becoming one more source of a new denomination?

What relation, if any, does the Administrative Board of the East Harlem Parish have to the extension of the East Harlem plan?

Early in the century a great social worker said, with regard to what we now call social action, "We must wait our chance, and then we must strike hard; we must work unstintedly and cumulatively when the chance comes." In East Harlem, in Chicago, in Cleveland, this maxim has been echoed. "We know that if the ideals and purposes of the Parish are to reach beyond East Harlem they must be put into practice in many different situations." But who are "we"?

Several boards have put thousands of dollars a year into this experiment in each of several cities. Are they prepared to keep this up? How far will they agree to go? Does a plan begin to emerge? Is the East Harlem pattern normative?

Perhaps the $64 question is just this: To what extent is this Parish pattern capable of duplication elsewhere? Can we Protestants afford the cost of widespread duplication of this pattern? Although "5,200 contacts in a given month" seems gratifying, how about a cost item of well over a dollar per "contact"? Must we face up to vastly increased costs if we are serious about evangelizing the urban slum in any thoroughgoing fashion? What would be the total cost of really tackling an adequate ministry to all American areas of urban blight? Should the anticipated size of such a sum close our minds to our duty and our privilege? Do we perhaps need greatly to raise our sights and revise our whole missions economy? Have we ever seriously tackled a total strategy for co-operative action in urban America?

It is particularly to be hoped also that the field research activities of the new department of the Protestant Council of Greater

New York, building on the careful foundations laid by the Path-finding Service of the New York City Mission Society, may provide new knowledge, within a metropolitan frame of reference, which will enable Protestant strategists to see East Harlem in the light of Greater New York's total needs and aggregate resources. One phase of this larger problem is the development of some system by which those won for Christ in East Harlem, or other interdenominational parishes, can be made to feel at home in neighborhood churches in areas to which they migrate. (This is all of a piece with a similar problem in "mission lands.")

One rejoices that "the initiative for social action" has been taken by the people of East Harlem themselves. One rejoices that the Parish continues to identify itself with their problems, that young people coming into one of the churches took as their first task assisting the District Health Committee in carrying through a chest X-ray drive. One is eager to be a party to making religion "relevant." Yet one has to raise the question as to the relative importance of social action and evangelistic appeal, in the long run.

One can readily understand the impatience of the staff in the field of social action. To attempt to operate through "channels" —whether political, social work, or ecclesiastical—often means that the whole process is slowed down to the point where the most conservative can effectually block any significant progress. To break through the web of checks and balances, to spotlight a particular issue, sometimes accelerates progress widely desired but long stymied. Often, on the other hand, everything comes down at long last to some item of tax-supported expenditure, e.g., the cost of additional inspectors to enforce ordinances; and particular issues must be won not only in principle but in terms of appropriations, and adequate budget resources. Sometimes even unsuccessful attempts at direct action at least "stir up the animals" too long somnolent.

To what extent has the social action emphasis affected the

life of the sponsoring denominations? What have been its results in terms of commitments to the Church? Certainly this Group Ministry has been left free to act in fields regarded as controversial by many members of the supporting denominations. Probably the staff of the Parish have been more free to battle for social justice than many a pastor of a middle-class church would be. Denominational support has certainly not throttled social action.

One rejoices too that after long preparation a special April, 1954, "Newsletter" (six mimeographed pages) effectively featured housing. To be intimately involved in the long "uphill fight against landlord irresponsibility, inspection inadequacies, and legal loopholes" is to be steeled with continuing purpose. Here, as in Chicago and elsewhere, it does something to the souls of sympathetic parish workers to find "three families where there had been one before," and to note a 59 per cent population increase in thirteen years, during which there had been practically no construction, while people were "packed close to the bursting point several years ago." One cannot live in the midst of overcrowding without becoming a housing enthusiast. If one were not, would one be worth his salt?

Ought now the basic claims of evangelism to be newly examined? Following the publication of *Alleluia!* (the Parish song book) is there a place for leaflets, posters, larger use of outside bulletin boards, and other media of communication within the Parish? Can the effective use of drama now be supplemented by carefully organized visitation evangelism? If not now, can it be undertaken later, after careful preparation? Is the situation in East Harlem any more difficult than that confronting the Indian churches in their effort to reach outcasts and poverty-stricken villagers? (Cf. A. Ralla Ram, who says, "The cart of evangelism goes squeaking along, propelled and pushed forward by gigantic foreign financial resources." Is the situation so different in East Harlem?) Can others besides deacons be trained to help? Granting that "If the Church as the Body of Christ is a redemptive community, she will always enter into new areas where redemption is to be carried" [10]—such as social or even political action— is not the direct effort to build up "the redemptive community" both legitimate and necessary? Certainly the original, deeply theological convictions of the founders of the Parish looked in this direction from the outset.

To what extent has the "conviction that there is in the Christian faith a dynamic that can transform society" been justified? Are there evidences of social transformation in East Harlem? If the results are less than might be desired, what resources would be necessary to assure larger results? Is so massive a concentration of evils "too much for a divided church"? Is it more than an accident that in "liability areas" like East Harlem there is a widespread tendency to recognize the need for some form of united churches?

In East Harlem, for block after block there had been no church, either in the sense of a building or in the sense of an adequate program under competent staff leadership. The Parish had to start from scratch, sans members, sans facilities. Tens of thousands of people had no institutions of religion of the sort Protestantism wants them to have.

Such an area is an area of experimentation. To put any pattern into quantity production requires many modifications. In a human institution the most important and highest item of cost, until capital investment in buildings is required, is personnel—or salaries. To change a whole section of a city there must be new blood, new ideas, new example.[11]

[10] Rev. J. Russell Chandran on "Christianity and Social Planning," 1953.
[11] *An Undenominational Church.* The Church of the Savior, Washington, D.C., is an independent congregation, but accepted as a member of the local Federation of Churches. It seeks to reach the religiously unreached, having chosen this as the hardest task in the city. Its first workers were idealistic young people who were searchers for something more demanding than the requirements of ordinary society or its traditional churches. Basic

If you are going to leaven a big lump, even a little leaven is going to cost. Perhaps American Protestantism if it is to learn the skills necessary to redeem and reclaim areas like this, must be prepared to spend not less but more.

---

to its work is stewardship of both time and money. It has exceptional study and service standards. A small inner membership is surrounded by ten or a dozen times as many adherents. Beginning from scratch, Rev. Newton Gordon Cosby now administers a budget of approximately $100,000.

## Chapter IX

## Summary Interpretation

### Church Reactions to Social Change

Where there are no people, there need be no churches. This is the same as saying that where there are no boys and girls, there need be no elementary schools. But for the most part even the inner city still has plenty of people in it. Occasionally a whole neighborhood is zoned for nonresidential use. The number of churches can and should shrink with population loss—and one of our major problems is how to agree co-operatively on who should stay where. By and large, however, we are not quite at that stage. We are still in the habit of running away, helter-skelter, pell-mell. Clearly it is time for the exodus of panic and of selfish institutionalism to be halted.

Maritain has said, "We are not cooperators with change; we are cooperators with God." Often we Protestants have acted as if we were wholly the victims of social determinism. As reported by Lucien Price, Whitehead asks: "Why talk about 'the laws of Nature' when what we mean is the characteristic behavior of phenomena within certain limits at a given stage of development in a given epoch—so far as these can be ascertained?" Does the urban church face an immutable "natural law" of city life, or have we often merely described the actual behavior of city churches, as if they were driven by some unavoidable necessity? Perhaps the time has now fully come when we can see that the Church does not need to run away just because the kind of people living in the community has changed.

Twenty-two years ago it was easy to write, "Where there are

no people of the type served by the church within reach of its building, the church cannot survive." Doubtless that was a correct description of the facts, but the statement itself was also a judgment on urban churchmanship. Obviously a church of that kind, serving only that kind of people, could not survive if the people in its neighborhood began to be wholly different; but within the last quarter of a century it has slowly been dawning on the Church that as neighborhoods change, churches must change also. They can take the initiative in areas and times of transition. At the very worst, they can stand their ground. If, "having done all," they cannot do more, all honor to them; but how many have resolutely faced up to the mandate of social change?

Queen and Carpenter in their recent volume, *The American City*,[1] say:

When a church is declining, its members moving to other parts of the city, its area being invaded by new population elements or by business, the question of what to do is very pressing. Generally speaking there are five alternatives:

1. An effort may be made to adapt the program to the changing characteristics of the district.

2. A new location may be sought which will be more convenient to the membership.

3. The congregation may disband and sell the property.

4. What often happens is that a few of the faithful hold on, vaguely hoping that something may enable them to preserve the organization.

5. Under favorable circumstances of finances and leadership, a metropolitan church may develop.

It will be noted that alternatives 1 and 5 are not mutually exclusive, and that this report has had something to say about the sort of adaptation suggested in 1.

Or the situation may be as described by William A. Dudde in the Lutheran Interracial Service memo of February 11, 1953:

[1] New York, McGraw-Hill, 1953.

"Many churches, vainly trying to follow their old members, moved out to the suburbs; others stayed, tried to keep going with the old members now living far away, and eventually collapsed. But some parish leaders advocated a third choice, based on the congregation's continuing mission to its community, which they saw as a Christian imperative. That choice was to broaden the church's fellowship to welcome their new neighbors."

To which Pastor Schroder of the Bronx adds: "Certainly moving does no good to the community that has been left."

In seeking to understand the situation in East Harlem, a representative of the World Council of Churches found the traditional Protestant churches following three patterns:

1. Failure to adapt to changing population, as waves of immigration changed the neighborhood, has left some churches virtually empty as the original members have moved into better neighborhoods. These churches make a negative impression on the community that the church is a failure and is outmoded.

2. Some of these churches do not differ greatly from the pentecostal storefronts in evangelical content. That is, the gospel preached has little relevance to life lived here and now in this community.

3. A third pattern is the church which provides extensive recreation and welfare services to people of the community with little attempt to proclaim a gospel relevant to the conditions of life which create the need for welfare.

In a brilliant thesis, "An Analysis of Protestant Churches in the Brooklyn Heights," Robert Lee of Union Seminary has presented a convincing "Study of Adaptation to Transition in Ethnic Composition and Social Class Status." He points out that while "the church is a function *of* its neighborhood, [it] also functions *in* the neighborhood and is not exclusively a product of its environment." Surely here is churchmanship at long last realistically reckoning with sociology.

Lee shows that there are various types of transition: Land may be differently used, or cultural change may take place among residents, in terms of ethnic, religious, or social-class status. By the same token, churches caught in these changes may make various adaptations. Over-adaptation can turn a church into a settlement house rather than a place of worship. Where "it takes about four of the new families to equal one of the older families in the amount of contributions to the budget," adjustments are obviously necessary. Three sources of income appear: giving, subsidy, and endowment. In a changing area, a church can ignore its new neighbors and serve a city-wide selective parish, or it can serve part of its new neighbors (white persons of lower income, except Puerto Ricans, for example), or it can try to serve everybody. "The responsible church is more than a social institution, [it] has no vested interest in mere survival." (Our Lord went to the suburbs for overnight, but he came into the inner city for his last great battle.)

From another metropolis an experienced researcher wrote of an area which is sociologically "one of the most complex, amorphous sections in the city. It is made up of social, economic, and cultural groups at the extreme poles from each other. Students, professors, doctors, nurses; patients in hospitals, homes for the blind, or for convalescent aged; Negroes, whites, and foreign constituencies—these compose the hodge-podge. At one time at least nine white churches served the community. At the present six remain, of which two are seriously contemplating withdrawing before the Negro invasion. The remaining churches are merely existing." (This could be in any one of a number of cities.)

In the South End of Boston, to the Settlement House workers half a century ago "the church societies from a local social point of view were divisive." Under conditions of declining Protestant opportunity and increasing responsibility, can we afford the luxury of so many divisions? It was the conclusion of the observer quoted in the previous paragraph that there must be a better and more co-operative way of meeting this sort of need.

There is increasing dissatisfaction with a merely statistical, descriptive approach. As J. C. Hoekendijk said in *The Ecumenical*

*Review* (Winter, 1950—"The Evangelization of Man in Modern Mass Society"), "Statistical estimates are only a preliminary to the real work. We have to ask *why* the statistics about the churches are as they are today."

Or, as David W. Barry puts it, "We Protestants have never learned—sometimes I think we have never even really tried—to evangelize people who do not speak the language of our own cultural group." He goes on to point out, "City churches are chronically involved in a series of crises due to population movement, and at any time as many as one-third of a city's churches will show symptoms of trouble." Yet, he insists, "The crises of Protestantism that have been progressively pushing many denominations out of the inner city do not derive basically from the physical or economic deterioration of the inner city; they derive from our inability to make a vital contact with the people who live there." We have been "too easily diverted by the quicker and easier profits of suburban church extension" (from an address at Cleveland, December 14, 1953).

## A Quickened Social Conscience

Human welfare is increasingly a first charge on the conscience of all Christians. Out of the Church has come a high proportion of the entire social welfare enterprise. Just now American Protestantism is girding itself for a new appraisal of its social work achievements and responsibilities. In this study the role and function of the Church in the field of social welfare has been touched lightly here and there, but never more than a glancing blow has been struck at a subject soon to be competently explored in another National Council of Churches study. We must all wait on an approaching conference in that field both for long-range Protestant strategy, as yet only dimly glimpsed, and for more immediate tactical blueprints.

Bilingualism and race relations have emerged, contrary to any adequate expectation, as the very stuff of the life of the changing city. Incidentally, it may be that the end of the foreign-language church has in some quarters been prematurely announced. Yet Bishop Horace W. B. Donegan said recently to a New York dinner gathering: "No part of Christ's Church has any permanent mission if its ministry is to one particular group or class." Seen in this light, cultural distinctions cease to be a matter of pride, and even become an index of cultural illiteracy. The bishop seems to be saying, with St. James, that sociological and cultural factors must not be permitted to prevent "the man with a gold ring, in goodly apparel" from worshiping side by side with "the poor man, in shabby apparel."

## A New Settlement Movement?

J. Archie Hargraves, in a recent memorandum about the Chicago West Side Christian Parish, writes: "Much like the old *settlement house movement*, the Parish feels that much of the apathy and helplessness can be changed by being out here, immediately available for service." This is merely to make articulate what soon became evident to the writer of this report, as he moved from case to case and city to city. Whatever the denomination, whatever the pattern of churchmanship, here in these varied ministries to the changing city is a new ripple of the settlement tide, less secular, more theological, but in its motivation, attitudes, and dreams strikingly similar to those of the great founders of a vast social work movement now less conspicuous because so widely accepted. Perhaps it is this outgoing spirit which makes all these various enterprises so *en rapport*. In terms of human service they talk only one language: the idiom of the gospel is common to them all.

In 1884 Samuel Barnett, founder of Toynbee Hall, talked of "education by permeation," Thomas Chalmers' "principle of locality" was utilized to offset the sterility of parish life and the consequences of the industrial revolution. "Settlements," said Paul U. Kellogg, in a 1934 article in the *Encyclopedia of the Social Sciences*, "have revived the spirit of the pioneering in decades which have seen the frontier shift to urban centers."

In assaying the present new Protestant interest in the changing city, one needs to recognize the motives and techniques of these social work pioneers of the close of the nineteenth century. Unfortunately their task was harder than was realized. The social work prophets of those early years were flaming apostles of social change. Their successors have often found themselves busy with this particular social service or that—to childhood or old age—and in all their massed strength still incapable of doing much to reduce "the shame of our cities" that still remains. Robert A. Woods found Boston's South End "one of the half-dozen most notorious city districts in the United States where a change was almost too much to be thought of" (p. 354 of his wife's biography of him). In spite of "the most remarkable cluster of progressive municipal philanthropic agencies to be found in any such district throughout the whole world" (p. 262), despite the fact that "after we get our house there will be eight different centers in this neighborhood for whose establishment [South End House] may be credited" (in the years from 1892 to 1902), nevertheless the South End still leaves much to be desired.

However, the Church pot is in no position to call the social work kettle black. Protestantism's flight from Boston's South End has been noted (see Chapter IV). Similarly Josiah Strong testified: "As the tenement-house has been substituted for the comfortable home, the churches working on the old lines have either died or have followed the well-to-do class up-town. Thus in New York, while 200,000 people moved in below Fourteenth Street, seventeen Protestant churches of the old type moved out." [2] They didn't change; they couldn't survive.

There is no room here to discuss the Wesleyan Revival, or the great names (Kingsley, Maurice, Arnold, Ruskin, Freemantle, et al.) associated with the memory of Arnold Toynbee. All this was set forth in 1922 in The Settlement Horizon by Woods and Kennedy (op. cit.). Suffice it here to point out that this impulse to

[2] Religious Movements for Social Betterment, New York, Baker & Taylor, 1900, p. 46.

identify oneself not with privilege but with underprivilege is an urge of long standing. In America one must remember the influence of Tucker (who conceived of Andover House "as a field laboratory for the seminary"), Peabody, Graham Taylor; of the Neighborhood Guild (1886), Hull House (1889), and Union Settlement (1895) in East Harlem itself.

There were pioneers in those days too, who blazed new trails without kowtowing to contemporary ways of road building. "Conferring but little with established forms of charity or education, unable in advance to make sure of working colleagues, with even the outline of their method lying vaguely in the future, they took their courage in their hands and adventured. Cherishing merely a hopeful prospect of meager financial assistance, carrying with them moral support of only a trusting few, almost sure to encounter recoil against their overtures, they none the less pressed forward. All these difficulties, partly because they had not been fully faced, seemed but to stiffen the youthful confidence of the pioneers, nearly all in their mid-twenties. They possessed assurance of faith in the human value of what they had to bring; in the kindly, considerate goodwill of many of the people among whom they were to live; in the simplicity, freedom, not-to-be-denied validity of the neighborly relationship." [3]

Moreover, these early settlement workers made two discoveries which are still most timely: "the centrality of the group" and the necessity of proceeding "without a preconceived program." Further, their idea of rebuilding a city by "taking one neighborhood at a time," "with minute attention to the special problems of each neighborhood, each block, each family," but at the same time acquiring "an increasing capacity . . . to enter into new combinations for the public welfare regardless of economic conditions, nationality, or religious affiliations" is an obvious prerequisite to any sound urban strategy, ecclesiastical or civic. If American Protestantism is too timid even to face up to "Faith and Order"

[3] Woods and Kennedy, *The Settlement Horizon*, New York, Russell Sage, 1922, p. 52.

in its national implications, how can it hope to help bring order out of civic chaos? "Of one thing the settlement worker is sure: if you cannot live in love and peace and understanding with your neighbor, you cannot even begin to talk of living in peace in united nations" (David Rosenstein, Presidential Message, National Federation of Settlements and Neighborhood Centers, 1953).

On the other hand, it is easy to be too critical of the Church. Those who now, with great resources of money and devotion, seek to recall Protestants to a more inclusive service may well remember that there are men and women still living "who have devoted an entire lifetime to implementing precisely the kind of ministry across cultural lines that we [now] keep stressing." For example, one father confesses to his son, "Your logic and your vision of the inner-city church is a clearer one than I had in those days (25 years ago and more), but it was exactly what I wanted the Church to do."

It is a matter for rejoicing, however, that there seems now to be on foot a new crusade, which goes deeper, and is unapologetically more religious, or at least more churchly, than the "college" settlement often dared to be, and adds a plus, in a generic sense more frankly sectarian, on the rebound from excessive secularism.

## Debatable Matters

This study is not prepared to conclude that the inner-city church must be large. Undoubtedly there is a place for small city-wide groups, however tiny, which want to be different, and maintain a peculiar witness. Moreover, "All social scientists recognize that promoting participation is a key problem in a democratic society which rests finally 'not on isolated individuals, but on groups small enough to express the spirit of neighborhood and personal acquaintance.' " [4]

[4] Murray, Bowens, and Hogrefe, *Group Work in Community Life*, New York, Association Press, 1954, p. 67, quoting G. D. H. Cole in *Essays in Social Theory*.

Furthermore, there are small churches and small churches. Some are small because ineffective. Some are small and very effective. Ruoss, in his study of Puerto Ricans in New York ("Mid-century Pioneers and Protestants," 1953), found that certain "small churches bear little resemblance to the typical 'denominational' small church which is slowly fossilizing on central agency handouts. The Puerto Rican's small church is indigenous and dynamic. It is self-starting and self-supporting. It is evangelical and missionary-minded. It may meet in a structure no more imposing than a converted storefront, and its pastor may be giving only part-time service, but there is a high rate of lay leadership and responsibility. Tithing is a common practice of high percentages of the smaller church memberships. It is not uncommon for churches of 100 members or less to support a full-time pastor, a part-time missionary in New York City, and contribute substantially to the support of one or more missionaries in the Caribbean area." [5]

But many are sure that churches which hope to attract and to count vigorously must be big enough to have some momentum. They will require personnel, facilities, program, organization, and money. Within their membership, to be sure, there will be the continuing necessity for small, face-to-face, more primary groups. If facilities are lacking, homes may be used to advantage. If loyalties are to be built up and conserved, it is of the utmost importance that individuals be attached to groups. Unrelated persons constitute too high a membership hazard.

Physical facilities, however simple and inexpensive, are absolutely essential—for worship, for education, for sociability. While in highly technical matters relatively remote referrals may be necessary, even these presuppose and require specialized competence. Adequate contacts with community resources, such as welfare agencies, are a necessary part of liaison service. If counseling service is to be competent, the counselors will usually need spe-

[5] Cf. also "No Room in the Church," in *The City Church*, September, 1952.

cialized training. If case work or group work is to be attempted or utilized, the staff will need to understand the basic requirements of such techniques. If the services of councils of churches and councils of social agencies are available, they should be used to the full.

The greater the human needs, the stronger should be the enterprises seeking to meet the needs. Where people are self-reliant their religious institutions need not necessarily be very complex. Where needs are many and varied, churches should be sturdy and resourceful, rather than weak and precarious. And what the Church is is more important than what it does. Institutional activities should never be permitted to wag the church dog.

What is true of size is true of other debatable issues.

*Some Major Findings*

1. *Church work*, especially in the changing city, *must be organized in terms of neighborhood need.*

"Every community must make its own program, and the making of the program is itself one of the most important phases of community organization," said Robert A. Woods at Andover-Newton in 1912.[6] When homes lacked baths, Morgan Chapel put them in. When recreation is not organized, alert churches provide it or get it organized in the community. Where social services are absent, churches supply them, at least on an emergency basis. Just what the permanent social work functions of the Church are, whether institutional or in terms of staff, is a question on which there are wide differences of opinion.

There seems to be little question that the supreme function of the Church is to meet continuing basic religious needs. As a consequence there is an observable re-emergence of theology and an increased emphasis on churchmanship. This means a new appreciation of the church edifice, both instrumentally and as a place

[6] *The Neighborhood in Nation Building*, Boston, Houghton Mifflin, 1912, Chapter XII, "The Recovery of the Parish," p. 139.

for spiritual experience. Education in the faith, sometimes called indoctrination, regains its place.

If the need is great, the response must correspond. If equalization of educational opportunity is a sound urban principle, equalization of spiritual opportunity deserves more serious attention.

2. *Inclusiveness is an unavoidable goal.* This applies to social and economic status, to vocation, to all ethnic backgrounds. Congeniality is a normal principle of association, but inadequate in itself. Interest groups have their proper place; but all interests must be served, and all must be constructively related. The best church is one which serves all sorts and conditions of men.

Bilingualism must be regarded as temporary and on the way out. The formation or continuation of nationality churches in America is no longer justified as permanent policy. Continuing external subsidy for any organizational process which deliberately delays assimilation is doubtless unwise. Yet the needs of certain vestigial or emergency groups must be recognized. Just now the Chinese in America constitute a special opportunity. While Italian or Armenian may be decreasingly necessary as a language requirement, it is perfectly natural for birds of a nationalistic or linguistic feather to want to flock together. Only they must learn not to be closed societies; and they need no longer be mendicant. There will be later newcomers.

Now that the Supreme Court has spoken about segregation in education, urban Protestantism will have to begin more seriously to mend its ways.

The geographical parish is a continuing responsibility. If no church can serve everybody, all of the churches working together must see that everybody is somehow served. "Whosoever will may come" is a counsel of evangelism, not merely a sentiment in a gospel song. Whatever the social distance that separates Christians, they are members one of another in Christ.

3. *The Group Ministry idea marks a definite advance and meets an urgent vocational need.* Comradeship, the aggregation

of specialized functional abilities, and mutual support are invaluable. Recruitment, training, and administration of multiple staffs are still in their experimental infancy. Few senior pastors know how to serve effectively as chief-of-staff. On the other hand, to have no head seems wasteful of time and energy, and as yet dubious or of unproved value.

Not every group will succeed. Group living has failed in the past, it doubtless will in the future. The essentials of success in Group Ministry are now being forged on the anvils of experience.

Perhaps the size of a staff must vary directly with the degree of underprivilege. In any case, the number of members per ordained staff member varies greatly among the cases studied. By and large, churches (like public education) have too high a ratio of persons served to persons serving. Private education does far better but costs far more.

4. *Connections with educational institutions, especially theological seminaries, are valuable where possible.* Unfortunately there are many cities where schools of theology do not exist. Almost everywhere, however, there are institutions of higher learning—municipal universities, teachers' colleges, technical schools, and the like. Whole institutions have grown out of service ministries to inner-city neighborhoods—e.g., the School of Social Service and the Department of Religious Education at Boston University, not to mention the general area of development of the social sciences. The student body can still be reached in terms of *noblesse oblige.* The best trained have something to share with the most needy.

On the other hand, the absence of theological seminaries in some cities may alter some too professional parish patterns for the better, through the larger use of lay volunteers.

5. *Adequate support is imperative.* Effective church work in the changing city costs money, a lot of money. The total costs of the cases studied would be a staggering sum. Subsidy per member is a rather terrifying figure when the question of reproducibility is

broached. But it must be remembered that all urban costs are high, including church expenses in the most fortunate parishes.

*Endowment* is one way of building up reserves against times of special need. In such a situation as that confronting the Church of All Nations in Boston, capital funds might be multiplied ten times without risk of discouraging the regular giving of members.

Wherever possible, cash *subsidy* is to be avoided. The provision of specialized, functional services that could not otherwise be afforded seems less objectionable. When a parish is legitimately receiving outside financial assistance, as often seems necessary, "paternalism must be guarded against, by close association of clergy, staff, and people in their way of life; dependency must be guarded against by developing a sense of financial responsibility in the parish itself" (from a statement of Urban Mission Priests for discussion with laymen). Particularly are members of city parishes to be urged to contribute or otherwise secure all maintenance costs, and to manage the matters of local expense; and no people should be regarded as too impoverished to be missionary.

*Public contribution* (through community chests, for example) is legitimately sought for social services rendered on a nonsectarian basis, but not at the price of unfair policy control. A recent word of Walter Lippmann's with regard to education is equally pertinent here: "There is an enormous margin of luxury in this country against which we can draw for our total needs." [7] The better churching of the city, and its better service, are a proper claim on personal and corporate generosity. Moreover, there is increasing evidence that the appeal of the changing city to the suburban church pocketbook is being made with increasing effectiveness.

*Fees*, and member support, need to be adjusted according to changing dollar values, and "good interpretation and active promotion" are as essential in church work as in such agencies as the Y.M.C.A. Yet there is also an obvious danger of over-publicizing, which has been felt by more than one worthy enterprise.

[7] In *Atlantic Monthly*, May, 1954.

*Indigenous financing,* or member giving, is to be pushed without apology, whatever the economic status of the constituency of the city church, or the rural church. A study made by Meryl Ruoss, then of the Pathfinding Service of the New York City Mission Society, already cited, "shows that the great growth of work among the Puerto Ricans in New York is generally where its financing and leadership is indigenous."

Alleged fright of local people, when budgets involving thousands of dollars are concerned can be seriously discounted. Whatever the polity of the communion involved, democratic financial controls are of demonstrated value.

Not only is the contribution of money important, but *intelligent understanding and support of program activities* is imperative. Participation needs to be on as broad a membership base as possible. Wide geographical and vocational inclusiveness are desirable, perhaps essential. The discovery and training of *indigenous leadership* is everywhere imperative.

6. *Continuity and duration of effort are essential.* Short pastorates get nowhere in the inner city. Institutional development and functional differentiation are often the slow evolution of decade after decade. New ministries to the underprivileged need not start from scratch, but they must not be impatient of results. In 1892 Robert A. Woods was sure the settlement "must not hurry." In church work too, in the changing city, "haste makes waste."

Yet, if one is to quote proverbs, one must also remember that "the King's business [often] requires haste." That is to say, the time element must not be permitted to serve as an alibi for too little and too late. Bishop Newbigin has recently called attention to the observations made by Roland Allen in *Missionary Methods, St. Paul's or Ours?*" [8] Says Allen: "St. Paul leaves behind him in Ephesus, after only two years of missionary work, a fully established Church provided with its own ministry, able to stand entirely on its own feet. Two centuries would be regarded as a more reasonable period by a missionary of the modern era, and

[8] New York, World Dominion, 1953.

during most of that period the young Church would be treated as a charge on the personal and financial resources of the home base precluding further advance into new regions. The contrast is startling and becomes more so the more it is examined in detail. Our present methods show little sign of being able to achieve the enormous new advances which are necessary if the vast unevangelized regions are to be reached."

What goes for unevangelized peoples goes for the pagan inner city also. Does it not need some Kraemer to tell even the Babes in Christ, "YOU ARE the Church, and you must shoulder its responsibilities"?

7. *Religion should function co-operatively rather than competitively*—"the changing city," Bishop Brent might say, "is too much for a divided Church." Churches should integrate the community rather than divide it. All too often, Woods said, the local church remains "a divisive and disintegrating influence, instead of a center for the promotion of catholic human fellowship and cooperation in its neighborhood, in the local community, for whose democratic progress it stands in the most solemn of all conceivable responsibilities." [9]

Where it is desirable for churches of different denominations to federate or otherwise associate their efforts, the need of new and more inclusive interdenominational "overhead" may be indicated. Successive *ad hoc* arrangements may become wasteful of time and destructive of adequate strategy. Ecumenicity may need to come to grips with the better churching of the changing city and the ecclesiastical administration involved. Neighborhoods were not made for denominations, but denominations to serve people in their natural groupings. If we need new ecclesiastical mechanisms to meet community needs, why not create them? Some of the talk about not developing a "superchurch" seems to betray a fear of greatness. It might be that in the exigencies of the changing city situation we might discover the seeds of greater Christian unity.

[9] Woods, *op. cit.*, p. 136.

*Some Personal Conclusions*

To dwell in thought, as well as physically, month after month, in the changing cities of America does something quite unexpected to one's mind and heart. At the conclusion of his writing this writer found himself automatically erupting in the following perhaps entirely too cryptic paragraph, the expansion of which into a reasoned argument would require more pages.

As one sets the changing city over against the problem of the planet, one is forced to the conclusion that *poverty is too expensive,* that we simply can't afford a world that is partly rich (and a small part at that) and partly desperately poor. Doubtless the hardheaded realist will be appalled at such radicalism. Very well, then. Let unredeemed human nature take its course. That way the problem of the inner city will soon be shelved, for all our cities will be deprived of their insides, and most of their outsides. We walk by faith, or we don't walk.

Suppose we step this down to two less extreme statements.

*The city as a whole needs reconstruction and redemption.*

To Abbé Michonneau, Paris seemed a "de-Christianized community." Are some American cities any better? How can they be changed?

Robert A. Woods, in the seminary address already cited, declared: "The true point of attack for the Church is the local neighborhood. This is also where the structural upbuilding of society has to begin. This is the distinctive unit and organ of social reconstruction. The neighborhood is the very pith and core and kernel and marrow of organic democracy. Democracy is a cooperative society made up of *people just as they come*; and so far as there is democracy, people must be taken precisely that way, just as they come. Likewise, in its fundamental meaning, the parish is simply a downright practical contrivance for seeing to it that the gospel is imparted to every creature, taking them all as they come, seeing that none is overlooked, and that none get away from the range of the spiritual power of the gospel." [10]

The neighborhood is hard to maintain in the city. If it be lost there, and the Church lose faith in the neighborhood, while more than half of the people live in cities, can democracy survive?

Churches that mean business about the needs of their neighborhoods will understand why St. Margaret's Episcopal Church (940 East 156th Street, New York) devoted its February, 1954, issue of "The Militant" (ten mimeographed pages and cover) to "Christian Concern for Housing," at the same time that it featured a Gospel Preaching Mission during Lent. Neighborhood improvement is a natural clinic in general social reconstruction. The Church will inevitably be concerned with *redevelopment*, if it is interested in people in slum areas.

The truth is, blighted areas were long ago proved to be *too expensive*. The 1952–1953 Annual Report of the National Federation of Settlements and Neighborhood Houses succinctly described how downtown residential areas deteriorate:

"As the growth of the city creates a demand for additional commercial, light manufacturing, warehouse, governmental, and cultural institutions, adjacent residential areas are absorbed. The demand on the part of the city and suburbs for convenient and quick transportation to the central areas brings about the construction of new transportation lines and highways. These throughways disrupt the pattern of old residential areas and render even the most desirable of such neighborhoods noisy, dirty, and dangerous.

"During the past two decades it has become clear that the economic cost of these neighborhoods is beyond the capacity of the city to bear."

But it is not merely the physical city that needs rebuilding at its heart. As Robert Woods put it, "The apparently reckless pouring of its energy out into the open life of the community on the

[10] *Ibid.*, p. 135.

part of any particular local church, with careful avoidance of any appearance of seeking to glorify itself—the stirring of other churches in the vicinity to like action—would mean a new moral and spiritual life in any local community." [11]

And he went on to cite "the great principle upon which the foreign missionary service of the Church has won its amazing triumphs—that *an outlet of service is the essential precursor of an inlet of grace.*"

Accordingly, "we must be fully satisfied with the fact that the leaven is permeating and doing its work. We must avail ourselves of all existing groups, and be prepared to let all the honor and glory be theirs provided the Kingdom of God be advanced. The Church which seeks to label its service or attach to itself the results of its work, or do anything other than freely cast its bread upon the waters, will by just so much fail of its true reward." [12] That is hard doctrine. Is it untrue?

The church in the changing city must be interested in the redemption of persons, of families, of neighborhoods, of the inner city, of the outer city, and of all urban society. Reconstruction is its reason for existence. For this redemption was it founded.

8. Finally, *we must abandon the idea of the impossible.* It is no accident that a former Marine should be found at work as rector of an inner-city church in a situation of extreme difficulty. He asked for it. Does not the Marine Corps "specialize in the impossible"?

There has been some ground for saying that there can be no such thing as an urban neighborhood. Great housing builders, where they can start new, are now deliberately building for small neighborhood contacts, self-contained, unhampered by traffic hazards. Under favorable conditions the neighborhood may stage a comeback.

Can it do so under the most unfavorable?

[11] *Ibid.*, p. 137.
[12] *Ibid.*, pp. 144, 145.

The settlement movement was a wager that it could. Neighborhood houses sought to re-create the neighborhood, under difficult circumstances. It takes more than good houses to make a neighborhood; it takes a better spirit. Where the housing is bad, so much the harder is it to stir up the better spirit. That is just what East Harlem affords the chance of doing.

As college and university men went into slums to build homelike institutions, so the workers enumerated in these case studies have gone into slum after slum, to live there, to make them *their* neighborhoods, and to help transform them. This is a primary function of the Church. To *live* where one's parishioners live adds to one's testimony, whether of life or of pulpit.

Any ecclesiastical administrator could list for the protection of anybody's pocketbook all the reasons why the city is hopeless. Chief among them is the fact that the administrators' budgetary commitments must be protected, and any wild ideas of mythical sums to be raised by nonexistent "friendly citizens" must not be allowed to run rampant. Fortunately inventive youth has always been willing to tackle the impossible, to smash the stereotypes, to upset the applecarts carefully inscribed "It can't be done."

In an ecclesiastical order whose very burgeoning ecumenicity could easily be satisfied with sanctifying the ecclesiastical *status quo*, there is no need greater than that of *inventiveness*. Nowhere is inventiveness more needed than in the local parish, in the changing city. Paul G. Hoffman, chairman of the Board of the Studebaker Corporation, quotes his father, a successful inventor, as saying, "Many of our greatest inventions came from the minds of men who had not learned too well what can *not* be done." What we are beginning to witness now, in parish, in board offices, and in councils of churches, is a new, heart-searchingly profound refusal to believe that the church job in the changing city cannot be done.

The urban world is surely upside down, and the desire to help set it right side up is more than youthful bravado; it partakes of the New Testament apostolate, based on the heritage of Old Testament prophecy, and strengthened now by centuries of cumulative Christian experience which need not accept the *status quo* as unredeemable.

Impossible? In their various ways, these cases rise up, smiling, to say, "Sorry, brother, but we are *doing* it."